Creaturely Forms in Contemporary Literature

New Horizons in Contemporary Writing

In the wake of unprecedented technological and social change, contemporary literature has evolved a dazzling array of new forms that traditional modes and terms of literary criticism have struggled to keep up with. *New Horizons in Contemporary Writing* presents cutting-edge research scholarship that provides new insights into this unique period of creative and critical transformation.

Series Editors:
Martin Eve and Bryan Cheyette

Editorial Board: Siân Adiseshiah (University of Lincoln, UK), Sara Blair (University of Michigan, USA), Peter Boxall (University of Sussex, UK), Robert Eaglestone (Royal Holloway, University of London, UK), Rita Felski (University of Virginia, USA), Rachael Gilmour (Queen Mary, University of London, UK), Caroline Levine (University of Wisconsin–Madison, USA), Roger Luckhurst (Birkbeck, University of London, UK), Adam Kelly (York University, UK), Antony Rowland (Manchester Metropolitan University, UK), John Schad (Lancester University, UK), Pamela Thurschwell (University of Sussex, UK), Ted Underwood (University of Illinois at Urbana-Champaign, USA).

Volumes in the series:

Thomas Pynchon and the Digital Humanities, Erik Ketzan
Northern Irish Writing After the Troubles, Caroline Magennis
Jeanette Winterson's Narratives of Desire, Shareena Z. Hamzah-Osbourne
Transatlantic Fictions of 9/11 and the War on Terror, Susana Araújo
Life Lines: Writing Transcultural Adoption, John McLeod
South African Literature's Russian Soul, Jeanne-Marie Jackson
The Politics of Jewishness in Contemporary World Literature, Isabelle Hesse
Writing After Postcolonialism: Francophone North African Literature in Transition, Jane Hiddleston
David Mitchell's Post-Secular World, Rose Harris-Birtill
New Media and the Transformation of Postmodern American Literature, Casey Michael Henry
Postcolonialism after World Literature, Lorna Burns
Jonathan Lethem and the Galaxy of Writing, Joseph Brooker
The Contemporary Post-Apocalyptic Novel, Diletta De Cristofaro
David Foster Wallace's Toxic Sexuality, Edward Jackson
Wanderwords: Language Migration in American Literature, Maria Lauret

Forthcoming volumes:

Contemporary Fiction, Celebrity Culture, and the Market for Modernism, Carey Mickalites
Encyclopaedism and Totality in Contemporary Fiction, Kiron Ward

Creaturely Forms in Contemporary Literature

Narrating the War Against Animals

Dominic O'Key

BLOOMSBURY ACADEMIC
LONDON • NEW YORK • OXFORD • NEW DELHI • SYDNEY

BLOOMSBURY ACADEMIC
Bloomsbury Publishing Plc
50 Bedford Square, London, WC1B 3DP, UK
1385 Broadway, New York, NY 10018, USA
29 Earlsfort Terrace, Dublin 2, Ireland

BLOOMSBURY, BLOOMSBURY ACADEMIC and the Diana logo
are trademarks of Bloomsbury Publishing Plc

First published in Great Britain 2022
This paperback edition published 2023

Copyright © Dominic O'Key, 2022

Dominic O'Key has asserted his right under the Copyright, Designs
and Patents Act, 1988, to be identified as Author of this work.

For legal purposes the Acknowledgements on pp. vii–viii constitute
an extension of this copyright page.

Cover image design by Namkwan Cho
Cover illustration © Rawpixel.com/shutterstock

All rights reserved. No part of this publication may be reproduced or
transmitted in any form or by any means, electronic or mechanical, including
photocopying, recording, or any information storage or retrieval system,
without prior permission in writing from the publishers.

Bloomsbury Publishing Plc does not have any control over, or responsibility for,
any third-party websites referred to or in this book. All internet addresses given
in this book were correct at the time of going to press. The author and publisher
regret any inconvenience caused if addresses have changed or sites have
ceased to exist, but can accept no responsibility for any such changes.

A catalogue record for this book is available from the British Library.

A catalog record for this book is available from the Library of Congress.

ISBN: HB: 978-1-3501-8962-1
PB: 978-1-3501-8967-6
ePDF: 978-1-3501-8963-8
eBook: 978-1-3501-8964-5

Series: New Horizons in Contemporary Writing

Typeset by Integra Software Services Pvt. Ltd.

To find out more about our authors and books visit www.bloomsbury.com
and sign up for our newsletters.

Contents

List of figures	vi
Acknowledgements	vii
Introduction	1
1 The war against animals: reading for creaturely life	11
2 W. G. Sebald's creaturely melancholia	41
3 J. M. Coetzee's creaturely trouble	83
4 Mahasweta Devi's creaturely love	123
Conclusion: from anthropological machines to creaturely forms	157
Bibliography	179
Index	197

Figures

1. A red herring? © W. G. Sebald, *The Rings of Saturn*, 1998. Reproduced with the permission of the Wylie Agency and the W. G. Sebald Estate — 63
2. Connection or comparison? © W. G. Sebald, *The Rings of Saturn*, 1998. Reproduced with the permission of the Wylie Agency and the W. G. Sebald Estate — 65
3. Comparison or connection? © W. G. Sebald, *The Rings of Saturn*, 1998. Reproduced with the permission of the Wylie Agency and the W. G. Sebald Estate — 65
4. Returning the gaze © W. G. Sebald, *The Rings of Saturn*, 1998. Reproduced with the permission of the Wylie Agency and the W. G. Sebald Estate — 74

Acknowledgements

This book began its life as a doctoral thesis at the University of Leeds. There, I benefited immensely from the guidance, encouragement and meticulous commentary of my supervisors, Helen Finch and Sam Durrant, as well as from the incisive criticisms of my examiners, Bob McKay and Graham Huggan. I am grateful to Stuart Taberner for his insightful reflections on early drafts. I also extend my gratitude to Jane Featherstone, whose generous donation to the university funded my studies.

The ideas and arguments of this book have grown out of countless critical conversations with many teachers and intellectual comrades. At Leeds, I want to thank everyone who joined my Creaturely Life reading group. To Ian Fairley and Nick Ray, for listening intently. To Jane Taylor, for your playful curiosity about the subject-object continuum. To Daniel Hartley, for energizing the intellectual atmosphere. And to Stefan Skrimshire, for your collaboration and mentorship. For friendship and solidarity along the way, especially during two rounds of strike action in the snow, I thank Angelos Koutsourakis, Anna Fleming, Arunima Bhattacharya, Asa Roast, Carlos Navarro González, Danny Evans, Dave Gould, David Wylot, Dima Barakat Chami, Elspeth Mitchell, Emily Timms, Georgia Walton, Jason Allen-Paisant, Jivitesh Vashisht, Lenka Vráblíkova, Liz Stainforth, Marlo de Lara, Nathan Brand, Oliver Thurley, Rachel Johnson, Ruth Clemens, Ruth Daly, Sam Perks, Sam Rae, Sreya Mallika Datta, Tim Joubert, Tristan Burke and Xiaolei Sun. For helping to create an Animal Studies community at Leeds, I am grateful to Caitlin Stobie, Ryan Sweet, Sophie Nicolov and Tom Tyler. For our discussions in Johannesburg, Cape Town, Copenhagen, Stockholm, Utrecht and London, I thank Ian Ellison, Jade Lawson, Maya Caspari and Rebecca Macklin. To Kasia Mika and Ryan Topper, for your ever-perceptive readings and close friendship.

Beyond Leeds, I want to thank the many interlocutors whose advice and provocations helped me to refine this project during and after the PhD. Special thanks must go to Susan McHugh, Kári Driscoll, Arthur Rose, Pieter Vermeulen, Stef Kraps, Ben Hutchinson, Francesca Orsini, Stefan Helgesson and Elisabeth Herrmann – each of you offered thought-provoking feedback at crucial junctures. I'm grateful, too, to those who have been thinking-companions since the beginning. Thank you especially to James Thurley, Lily Dessau, Louis Fletcher and Patrick Jones for reading draft chapters. Thanks also to Joana Formosinho and Michelle Bastian for our weekly writing accountability sessions. At Bloomsbury Academic, Ben Doyle, Laura Cope and Lucy Brown guided this book to publication. Thanks to the series editors, Bryan Cheyette and Martin Eve, for giving my work a home. Thank you also to Barney the cockapoo and Hornby the cat, and to the many nuthatches and songbirds who unknowingly saved me from pandemic hell.

I dedicate this book to my families: O'Key, Ellis, Sharp and Sehmbi. Finally, I want to thank Vineeta – who was with me, and knows how it is.

Elements of this book have been published in different forms elsewhere. I'm grateful to the publishers for allowing me to expand on the ideas of the following essays: Dominic O'Key (2019), 'W. G. Sebald's Zoopoetics: Writing After Nature', in Frederike Middelhoff, Sebastian Schönbeck, Roland Borgands, and Catrin Gersdorf (eds), *Texts, Animals, Environments: Zoopoetics and Ecopoetics*, 217–27, Freiburg im Breisgau: Rombach; Dominic O'Key (2019), 'Herring Fisheries, Fish-Eating and Natural History in W. G. Sebald's *The Rings of Saturn*', in Seán McCorry and John Miller (eds), *Literature and Meat Since 1900*, 125–42, Basingstoke: Palgrave; Dominic O'Key (2020), '"Entering Life": Literary De-extinction and the Archives of Life in Mahasweta Devi's *Pterodactyl, Puran Sahay, and Pirtha*', in *LIT: Literature Interpretation Theory*, 31 (1): 75–93. I also gratefully acknowledge the Wylie Agency (UK) Ltd. and the W. G. Sebald Estate for granting permission to reproduce four images from *The Rings of Saturn* (1998) and *Austerlitz* (2001).

Dominic O'Key, April 2021

Introduction

In her 1962 book *Silent Spring*, the marine biologist and writer Rachel Carson condemned American industry's indiscriminate spraying of pesticides as a 'war against nature'. These sprays, dusts and aerosols, she says, 'have the power to kill every insect, the "good" and the "bad", to still the song of birds and the leaping of fish in the streams' (2000: 24–5). *Silent Spring* is a quietly apocalyptic text, a document of environmental degradation written against a backdrop of chemical ecocide and possible nuclear war. Carson writes as if the entire planet is at stake. She expresses how the exploitation of nonhuman life has gone unchecked, emphasizing how modernity rapidly reorganizes and impoverishes habitats that have taken shape over millions of years. Although a work of environmental science, it has not gone unnoticed that *Silent Spring* is also a text of literary innovation, experimenting with genre and realizing a polemic lyricism through its composition of haunting descriptions, emotive imagery and rhetorical forcefulness.[1] Indeed, in the book's opening chapter, 'A Fable for Tomorrow', Carson adopts a subjunctive mode in order to imagine an idyllic town, once 'in harmony with its surroundings', but now overcome by a 'strange blight' (21): vegetation withers, rivers turn lifeless and the animals – robins, catbirds, doves, jays and wrens – grow silent. This fairy tale of speculative nonfiction feels nostalgic in its tragic opposition between a pristine past and a ruined future. But Carson goes on to trouble the incipient dualism. 'This town does not actually exist', she states, shattering the Edenic fantasy. And yet it has 'a thousand counterparts in America or elsewhere in the world… Every one of these disasters has actually happened somewhere' (22). Carson's despairing prolepsis thus returns us to the present, metonymically extrapolating from one town to thousands more so as to underline, yet also imagine anew, the scale of environmental impacts on human and nonhuman communities.

As much as *Silent Spring*'s ethics of ecological care continues to inspire environmental movements and nurture ecocritical thinking, its poetics is also symptomatic of a puzzling literary form-problem which accrues new meaning and intensity in the decades following the Second World War: How to communicate this war against nature? How to write, which is to say, *give form to* the deforming of planetary ecologies and the domination and exploitation of animal life? If these questions are already complex enough for a work which stretched the assumed generic boundaries of public science writing, they become differently difficult when the object of our attention is prose fiction, a form of writing in which the aim is not simply to communicate ideas or put forward particular arguments but to tell stories, build worlds and dramatize the experience of invented characters through narrative twists and turns. Carson is, of course, a storyteller in her own right. And fiction writers often do wish to develop claims and intervene in debates, as we will see throughout this book. But, fundamentally, fiction creates, sustains and posits its own truth, a truth that can simultaneously register, challenge and reimagine real conditions that persist outside of the text.[2]

This book therefore sets out to interrogate how fiction grapples with this form-problem. Focusing especially on contemporary writers who narrate the destruction of fellow creatures, I will ask: How does fiction express and thereby *formalize* modernity's planetary impacts on human and animal life? What capacity does literature have, both formally and thematically, to write the relations between humans and other creatures? And what role does contemporary literature play in imagining different human–animal futures? Literature, and the novel form especially, is often said to shape and sustain our conceptions of human subjectivity. If this is true, then literature's construction of 'the human' must also be implicated in the ways we think about animal life, and of those lives that are judged to be nonhuman, inhuman or creaturely.

This form-problem is by no means exclusive to contemporary literature. As the field of literary animal studies teaches us, the history of world literature is, in a sense, also the history of human–animal relations; epics, fables, poetry and science fiction all attest to and enable different ways of engaging with animals (Ortiz Robles 2016: xi). Yet one of my central arguments in this book will be that the question of literature's relationship with animals, by which I mean the very idea of writing animals within or into fiction, has taken on renewed significance in the contemporary moment. The period between Carson's *Silent Spring* and today has seen a deepening ecological rift, a time of 'unprecedented planetary change' according to the World Wide Fund for Nature's most recent *Living Planet Report* (Grooten and Almond 2018: 6). This rift is emblematized by two interrelated forces of mass death – the global mass production and mass extinction of animal lives – that I will theorize below, adapting Carson's formulation, as constituting a *war against animals*.

But this period has also inspired struggle and resistance: animal liberation activists, advocates for nonhuman personhood, anti-capitalist environmentalists and indigenous land sovereignty groups have, in spite of their differences and disagreements, all organized against this domination of nature. The academic discipline of animal studies is at once a product of and a direct contribution to this conjuncture of ecological contestation. Emerging out of critical theory's ethical turn and the mainstreaming of animal rights discourse, learning from (eco-)feminist and postcolonial studies' critiques of liberalism's normative concept of 'man' as a rights-bearing and autonomous person, and working towards the posthumanist assignment of interrogating 'that thing called "the human" with *greater* specificity, *greater* attention' (Wolfe 2010: 120),[3] animal studies has developed a wide-ranging analysis of the ahistorical dichotomy between 'the human' and 'the animal'. By deconstructing and denaturalizing this supposedly fixed dualism, the field of animal studies investigates the historical conditions under which dominant knowledges of species difference are created, disseminated and maintained.

One of the key intellectual advances of animal studies is its insistence that not just human–animal relations but also the borders that supposedly separate humanity from animality are under constant negotiation, navigation and contestation.[4] Animal studies thereby aims to fracture the image of a timeless and hierarchical distinction between the ontological and identity categories of human and animal. It reminds us that, underneath it all, there is no 'animal' as such, only *animals*: humans, rats, octopuses, grasshoppers, buzzards. The field's dedication of thought towards *the animal* thus calls into question the material (economic, social, institutional) and ideological (discursive, theoretical, methodological) practices of power which sustain the normative supremacy of human over animal, which protect this universal category of the 'human' and sanction the 'non-criminal putting to death' (Derrida 1992: 278) of life defined as not sufficiently human. Animal studies, in sum, articulates an epistemological and methodological intervention into the prevailing practices of the war against animals.

Animal studies' literary wing teases out how this problematic is represented within and contested by literature, asking: *how do we read for animals?* At stake in this question is not just an understanding of how animals feature semantically and symbolically within novels and poetry. It also prompts an analytical intervention into the assumed humanisms of literary criticism as such.

By reading *for* animals, in other words, literary animal studies develops new reading practices which study how animals function within literature and foreground the urgency – political, ethical, ecological – of transforming the actually existing relationships between humans and other animals. Yet still, despite its long-standing analysis of literary animals' ubiquity and invisibility, what Susan McHugh calls the 'representational problems of animals' (2009: 491), literary animal studies has less rigorously interrogated the interplay of representation, politics and literary form. There is, I will argue, more work to be done to investigate how the ideological production of species difference functions within the parameters of the novel form. There is more to be said about how fiction, ostensibly a machine of humanization, can also plot against the exceptionalism of human subjectivity. And there is room within literary criticism for a sharper theorization of how constructed oppositions between the human and the animal are necessarily conjoined with other modalities of human marginalization.

This book, *Creaturely Forms in Contemporary Literature*, is my attempt to develop such an analysis of the interrelation of literary form and species difference in a time of staggering animal death. It will be my contention throughout that literature constructs particular ideas, or genres, of the human subject and that this process necessarily involves the figure of the animal. Literature, to repurpose a concept from the Italian philosopher Giorgio Agamben, is an *anthropological machine*, a 'device for producing the recognition of the human' (2004: 26). At stake in this anthropological recognition is the ongoing sociocultural partitioning of the species boundary.

But as I will argue below, this need not lead us to conclude that literary forms are always already humanist or 'anthroponormative' – a term I will unpack in Chapter 1. For there are authors out there whose texts intriguingly trouble literature's recognition of the human. There are writers, in other words, whose stories unmake the 'human'. Many people today think that large-scale animal farming, scientific and commercial testing on caged animals and the globalized pet industries are either normal, necessary or unfortunate but inevitable components of modernity. But there are some writers, and some works of literature too, that consider the human use of animals to be deeply disturbing. Where some see peace, then, these writers see conflict. It becomes distressing and shameful for these authors, and for some of their invented characters, that the experience of everyday life is in many ways founded on the suffering of other creatures. Indeed for them literature itself is complicit in a vast system of meaning-making which sustains fictions of human superiority.

And yet, rather than abandoning the realm of fiction, these authors grapple with it internally, immanently, experimenting with the formal potentialities and limits of literary writing. In other words, rather than simply producing anthropological machines, these authors craft what I will call *creaturely forms*, texts that are newly attentive towards animal life. Attentiveness, deriving from the etymology *to stretch*, denotes here a form of textual stretching-out towards the animal. My book's title therefore calls attention to those texts that, in their narration and literary formalization of the war against animals, affirm a less narrowly 'human' and hence more creaturely form of life. Creaturely forms, I argue, are works that make creaturely life narratable. Creaturely forms push up against the very limits of a form that prioritizes and produces human subjectivity, repurposing and remaking forms in order to re-form human–animal relations. They critically rewrite literature's recognition of the human, emphasizing the human's connections with and responsibilities to the nonhuman, thus envisioning what Sylvia Wynter describes as 'new genres of the human' (2003: 331).

What this book proposes, then, is both a mode of reading and a more formalist iteration of literary animal studies. My aim? To scrutinize how literature consolidates and remakes the arena of political subjectivity – to closely read formal patterns, generic structures and narrative possibilities in order to reveal how literature's imagination of subjectivity conceives of human and animal liberation as being interlinked. In short, *Creaturely Forms in Contemporary Literature* pushes for a renewed understanding of the relationship between politics and aesthetics in light of our obligation to other creatures. I use the pluralized term 'creaturely forms' as a way of making sense of how certain texts dramatize, and how certain literary strategies navigate, the form-problem of literature as an anthropological machine.

To make these arguments I will turn to the work of three world-renowned authors whose literary projects develop abiding preoccupations with the war against animals: W. G. Sebald (1944–2001), J. M. Coetzee (1940–) and Mahasweta Devi (1926–2016). Writing with an acute historical awareness that they stand on the threshold of a new millennium, looking back over a century of world wars, genocides, anti-colonial struggle, nuclear explosions and environmental devastation, Sebald, Coetzee and Mahasweta[5] are each alert to the ways in which life – not just human but nonhuman too – has been colonized, dominated and exploited across modernity. Sebald's work bears witness to a *longue durée* of colonial expansion into nature, utilizing its distinctive first-person narration in order to show how animals are simultaneously eliminated and exhibited across modernity, driven to extinction yet displayed in museums, stripped of their habitats and put on show in zoological gardens. Coetzee's writing is deeply concerned with the twentieth-century growth of industrialized agriculture, the rationalist-scientific instrumentalization of animals and the obsolescence of 'racist' guard dogs in a post-apartheid era. Mahasweta's texts thematize how the developmental projects of postcolonial India mark a new form of violence against indigenous tribes and nonhuman communities, as forests are destroyed for logging and infrastructural projects.

Throughout these three writers' works, the figure of the animal stands not only as a representation of nonhuman species. It also comes to imply the animality of the human subject, an animality that is fundamentally shared between species but is all too often projected and displaced onto subordinated human others. Within literary studies, all three of these authors have tended to be interpreted through a humanist register that overlooks how their fictions dramatize encounters with and tensions between different figurations of animality. But what is critically important and immensely complicated about these authors, I think, is that they might be said to actually arrive at an ethics of animality *through* their writing of how subjugated humans are treated 'like' animals. Far from endorsing a humanist horizon in which dehumanized communities are elevated to the status of 'the human', their works unsettle the exclusionary and normative category of the human itself. As I hope to show across these chapters, their fictions suggest that human emancipation requires a reconciliation between humanity and animality.

Sebald, Coetzee and Mahasweta also share a criticality about and reflexivity towards literature's own role in mediating these relations between humans and other creatures. Each author is differently vigilant about how literary forms contribute to the self-fashioning of human subjectivity and exceptionalism. And because of this, their literary projects can be read as three thematic-formal negotiations of literature's humanist tendencies. In some works, Sebald, Coetzee and Mahasweta test out whether time-honoured novelistic forms can accommodate animals as figures and characters. In Sebald's *Austerlitz*, Coetzee's *Disgrace* and Mahasweta's long story *Pterodactyl, Puran Sahay, and Pirtha*, each author works through the interrelation of dramatic plotting, human or character development, and nonhuman incorporation, simultaneously narrating and dramatizing the war against animals. In other, more experimental texts such as Sebald's *The Rings of Saturn* and his prose poem *After Nature*, Coetzee's *The Lives of Animals* (first delivered as lectures in 1997, published as two short stories in 1999, and later re-published in 2003 as the metafictional novel *Elizabeth*

Costello) and Mahasweta's short stories, these authors experiment with and combine minor genres and forms in order to allow for different engagements with creaturely life. Under my reading, Sebald's poetics of connection and idiosyncratic use of images, Coetzee's interrogation of realism and developing recourse to metafictional strategies, and Mahasweta's mobilization of the short story form and free indirect discourse all become part of a repertoire for addressing the form-problem of narrating the war against animals. These three writers adopt literary forms in order to blur the boundaries between human and nonhuman, thus calling attention to a shared animality, or creatureliness, between their human and nonhuman characters.

But what of this concept, the 'creaturely'? What does it mean? Where does it come from? With this, I seek to mobilize a term which, in its interruption of the dualism of the human and the animal, simultaneously deconstructs an exclusive anthroponormativity (the norms that produce a 'proper' human subject) and opens up the possibility of new human–animal relations. As I will explore in Chapter 1, the creaturely stands today as a paradigmatic and polysemous keyword of contemporary theory. It is a word which carries a complex history of contradictory valences that have rendered it overdetermined, even troublesome. In fact, one of our foremost thinkers of human–animal relations, Donna Haraway, describes the creaturely as a 'semiotic barnacle', a word so tainted by its humanistic and theological connotations that it must be 'scraped off' of our vocabulary (2016: 169 fn. 1). But there is a crucial distinction to be made between Haraway's preferred substitute word, 'critters', which connotes real organisms, and creatures, which I will think of here as fundamentally literary creations. Creatures are aesthetic mediations of animals rather than *the* animal itself. After all, the OED has it that creatures are 'created things or beings; a product of creative action; a creation' (2020: n.p.), thus neither explicitly human nor nonhuman.

The creation of animal characters, the description of animals as part of a novel's environment or setting and human characters' ruminations *about* animals – all of these are deliberate incorporations of animals into the given text, and deserve to be read as such, in conjunction with the text's specific formal and generic articulations. To turn Haraway's warning back in on itself, in this book I intend to *stay with this trouble* of the creaturely, offering critical explication of how literary creatures and forms rethink interspecies social relations. The creaturely is multivalent, a concept that I even want to generatively overdetermine through my engagement with different literary texts. In these fictions, the creaturely variously signifies a negative *and* positive diminishment, a dehumanization and an animalization of the human subject; by imagining modes of lived indistinction, of creaturely life, these texts differently reveal the paradoxes and limitations of human subjectivity, all the while articulating a new relationality between species.

As its title suggests, *Creaturely Forms in Contemporary Literature* will make claims about how contemporary literature narrates the war against animals. Yet the texts I read stretch back to the late 1970s, a time that many would not immediately think of as 'contemporary'. Although some literary critics have periodized contemporary literature as being any works written after 1945,[6] and others have suggested that 'our' contemporary moment actually begins with the tightening of neoliberal orthodoxies in the 1980s,[7] it remains an open question whether it is more useful to understand 'contemporary literature' as a historically specific socio-temporal period or a collection of works published in the previous five or so years.[8] Because of this, I have found it helpful to conceive of the contemporary as a critical category and conceptual problem. Perhaps the contemporary is not the temporal moment that we simply inhabit but 'a moment that we must first conceive *as* a moment' (Martin 2017: 5). To describe a – not *the* – contemporary means embarking on a process of identifying, clarifying and hence denaturalizing a particular conjuncture that envelops us, structures our experience and creates paths towards specific futures.

The massified production, slaughter, exchange, consumption and extinction of animals is one such contemporary, a reality that underpins capitalist modernity broadly but has become more deeply entrenched and extended, more paradoxically ubiquitous and invisible, and still more widely resisted in the decades following the Second World War. The literature I read is therefore *contemporary to* the war against animals. In the chapters of this book, my argument will be that authors like Sebald, Coetzee and Mahasweta are each differently cognizant of the material and ideological dimensions of the war against animal. Writing from different locations and engaging with different literary traditions, they construct texts which contest and rethink human–animal relations, in turn responding to their own contemporary.

But what is at stake in their writing and rewriting of human–animal relations? And what is the real significance, or advantage, of using the word 'creaturely' to analyse works of literature that are attentive towards animals? I spell all of this out in Chapter 1. Here I lay the groundwork for my book's theoretical and methodological arguments, explicate my critical vocabulary and thereby develop my specific intervention into contemporary literary studies. Of real focus in Chapter 1 will be my adoption of the term 'war against animals', which I take from Jacques Derrida (2008: 29) and, more recently, Dinesh Wadiwel (2015). This idea, of a war being waged against animal life, might strike readers as hyperbolic and imprecise. Humans are not soldiers on the lookout for enemy animal combatants. Surely describing contemporary human–animal relations as a 'war' ignores the manifold ways in which humans and animals often live together in non-instrumental and kin relations. Surely the sheer diversity of animal life across the planet also means that any attempt to think through the contradictions of our love towards some creatures and exploitation of others will be ultimately reductive and unsuccessful. Does a claim like this, which collapses the multiplicity of human–animal relations in different corners of the world, risk a dangerous form of cultural projection? Maybe so, but as I will argue in Chapter 1 the upshot of adopting this rhetoric of conflict is that it forces us to confront the variegated and historically mutating totality of violence that has afflicted and continues to afflict nature. It compels us to take notice of capitalism's own totalizing desire to standardize human–animal relations and make them profitable. The phrase 'the war against animals' is thus utilized as a strategic abstraction that allows us to think analytically about the deliberate decisions, compulsions and imperatives of global capitalism, the continued growth of which is still wedded to practices of expansion, extraction and animal slaughter.

The three author-study chapters that follow offer critical readings of Sebald's, Coetzee's and Mahasweta's literary projects. In Chapter 2, I show how Sebald's paradigmatic melancholia is inseparable from an animal ethics; his connective prose bears witness to the innumerable ways in which modernity simultaneously eliminates and exhibits, destroys and preserves, creaturely life. In Chapter 3, I argue that Coetzee's 'animal turn' is also a stylistic or formal turn. Coetzee's growing preoccupation with animal rights, animal welfare and vegetarianism in the 1990s not only leads to literary works *about* animals but actually produces a literary experiment in which different literary genres are tested out, at a sentence-by-sentence level, in order to see how far they can dramatize an affinity with animals. Chapter 4 considers how Mahasweta's short fictions formally call into question the rights-bearing sovereign subject of postcolonial development through plotted encounters with indigenous communities and nonhuman life. Mahasweta's writing, I argue, conceives of the fight for indigenous recognition and redistribution as being inextricable from a fight to arrest environmental destruction.

Creaturely Forms in Contemporary Literature concludes by turning to a selection of other, more contemporary writers – including Amitav Ghosh, Indra Sinha, Jean-Baptiste Del Amo, Sarah Hall, Aminatta Forna, Arundhati Roy, Henrietta Rose-Innes and Richard Powers – who similarly negotiate literature's humanism as they strive to write in ways that are more attentive towards animality. Writing against the backdrop of centuries of human exploitation of creaturely life, authors like Roy, Rose-Innes and Powers articulate literary responses to the war against animals that imagine forms of surrender and repair in which human–animal relations might begin again. My readings uncover how literary forms, whether overarching plots, narrative strategies or sentence-by-sentence units of syntax, dialogue and characterization, at once figure and reconfigure our sense of what it means to live with and alongside other creatures.

Notes

1. Although Carson's contemporary critics dismissed her work as neither science nor literature, recent scholarship has recuperated and reappraised *Silent Spring* as a key text in the emerging environmental humanities corpus. See Garrard (2004), Foote (2007) and Twidle (2014).
2. I take the phrase 'posits its own truth' from Jonathan Culler, who, during a careful elaboration of Derrida's writing on the singularity of literature, argues that 'since literature, as fiction, does not presume a reality already given and to be represented but posits its own truth, it inscribes its own context, institutes its own scene, and gives us to experience that instituting' (2008: 14). I also derive the critical verb 'register' from the Warwick Research Collective (WReC). For them, 'register' means to record, to mark, but also to express, to display. This allows us to consider literary works' manifold ways of 'encoding… modernity as a social logic' (2015: 15).
3. Emphasis is in the original. Throughout the remainder of this book, emphases are reproduced exactly as in the original. Wherever I add or modify the text's emphasis, I will indicate this in parenthesis.
4. For more on this, see my introduction to a special issue of *parallax* (O'Key 2019: 352).
5. Mahasweta Devi, born Mahasweta Ghatak, is referred to across literary scholarship by her personal name, in part because her chosen name 'Devi' – literally, 'goddess' – is a common Hindu matrilineal honorific. I will retain this denomination throughout, thus referring to Mahasweta, not Devi.
6. See, for example, Eshel (2013: 4).
7. On this, see Huehls and Greenwald Smith (2017: 3). For a critique of their periodization, see Deckard and Shapiro (2019: 33).
8. Owing to this, critics like Hungerford (2008) have deliberated on the term's relevance.

1

The war against animals: reading for creaturely life

Thirty years on from Rachel Carson's condemnation of American industry's war against nature, the philosopher Jacques Derrida delivered a ten-hour conference address in Cerisy-la-Selle in which he too spoke of human–animal relations as a war. Inspired by a moment of naked vulnerability in front of his pet cat, Logos, during which Derrida considered himself to have been '*seen seen*' (2008: 13) by the animal, his lecture posits that humanity has long waged a 'species war' (101) against forms of life that are deemed animal, not normatively human, or inhuman. Throughout, Derrida articulates how the 'boundless wrong that we inflict on animals' (89) is both material and epistemic, a conjoined violence that encompasses ancient theological notions of dominion and sacrifice, the fact that numerous languages reduce the diversity of species difference into the singular and monolithic category 'animal', and the specific practices of cruelty that humans inflict upon our animal neighbours, from genetic experiments to species extinctions. Even the major philosophical thinkers of modernity, Derrida writes, speak about animals as if they were mere objects rather than subjects. Despite the many advances of Cartesian mechanical philosophy, the Kantian and Enlightenment articulations of human dignity and rights, Heideggerian *dasein*, Lacanian psychoanalytic theory and the Levinasian ethics of the other, Derrida says, each of these thinkers speak as if they have never been looked at by an animal. They make claims about human exceptionalism – about speech, reason, culture or technology as being what is exclusively 'proper to man' (5), and hence alien to animals – that rely on a misrecognition or disavowal of the animal's gaze.

Titled *The Animal That Therefore I Am*, Derrida's lecture marks an attempt to think philosophically from the understanding that the human is a fellow creature, an animal among other animals, rather than from a position of human superiority:

> To think the war we find ourselves waging is not only a duty, a responsibility, an obligation, it is also a necessity, a constraint that, like it or not, directly, or indirectly, no one can escape. Henceforth more than ever. And I say 'to think' this war, because I believe it concerns what we call 'thinking'. The animal looks at us, and we are naked before it. Thinking perhaps begins there.
>
> (2008: 29)

To think from this standpoint is to recognize the ways in which animals might address us, might make demands of us, just as Derrida's cat looks at him. But it also means thinking *against* the war against animals that continues to structure human societies. Derrida says that humanity's mastery over animals is 'probably ageless' (29). Although seemingly ahistorical, his primary hypothesis is that the war against animals has worsened, deepened, over the past two centuries, and that as he speaks in the final decades of the twentieth century, this war has entered a 'critical phase' (29), one of 'animal genocides' (26).

I first read *The Animal That Therefore I Am* as an undergraduate student, intimidated by Derrida's intentionally meandering, serpentine style, yet still struck by how his words clarified my evolving ideas about human–animal relations. In the years since I have made more sense of his claim that the war against animals has entered a new, critical conjuncture by thinking through how this age of mass production and mass extinction is also the age of its resistance, with various pro-animal social movements campaigning across the world for legally enshrined protections on behalf of other species. I have also come to think that the domination of nonhuman life is not monolithic but heterogeneous, having transformed throughout human history, under changing conditions and different modes of production and consumption. As Dinesh Wadiwel puts it in *The War Against Animals*, 'the genealogy of the war against animals is one of continual adaption and reworking of systems of domination to most effectively capture the agency, escape and vitality of animals' (2015: 16). I do not want to retread ground that Wadiwel has already covered in his book, a persuasive work of political theory that explicates how human sovereignty develops as an intersubjective, institutional and epistemic force wielded against so-called lesser forms of life. Even so, to understand what is at stake in contemporary literature's writing of human–animal relations, we must first attend to the specific conditions which lead us towards the present, a period of extreme environmental damage.

For millennia, human societies have long controlled and killed animals. Sacrifices, hunting, fishing, domestication and the instrumentalization of animals for labour (transport, ploughing and so on) might all be understood as developing forms of relations which tended towards pastoral forms of power being wielded against animals. With the Neolithic Revolution, some 10,000 years ago, sedentary food production came to replace nomadic lifeways. This transition to intensive agricultural methods, Ashley Dawson writes in *Extinction: A Radical History*, marks 'one of the most fundamental metamorphoses not just in human but also in planetary history' (2016: 26), as settled societies reorganized the land around them into agro-ecosystems. The impact on biodiversity was unprecedented, and civilizations such as the Sumerian and Roman Empires left in their wake considerable deforestation and defaunation.

Yet it is the capitalist mode of production, combined with the projects and imperatives of colonial expansion, which most intensively captures, exploits and extinguishes animal life. By 'transforming nature into a commodity that could be bought and sold', Dawson puts it, 'capitalist society shifted humanity's relations with nature into a mode of intense ecological exploitation unimaginable in previous epochs' (2016: 42). In 1524, as early forms of capitalist exchange and valuation began to take hold in northern Europe, the radical cleric of the early Reformation Thomas Müntzer lamented how animals were becoming increasingly commodified: 'all creatures have been turned into property, the fishes in the water, the birds in the air, the plants on the earth; the creatures, too, must become free' (Müntzer cited in Marx 1975: 172). Three centuries later, Karl Marx drew on Müntzer's words in order to explain what he called capitalism's 'real contempt for, and practical debasement, of nature' (1975: 172). Marx is rarely considered to be a pro-animal thinker.[1] But his foundational writings on the enclosure of the commons, private property and capitalism's appropriation of nature illuminate our understanding of the war against animals. Marx understood, for example, that capitalism depends on a separation between humanity and nature, a 'dissolution of the relation to the earth' (1993: 497). In texts like *The German Ideology*, Marx decried how industrialization destroys habitats: for freshwater fish, the river 'is no longer a suitable medium of existence as soon as the river is made to serve industry, as soon as it is polluted by dyes and other waste products and navigated by steamboats, or as soon as its water is diverted into canals where simple drainage can deprive the fish of its medium of existence' (1998: 66). And in 1851, two years after a Whig government passed the Cruelty to Animals Act, Marx wrote in a notebook that box-feeding, the practice of confining livestock to stalls for fattening, was a 'disgusting… system of cell prison' in which 'animals are born and remain there until they are killed off' (Marx cited in Saito 2016: n.p.). To stretch a concept that Marx himself only applied to humans, the war against animals profoundly estranges creatures from their *species-being*, their specific desires to live out their lives.

Capitalist modernity intensifies and extends the war against animals. Under today's conditions of industrial production, commerce and finance, nonhuman animals do not possess subjective experiences and desires, nor are they sacred beings. They are either propertied objects, super-exploited organisms whose bodies are maximized for value extraction, or they are worthless, and hence can be collateral damage of profit-seeking. Even within the apparent domains of animal care, from the pet industry to conservation tourism, animals remain commodified as *valuable assets* rather than individual beings. Modernity has seen the institutionalization of numerous forms of knowledge – zoological, ethological and biological – that enable deeper interventions into the lives of animals, whether through genetic experimentation, genome manipulation or artificial insemination. Yet one of the peculiar features of the war against animals is that it is increasingly made invisible. In his path-breaking essay 'Why Look at Animals', John Berger suggests that modernity symbolically and materially 'marginalized' animals (2009: 13). For him, modernity's urbanization, its new media technologies and its zoological gardens all peripheralize real animals. In the decades since Berger's essay, those companies who wage a war against animals have also sought to obscure and conceal it: the raising and slaughtering of animals mostly takes place on the peripheries of societies, hidden behind the closed doors of laboratories and slaughterhouses and protected from whistleblower scrutiny by law.[2]

Much of this has been propelled by the vested interests of the meat industry's production and slaughter of animal lives for consumption, so much so that modernity has been described a period of 'meatification' (Weis 2016: 8), in which animal flesh moves from the periphery to the centre of diets, disproportionately consumed and wasted by the world's richest few. Indeed this industrial-capitalist food regime accelerated in the twentieth century through the roll-out of Concentrated Animal Feeding Operations in the United States poultry industry in the 1930s and intensive mono-cropping – immense amounts of grain were now produced for feeding livestock rather than people. Through the invention of the CAFO, which sought to regulate the feeding of hundreds of thousands of chickens for maximum efficiency, farms became factories, creating the conditions for the US's increasing domination of global meat production.

Today, the war against animals is characterized by two interrelated forms of mass death: mass production and consumption on the one side, mass extinction on the other. The decades that followed the Second World War saw the consolidation of mega-agribusinesses who could mass produce meat products like never before. The so-called 'Livestock Revolution' of the last half century has matched growing global demand for meat proteins by creating increasingly extreme methods for raising and slaughtering chickens, pigs and cows in the quickest time possible. Between 1970 and 2008, beef production doubled, poultry increased sixfold and pork tripled (Keiffer 2017: 8). From 1961 to 2010, the global population of slaughtered animals leapt from roughly 8 to 64 billion (Weis 2013: 2). The United Nations predicts that, if demand continues, humans will devour nearly 450 million tonnes of animal flesh per year by 2050, roughly double the amount for the year 2000 (Keiffer 2017: 8). The meat and dairy sector is now dominated by just a handful of powerful and commercially expanding multinational companies. Combined, these companies' production of animal lives and deaths uses over a quarter of the earth's land surface. Inside their factories, animals are genetically bred to be bigger, faster-growing and more heat-tolerant, fed antibiotics to ward off illness. Existing and dying within cramped and stressful conditions, these animals often nurse broken bones, clipped beaks and severed tails. In her writing on the links between animal and disability liberation, Sunaura Taylor calls on us to think of mass-produced animals as disabled (2017: 31), both physically deformed and deprived of autonomy.

But this focus on industrial agriculture only tells half the story. During the same time as the Livestock Revolution, industrial capture fisheries around the world attracted major government subsidies in order to conduct a threefold expansion into the seas: horizontally, from coastal waters to open oceans, especially new commodity frontiers in global south waters; vertically, from shallow to deeper waters, made possible by the development of supertrawler ships and new onboard technologies such as longlines, which generate enormous amounts of wastage through incidental catch; and taxonomically, in that they catch, process and create commodity value around fish species that, for previous generations of fishers, were undesirable or simply not considered seafood (see Pauly 2009: 217). Beginning in the 1950s, this threefold expansion has led to decades of global over-fishing, regulated as well as illegal, unreported and unregulated. The Food and Agriculture Organization of the United Nations (FAO) concludes that, currently, almost a third of the global fish stocks are overexploited, and almost two-thirds are fully exploited (2018: 6), pushed to the brink of collapse. Although a handful of (trans)national moratoria have been called and observed around the globe, the industry's main response to fishing's ecological limits in more recent decades, under economic conditions of neoliberalism, has been to establish catch quotas and develop aquacultural fishing practices, the latter of which controls the breeding, raising and harvesting of numerous fish species in enclosed rings. Neither regulatory quotas – such as Individual Transferable Quotas or Total Allowable Catch – nor aquacultural methods will save endangered marine species from extinction. The former rests on the logic of capitalist sustainability, a fantasy that thinks of each species as producing a harvestable surplus population that can be extracted forever; the latter effectively creates a new offshore monocropping in which biodiversity plummets for the sake of stable commodity flows.[3]

At one level, then, the war against animals is being waged against wageless animals, those beings whose bodies have increasingly become 'living factories', to adopt Kenneth Fish's formulation, 'harnessed as a force of industrial production' (2012: 5). Faced with this knowledge of the daily torments of farmed animals, the novelist Jonathan Safran Foer became a vegetarian and wrote a book of animal advocacy, *Eating Animals*. He writes: 'we have waged war, or rather let a war be waged, against all of the animals we eat' (2009: 33). And yet, precisely *because* of intensive farming and fishing's continued reproduction and extermination of animal life, the war against animals also impacts upon those wild animals whose lives are not considered profitable, or who have not yet been incorporated into the logics of value. The environmental burdens of global agro-capitalism are by now well known. The industrial organization of animal production is predicated on staggering land-use, mass deforestation and soil degradation. In 2018, the UN's International Panel on Climate Change concluded that livestock supply chains – from feed production to enteric fermentation, and from transport to slaughtering, processing and shipping – account for around 15 per cent of global greenhouse gas emissions (Masson-Delmotte et al. 2018: 327).

Intensive animal industries, in their quest for value extraction and geographical expansion, also create the ideal conditions for the emergence of deadly zoonotic diseases which can result not just in human fatalities but also in the mass extermination – euphemistically termed *depopulation* – of farmed animals. The bovine spongiform encephalopathy (BSE) epidemic of the early 1990s is thought to have been caused by the deliberate recycling of animal tissue within feed. In the UK alone, millions of cows have been slaughtered in the fight to eradicate BSE. The emergence of deadly diseases such as H5N1 and coronaviruses like SARS-CoV-2 is inextricable from human encroachment, industrial agricultural expansion and wildlife trading, as Mike Davis reveals in *The Monster at Our Door*.[4] By razing old-growth forests for ranching and plantation, animal agricultural industries have shrunk, if not already destroyed, the habitats of innumerable wild species, forcing creatures like bats into closer and more sustained contact with farmed animals and other humans, thus dramatically increasing the likelihood of a pathogen spillover event.[5]

Because factory farming is an expanding, fossil-fuel-intensive and climate-warming phenomenon,[6] the mass production of farmed animals is closely related to, even a direct cause of, the mass extinction of wild animals. According to a WWF report, there has been a 60 per cent decline in the population size of mammals, birds, fish, reptiles and amphibians since the Livestock Revolution (Grooten and Almond 2018: 6). The Intergovernmental Platform on Biodiversity and Ecosystem Services states that biodiversity – meaning the diversity within and between species and ecosystems – is 'declining faster than at any time in human history' (IPBES 2019: 10), while biologists warn that, as things stand, as much as half of the planet's flora and fauna are expected to be lost by this century's end.[7] This dramatic disappearance of wildlife has been termed the 'Sixth Extinction' (Kolbert 2014). The war against animals is a mass extinction event whose scale and intensity rivals the natural disasters of millions of years ago, comparable in scale to a toxic algae bloom, an immense volcanic eruption or an asteroid crashing into the earth's surface. It is a kind of 'biological annihilation' (Ceballos et al. 2017: E6095).

A time, then, of mass production and mass extinction. This is the context in which the war against animals might be said to enter a critical phase. And it is this context, I will argue, that becomes unignorable for writers such as W. G. Sebald, J. M. Coetzee and Mahasweta Devi, whose literary projects seek to 'think' this war.

The war against *the* animal

But the war against animals is not merely a war against nonhumans. It is a war against *the* animal, against the figuration of animality, the subject's own animality *and* its perceived animal others. When I say 'the war against animals', then, my aim is to invoke simultaneously the extensive commodification and exhaustion of nature for profit *and* the ongoing epistemic-material production and allocation of 'humanity', which excludes other forms of life that are deemed animal, whether human or otherwise. To think the war against animals involves more than registering the systemic violence of factory farming, capture fisheries, animal experimentation, deforestation and habitat loss. As Derrida makes clear in an interview with Elisabeth Roudinesco, 'thinking' this war also means interrogating the 'image humans have of themselves' (2004: 64). For the ongoing construction or figuration of the animal is inseparable, Derrida writes, from the equally ongoing constitution of 'the ends of man' (2008: 12), that is, of precisely *who* is determined to be sufficiently or properly human, of 'a certain concept of the subject' (88) forged in Enlightenment modernity whose very humanization is structured in opposition to 'all the living things that man does not recognize as his fellows' (34). In other words, the shifting but ossifying dualism of the human and the animal also involves the 'appropriation of man by man' (101), enclosing and circumscribing particular ideas of what is politically counted as human.

This critique of the construction of man and the limits of personhood is by now well established. Michel Foucault once pointed out that the concept of 'man is only a recent invention, a figure not yet two centuries old' (2002: xxv). Feminist, postcolonial and critical race theorists have long held that humanity is not a universally inhabited category, and that the liberal conception of a rights-bearing person, inherited from Enlightenment thought and later developed and enshrined through human rights, is fraught with contradictions and exclusions. For Sylvia Wynter, the construct of 'Man' is a colonial invention that 'overrepresents itself as if it were the human itself' (2003: 260). By claiming the entire terrain of humanity for itself, this dominant construct of 'Man' draws the boundaries of political humanity, creating an order of subjectivity that forecloses alternative genres of being human. Judith Butler articulates a similar critique in her writing on the category of the human as a 'differential norm', 'a value and a morphology that may be allocated and retracted, aggrandized, personified, degraded and disavowed, elevated and affirmed. The norm continues to produce the nearly impossible paradox of a human who is no human… Wherever there is the human, there is the inhuman' (2009: 76). Not all humans equally occupy the space of human subjectivity and personhood. Founded on specific presumptions of rationality and autonomy, the institutionalized and intersubjective distribution of the human is exclusionary. My chapters on Sebald and Coetzee will trace how their texts thematize colonialism, antisemitism and apartheid as producing figures of inhumanity; my chapter on Mahasweta will explore how India's indigenous communities are obstructed from personhood and equated with 'nature' by colonial and postcolonial regimes of power.

Animal studies and posthumanism deepen this interrogation into the production and interrelation of taxonomies of difference, affording a new critique of human normativity through its attention to how the idea of 'species' is not a natural or essential given but a site of ongoing sociocultural contestation. The hierarchies of human subjectivity and speciation tend to be deeply ingrained and naturalized. However, as numerous thinkers have shown, what is counted and discounted, what is human and animal, shifts according to time and place, under different lived conditions, and is not reducible to biology alone. In her recent book *Infrahumanisms*, for example, Megan H. Glick explores how many abiding practices of human differentiation – from normative able-bodiment standards to sexualization to legal rights to the idea of childhood itself – are informed by biocultural 'hierarchies of speciation' (2018: 4) inherited from evolutionary frameworks. Animal studies began developing its critique of species categories at least as early as the 1980s, with Donna Haraway's (1989) analysis of primatology and Carol J. Adams's second-wave feminist account of the links between sexual violence and the meat industry (2010). In *Animal Rites*, a foundational work of posthumanist theory, Cary Wolfe develops these claims by pinning down how the dominant discourse of species difference that structures subjectivity is attached to modernity's projects of racialization and gendering. As Wolfe writes, 'the humanist discourse of species will always be available for use by some humans against other humans as well' (2003: 8).

In more recent years, scholars have advanced this inquiry by interrogating how the discourse of species – that is, the ongoing production of the human–animal dichotomy – is conjoined with specific modalities of human oppression. Within postcolonial studies, for example, writers like Bénédicte Boisseron (2018), Julietta Singh (2018) and Evan Maina Mwangi (2019) have focused on how cultural and literary artefacts are shaped by notions of animality that interlink with the racialization of colonized peoples. As Achille Mbembe puts it, the trope of animality was, in fact, a signature 'meta-text' of colonial conquest: 'discourse on Africa is almost always deployed in the framework (or on the fringes) of a meta-text about the *animal* – to be exact, about the *beast*' (2005: 8). Claire Jean Kim (2015), Alexander Weheliye (2014) and Lindgren Johnson (2017) have elaborated the yoking of race and animality in a US context, contending that 'race is forged in the crucible of ideas about animality and nature' (Kim 2015: 25). Weheliye especially, building on the work of Hortense Spillers and Sylvia Wynter, offers a useful way of thinking about race as 'a conglomerate of sociopolitical relations that discipline humanity into full humans, not-quite-humans, and nonhumans' (2014: 3). Elsewhere, Sunaura Taylor's *Beasts of Burden* vividly elaborates how dis/ability structures these sociopolitical relations, revealing across its pages how ableism and its assumed boundaries of normalcy are implicated with narrowly human-centred notions of whose lives matter.

Within these disciplines, 'anthropocentrism' has become the keyword for theorizing this dual domination of human and nonhuman life. Thought of by Donna Haraway as a 'fantasy of human exceptionalism' (2008: 11), anthropocentrism is often said to connote a patently false perspective that positions the human at the centre of all thought and life, thereby decoupling humanity from nature and laying the epistemological and ontological foundations for the domination of nature.[8] In a sense, anthropocentrism has replaced what used to be called *speciesism*, coined by Richard Ryder but popularized by Peter Singer across his foundational yet much-criticized writings on utilitarian ethics and animal rights. Yet there are crucial differences between these terms. While Singer has it that speciesism explains how humans permit the 'interests of their own species to override the greater interests of members of other species' (Singer 1975: 7), the term 'anthropocentrism' names a more exclusionary logic, institutionalized within societies, that makes and sustains dominant modes and practices of human superiority. If speciesism is, therefore, personal and prejudicial, anthropocentrism has been claimed as its systemic articulation. As Matthew Calarco has it, anthropocentrism gives a name to a network of 'systems of power that are in the service of those who are considered by the dominant culture to be fully and properly human' (2015: 25–6). Anthropocentrism's invocation thus calls attention to how human–animal relations are structured by systems – legal, economic and so on – that are built *for* particular humans.

Yet in this book I will be more interested in *anthroponormativity* than anthropocentrism.[9] Shifting the emphasis from one to the other is, I think, vitally important, primarily because enduring forms of human domination are not simply 'centred' but rather produced and reproduced as a norm. In other words, my problem with the term 'anthropocentrism' is that it lacks the very systemic focus that its exponents think it captures. Anthropocentrism has already received forceful criticisms for its ahistorical and idealist fixation on attitudes and individual behaviours, as well as its flattening of human difference into a generalized species-level vantage point that overlooks crucial inequalities *within* human communities. In her incisive book *What Is Nature?*, Kate Soper also raises the question of anthropocentrism's inescapability. Soper suggests that while many posthumanists call for a decentering of the human, there is in actual fact 'no way of conceiving our relations to [nature] other than through the mediation of ideas about ourselves. To suggest that it could be otherwise is to be insensitive to those ways in which the rest of nature is different, and should be respected as being so' (1995: 13).[10] Even the most reflexive and ecologically attuned human attitudes towards nature are, in the end, in some way, anthropocentric.

But it is anthropocentrism's inherently spatial logic that worries me, implying as it does that the war against animals might one day be overcome if the human is simply decentred, and/or if the animal is centred. This falls into the trap of extensionism, an ethical position – well known among pro-animal communities – that assumes that existing moral considerations and legal protections should or could be extended outwards towards nonhumans. It must be said here that it is often a major victory when nonhuman animals are recognized as sentient beings and afforded more rights under the law. But this cannot be the limit of our political imagination, not least because extensionism in the abstract tends to accept the law as it is, despite its norms being premised on historically contingent human principles such as individual freedom, and despite it being fundamentally insufficient not just for nonhumans but also for millions of impoverished humans across the planet who have no recourse to justice. Calls to decentre the human and centre the nonhuman therefore risk being absorbed within the 'pragmatic pursuits' (Wolfe 2008: 137) of a liberal humanism which is constrained, if not entirely contradicted, by its own imperfect compatibility with a contemporary capitalism that produces the hierarchizing of human and nonhuman life.

The analytical advantage of a term like 'anthroponormativity' is that it considers how the continued invention of 'man' is concomitant with the invention of an othered animality. By shifting the discussion away from spatiality and representation (who or what is centred?) towards more systemic questions (what produces this centring in the first place, when and how, under what conditions and to what ends?), anthroponormativity at once sharpens animal studies' interrogation of species hierarchies while also firming up the connections that link this critical pursuit to the critique of 'man' articulated by feminist, postcolonial and critical race studies. For me, anthroponormativity captures more clearly how dominant norms codify a particular idea of the sovereign human subject. It is a concept that helps us makes sense of how the alienation from and mastery of nature cannot be resolved without also thinking through the limits of subjectivity itself. And I therefore think that this concept also gets us closer to understanding how the projects of decolonization and feminism are also projects of animal liberation: all of these are, fundamentally, struggles against the de-wilding, the ongoing *anthroponormalization*, of planetary life.

Modernity has been a project of anthroponormativity, of human mastery and supremacy. Anthroponormativity is what guides the war against the animal while also being continually consolidated by it. Yet this does not mean that modernity exhausts all possibilities for interspecies compassion. Literature, I will argue, is able to imagine forms of deliberate and careful attention towards animals that interrupt this invention of man and open up new opportunities for cultivating a more-than-human ethics. Across contemporary literature there are not only *scenes* of human–animal interaction that depict or combat the war against animals. There are also *literary forms* that compel new ways of relating to other creatures.

Reading for animals

What would it mean, then, to narrate the war against animals? And how do our readings of literary texts change if we were to think of literature as being, at some level, an aesthetic registration of the social experience of the war against animals? With its call to read for animals, literary animal studies offers a valuable way into discussing these questions. Studying the ubiquitous yet often marginal presence of animals in literary texts, and placing special emphasis on the ways in which textual animals register and refract real relations between species, literary animal studies thinks through 'the ways in which animals appear in texts, are represented and figured, in and for themselves and not as displaced metaphors for the human' (Simons 2002: 6). To read the scholarship of Margot Norris (1985), Marian Scholtmeijer (1993), Philip Armstrong (2008), Susan McHugh (2011), Ortiz Robles (2016), Catherine Parry (2017) and Timothy C. Baker (2019) is to encounter a deep engagement with questions of how representations of animals transform across literary history. In an agenda-setting review essay that asks 'What Kind of Literary Animal Studies Do We Want, or Need?', Robert McKay encapsulates the key insights of a field gaining in methodological coherency: to read for animals, he suggests, is to 'conscientiously attend to the representational complexity of cultural imaginings of animals' lives and deaths, and of the manifold encounters with the humans that often mark the passage from one to the other' (2014: 637). Literature continuously inscribes specific and mutable human ideas and feelings about animals. Animal studies notices this inscription, indeed reads for it, thereby interpreting textual animals as 'disruptive presences that challenge our understanding of textual significance and figuration', as Colleen Glenney Boggs puts it (2013: 189).

Although literary animal studies has developed an important analysis of what Mario Ortiz Robles has called the 'demands animals place on literary representation' (2016: xi), it has been less rigorous in its articulation of the relationship between representation, form and the politics of literature. Indeed in the recent *Palgrave Handbook of Animals and Literature*, a flagship publication and distillation of the field's insights, the phrase 'literary form' appears just twice across the book's 636 pages. Despite its forty-two contributors' occasional analyses of how genre and forms transform across literary history, much of their analysis remains wedded to representational modes of interpreting animals. Something similar is at work in Timothy C. Baker's *Writing Animals*, a notable survey of how animals appear in and function within twenty-first-century fictions. Baker's guiding argument throughout is that nonhuman animals worry away at literature's own inherent humanism, thereby challenging species hierarchies. Despite literature's role as a linguistic site of inescapably *human* meaning-making, Baker argues, the textual presence of animals – whether central or peripheral – challenges 'the stability of linguistic representation, and the implied anthropocentrism of the novel form' (2019: 8). Yet for a book which sets out to trouble the 'inherently human paradigm' (5) of the literary artefact, Baker offers no conceptualizations of literature as a site of ontological production and no theorizations of the novel form. *Writing Animals*, like many other works of literary animal studies, therefore ends up challenging species hierarchies only at the level of representation, ultimately defanging its own proposed intervention into the boundaries of form and genre.

In this section, then, I wish to think more precisely about the necessary interrelation of literary representation and the politics of form, and to ask: How does literature intervene in the question of the animal? What is at stake in the narration, even formalization, of the war against animals? In other words, how do we read for animals and form simultaneously, and what critical insights are uncovered through such methods of reading? Asking these questions will be important, I think, not just because it will allow us rethink and revitalize the current predispositions and critical repertoires of literary animal studies. It will also generate new perspectives on the anthroponormative tendencies of literature itself, thereby articulating a specifically posthumanist challenge to dominant practices of literary criticism. In doing so, I wish to build on the work of scholars like Susan McHugh, whose book *Animal Stories* argues that the formal composition of texts themselves is pivotal sites in the ongoing ideological production of species difference. But where McHugh focuses specifically on the liveliness of animal agency, analysing texts – such as Virginia Woolf's *Flush* – that are animal-centred if not entirely animal-narrated, this book is concerned with human-narrated stories of human–animal relations.

My understanding of creaturely forms derives from a joint reading of critiques of the politics of literature on the one side and theorizations of human–animal difference on the other. I will focus first on the politics of literature, beginning with the work of French philosopher Jacques Rancière. For Rancière, the politics of literature does not necessarily correspond with the politics of individual authors. Instead, literature 'does politics' simply by being literature; literature has a fundamental stake in the political insofar as it simultaneously shares out and divides up what is sensible, sayable or perceptible. Rancière develops this idea through the formulation *'le partage du sensible'* (2011: 3), a phrase often translated as the distribution or partition of the sensible. Each and every literary text is political because its formal articulation recomposes what counts politically, what is sensible or intelligible. In contradistinction to what Rancière calls the classical Aristotelian dictum that great art imitates great men, the modern phenomenon of literature abandons hierarchical mimesis and, instead, carries 'new objects and subjects onto the common stage. It makes visible what was invisible, it makes audible as speaking beings those who were previously heard as noisy animals' (5).

When Rancière discusses the literature of modernity as a regime of visibility, he is talking about specific forms of writing that begin to circulate in Europe around the turn of the nineteenth century. His main points of reference are Madame de Staël, Flaubert, Balzac and Victor Hugo. By discussing literature's 'noisy animals', then, he is referring to none other than the working class, the proletarian labourers who not only began to feature within the novel form but also took to writing in order to form new political communities. Rancière's Marxist contemporaries, Pierre Macherey and Etienne Balibar, argued that the emergence of literature announces a restrictive 'bourgeois cultural revolution' (1978: 6). In contrast, Rancière thinks of literature as a democratic horizon for class consciousness, a horizon for the 'construction of a common world' (2011: 3) in which 'certain objects are posited as shared and certain subjects regarded as capable of designating these objects and of arguing about them' (5). Rancière thus sees literature as calling forth a new democratic chorus, a thought that echoes Mikhail Bakhtin's notions of heteroglossia and polyphony, of literature expressing 'the consciousness of real people' (Bakhtin 1981: 292). For Rancière, literature is a kind of apparatus, a logic and *dispositif* that recognizes previously unrecognized subjectivities, making them count politically. Literature reconfigures the archive of who is understood to be human.

Yet we must not lose sight of the ambivalence at the heart of Rancière's position. Literature might well be a profoundly democratic form in that it opens up new ways of writing, reading and responding to the world. But this does not necessitate that a given text's redistribution of the sensible is necessarily on the side of democracy, let alone on the side of the animal. While some literary works may well recompose the boundaries of the political, others might retrench or contract the political. Think, for example, of the prototypical English realist novel, which critics have long argued invented a narrow kind of autonomous, liberal personhood. Ian Watt's foundational study *The Rise of the Novel* details how the novel form erupts at the very moment in which eighteenth-century England crystallized its notion of individualism, assimilating Lockean and Cartesian philosophies of sensory perception alongside high marketplace capitalism and empire (1968: 17–18, 62). Nancy Armstrong's *How Novels Think* points out that 'the history of the novel and the history of the modern subject are, quite literally, one and the same' (2005: 3). For Armstrong, the early novel emerges as a form which fabricates a supposedly universal human subject and thereafter guards this rhetorical figuration as if it were the only type of humanity, invalidating alternative genres of subjectivity in the process. More recently, John Frow's rigorous study of literary character and personhood argues that, to this day, the novel form utilizes 'the affective and moral technologies of self-shaping inwardness that… inform much of our contemporary understanding of what it means to be a person' (2014: x).

Or perhaps we could take the classic *Bildungsroman* as another example of a genre that has functioned as a 'machine for producing… centred subjects', as Fredric Jameson puts it (1996: 182). In its prototypical form, the *Bildungsroman* stands as an ostensibly humanist novel of developmental subjectivization, one which articulates a tension between individual psychological depth and a broader social panorama as a protagonist, usually a young man, navigates the tensions between an emergent autonomy and responsibility. Foundational analyses have framed the form as typically humanizing, in which protagonists' education, meant broadly, leads them to 'identify with humanity' (Redfield 2006: 193). According to Jed Esty's (2012) and Joseph Slaughter's (2007) postcolonial critiques of the *Bildungsroman*, the form even cooperates with the 'Enlightenment project to modernize, normalize, and civilize' (2007: 5) the human subject. Because the *Bildungsroman* sought to announce 'humankind's coming of age – the *Bildung* of the species' (Slaughter 2007: 107), it defines its notion of the human against colonized humans and nonhumans who supposedly cannot be civilized. Looked at this way, literary forms like the early novel and the *Bildungsroman* become discursive formations of restricted humanization, in which a narrow subjectivity is forged in contradistinction to other humans and nonhumans. We will see in Chapter 4 how Mahasweta Devi rewrites the *Bildungsroman* into a more creaturely form.

Finally we might look to the Victorian realist novel and how its increasing thematization of domesticity and sentimentality came to rely on the presence of domesticated animal figures. As Ivan Kreilkamp puts it in *Minor Creatures*, 'the history of English domestic fiction is deeply bound up with that of the domestic animal' (2018: 1). Tracking the role of pet ownership and animal life in Victorian fiction, Kreilkamp observes that novels like *Wuthering Heights*, *Jane Eyre* and *David Copperfield* are works of domestication that symbolically humanize certain animals away from 'nature' into culture, doing so in order to imagine the home as a space of sentimental humanistic care. Yet these animals, because they are never granted protagonicity, are ultimately *minor creatures*, 'treated as *semi*human in the role of culture and *semi*characters in the realm of literature' (17). Thus Victorian literature participates 'in a process of dividing up the world in humans (individuals capable, ideally or supposedly, of becoming protagonists or full-fledged characters) and nonhumans (things and animals that fall below the threshold of the characterological)' (2). These novels' supposed domestic ethics of goodness is thematically and formally troubled by their only partial formal incorporation of other creatures.

This problem has not gone away. Indeed, the environmental crisis we face today has made the question of literature's humanizing tendencies ever more pressing. The Indian novelist Amitav Ghosh has explicated as much in *The Great Derangement*, his lecture series on literature and climate change. Here, Ghosh argues that because the novel form's historical development dovetails with modernity's disenchantment from nature, the 'contemporary literary novel' (2016: 27) – by which he means contemporary literature in its most dominant, celebrated and canonized forms – is structurally discouraged and formally obstructed from grappling with the urgency of a warming planet. As Ghosh puts it, 'it was exactly the period in which human activity was changing the earth's atmosphere that the literary imagination became radically centred on the human' (66). The novel form is thus founded on a suppression and alienation from nature and the animal. And this has real ramifications for the novel form's reckoning with climate catastrophe, Ghosh argues, first because the scale of climate change is almost incomprehensibly large, and second because the deeply ingrained tendencies of literary fiction are simply not used to doing this sort of comprehension, this sort of narration. I will have more to say about Ghosh's literary works in my conclusion.

We have arrived, then, at an understanding of how the politics of literature and the specific formal development of the novel relate to the invention of modern conceptions of human subjectivity. Looked at from this perspective, the institution of literature comes to appear to us like a machine that makes the human, that produces particular ideas of what it means to be human. In other, more critical words, literature functions as an *anthropological machine*, a creative contraption of biopower that forges and polices a border between 'human' and 'animal' life. I take this concept from Giorgio Agamben, who, in *The Open: Man and Animal*, describes the anthropological machine as an apparatus and tool for anthropogenesis that continually 'decides upon and recomposes the conflict between man and animal' (2004: 75). Agamben's work unfolds two models of this apparatus: an ancient machine, which humanizes the animal, and a modern machine, which animalizes the human. If for the ancients 'the slave, the barbarian, and the foreigner' appear as 'figures of an animal in human form' (37), then in the post-Darwinian world, the modern anthropological machine 'isolates the nonhuman within the human' (37), allowing for some humans to be ontologically cast as animal. The anthropological machine is thus 'an occurrence that is always under way' (79), recording and producing particular inclusions of the human, 'articulat[ing] nature and man in order to produce the human through the suspension and capture of the inhuman' (83). For Agamben, its modern iteration marks a new rift between humanity and nature, between the human and animality, that ultimately clarifies how we make sense of the colonial and genocidal impulses and projects of modernity, from the figure of the refugee to the Nazi persecution of Jews.[11]

By bringing literary theory and human–animal difference together in this way, I wish to think about literature's redistribution of the sensible as continually deciding between the human and the animal, between hegemonic anthroponormativities and other forms or genres of living, between speaking beings and noisy animals. Put differently, certain works and forms of literature are complicit with and sustain the modern anthropological machine. They discursively inscribe human exceptionalism against those other beings – inhuman, nonhuman – who are not determined to be sufficiently human. This gives us a new way of approaching the study of narrative form and ideology. In her development of a feminist narratology, for instance, Susan Lanser puts it well that literature is at once 'a means of communicating ideology', 'an ideological construct itself' and a means of 'resisting ideology' (1981: 100–1). There are fictions, then, that function as anthropological machines, producing the human they pretend only to describe, narrowing down the genres of the human and reinforcing the war against animals. From sentence to chapter to plot, narrative decisions are also decisions about which lives count, which lives are intelligible or sensible as lives.

But let me not be mistaken. My point here is not that novels are necessarily anthroponormative, nor is it that literary fiction is inevitably bound to reproduce the anthropological machine. Stuart Hall once wrote that any answer to the much-debated question of whether the novel is a bourgeois form 'can only be historically provisional: When? Which novels? For whom? Under what conditions?' (2019: 356). So too does this answer obtain when discussing literature's articulations and formalizations of human–animal relations, which are not predetermined but highly contingent. Moreover, although forms are historically produced and anchored, they also contain unexpected or latent uses that, down the line, might even be harnessed against their own original and continuing conditions of production. Critics have long pointed out that the prototypical forms of the novel exert a gravitational pull, the force of which compels the differential repetition of common tropes, figures, patterns and ideas. I would add to this that the war against animals, despite shifting and transforming across space and place, is also an abiding characteristic and condition of modernity that structures the very conditions under which literary writing has been conducted and constructed. And yet this does not prevent texts from self-consciously recognizing and tussling with literature's own participation in such processes of exclusive humanization, nor does it preclude the plasticity or elasticity of literary forms themselves, which – as I will suggest throughout this book – can be reconstructed in ways which undermine their apparent anthroponormativities.

What I wish to stress here, then, is that *Creaturely Forms in Contemporary Literature* is working towards a dialectical analysis of how literary form pertains to the subjectivation and narratability of life. Under this analysis, literary forms are understood as constraining and enabling a confrontation with, or re-thinking of, the war against animals. To put it modestly, I wish to argue that literature's distribution of the sensible is involved in the ongoing partition of species difference. Some texts function as anthropological machines that invent the human at the cost of the animal. Others, I will suggest, hesitate to make this decision; they wish, if anything, to interrupt literature's machinic production of anthroponormativity, and to express a creaturely concern for other animals. Agamben himself concludes *The Open* by envisioning a horizon of creaturely relations between species, one in which the anthropological machine is finally brought to a standstill:

> To render inoperative the machine that governs our conception of man will therefore mean no longer to seek new – more effective or more authentic – articulations, but rather to show the central emptiness, the hiatus that – within man – separates man and animal, and to risk ourselves in this emptiness: the suspension of the suspension, Shabbat of both animal and man.
>
> (2003: 92)

If the dominant conception of personhood is bound up with genocidal violence against other animals, human and nonhuman, then reconciliation will only be found inside creaturely emptiness, that is, inside the very ontological gulf that supposedly separates 'animal and man'. This is an enormous and enormously difficult task to realize out there, in the world. But less so in fiction, in which a given text's imaginative mediation of social relations between species can generate new ideas of how to live with and alongside animals. The work of narrative does not amount to a material contestation of socio-ecological catastrophe. Yet fiction can re-write our socio-ecological conjuncture. It can articulate, and hence formalize, different human–animal futures.

By turning to writers such as W. G. Sebald, J. M. Coetzee and Mahasweta Devi, I will explore works that are less anthropological machines and more creaturely forms. Creaturely forms, I propose, are those works of literature that do not want to decide between the two figures of animal and man. These are texts which stage human–animal relations in ways that seek to pause the anthropological machine's decisionist logic, coming up against and recomposing the limits of their particular literary forms in the process. It is not the purpose of this book to argue that texts like these divest literature of its anthroponormativities. Rather my focus is on those moments of generative contradiction in which literature's anthroponormativity is destabilized by writers who articulate an attentiveness towards animality, who adopt different literary forms to tell different stories about humanity's relationship with other animals. If I have been thinking of literature as an apparatus that formalizes notions of subjectivity in contradistinction to nonhuman life, then in this book I will be discussing authors whose works do not resolve but bear witness to this very problem.

The creaturely: a partial genealogy

The creaturely, I have suggested, is a concept which proposes to blur the supposedly fixed, supposedly settled categories of the human and the animal. But as I write today, the term is itself rather blurry. During the research and writing of this book, I created a growing list of newly published articles, monographs, edited collections and literary magazines which engage with the 'creaturely' for various, often contradictory critical ends.[12] This list included Pieter Vermeulen and Virginia Richter's essay on 'creaturely constellations', which itself notes how the term, despite its fluctuations, has tended to map 'the human's exposure to – and uncanny overlap with – their natural and supernatural others' in modernity

(2015: 2). Yet in spite of these recent publications, there are a host of significations and theorizations of the creaturely that still remain largely unaddressed. It is therefore worth spending a few pages with the creaturely, attending to its uses, locating some of its mutations and appropriations, and critically exploring its contemporary meanings.

By recovering the creaturely's genealogy, I aim to tell the story of a word, and to make the case that the creaturely is an instructive concept for those of us who think that human and animal liberation are bound together. In the end, I will offer a conceptual reconstruction of the creaturely, arguing that it denotes forms of life that are excluded from the genre of the human *and* offers a joined-up, solidaristic vision of reconciliation between different beings, human and nonhuman. At heart, the creaturely destabilizes the fixity of the opposing terms 'human' and 'animal' while also addressing a wider question of who or what is counted as fully human.

The creaturely derives from the late Latinate neologism *creatura*, from the verb *creare*, meaning 'to create'. With its *-ura* suffix, *creatura* implies something created, or something that is 'always in the process of undergoing creation... perpetually becoming created' (Lupton 2000: 1). We might think of creature alongside similarly suffixed words like 'culture', 'nature' or 'figure', all of which are phenomena that transform, move and hence resist easy categorization or ossification. For much of its usage as a concept, *creatura* has been associated with theological notions of creation, denoting the idea of both a created being and a world or environment. In the late Middle Ages, the adjectival form of creaturely, or *kreatürlich*, became synonymous with *Geschöpf*, meaning a being of God's creation. It was used in this context until the Enlightenment in the eighteenth century, when the more secular concept of nature began to dominate and thus demarcate a firmer distinction between social and biological life (see Hanssen 1998: 103–4). While 'creature' was still used to refer to other humans who might invoke pity or horror, it became more associated with signifying 'monstrosity' and 'unnatural' creations (Lupton 2000: 1).

Despite its waning usage in capitalist modernity, the creaturely's theological connotations nevertheless persisted into the twentieth century. Indeed the poet and philosopher Martin Buber saw the creaturely as a keyword of his German-Jewish intellectual project.[13] In 1926, Buber published the inaugural issue of a short-lived interdominational and socialist journal, *Die Kreatur*, writing in its opening editorial that he intended to create a new cross-faith dialogue founded on a 'common concern for the creature' [*gemeinsame Sorge um die Kreatur*] (Buber et al. 1926: 1). 'This journal', he adds, 'will speak of the world – of all beings, of all things, of all events of our contemporary world – in a way that reveals its creaturely nature' (1). By imagining the creaturely as an obscured foundation of contemporary life, Buber harnessed the concept as a universal that could foster a Christian-Jewish dialogue pointed towards the horizon of socialism.[14]

But it is one of *Die Kreatur*'s erstwhile contributors, Walter Benjamin, who would push the creaturely into new ontological and political directions, loading the term with more and more meanings. In Benjamin's breathless essay-report on his 1926 visit to the capital of the Soviet Union, submitted for publication in *Die Kreatur*'s second issue, he makes no explicit mention of the creaturely. But in a letter to Buber, sent in 1927, Benjamin defends his essay's inclusion in the journal on the grounds that it strives to 'give voice to the creaturely [*das Kreaturliche*]' by 'grasping and preserving this very new, strange language which loudly resounds through the acoustical mask of an environment that has been utterly transformed' (Benjamin cited in Buber 1996: 350). His essay, which pairs revolutionary fervour with a rapid, repetitive and anaphoric literary style, sets out to listen to this 'acoustical mask', noticing how 'Each thought, each day, each life lies here as on a laboratory table... No organism, no organization, can escape this process' (Benjamin 2003: 28). For Benjamin, the creaturely thus names something both aesthetic and ontological, at once capturing the seemingly total transformations, experimentations and improvisations of a society that is creating itself anew *and* the language or sound of this process as it reverberates around the city.

Benjamin's contribution to *Die Kreatur* marks just one instance of a wider intellectual engagement with the creaturely. Across two and a half decades of writing, Benjamin adopts the term for aesthetic, theological and ontological ends, often positioning the creaturely somewhere between Jewish Gnosticism and Marxist dialectics, at what Andrew Benjamin calls the 'curious intersection of theology and materialism' (2005: 109). On the one side, Benjamin turns to the creaturely when explaining the postlapsarian condition, sovereign power in epic theatre, the melancholia of created nature and secularization's 'reduction of the human being to the creaturely state' (Weigel 2013: 12). He argued that this pitiful reduction or exposure of the human subject to the elements was frequently expressed by the mourning play, or *Trauerspiel*, a dramatic form preoccupied with the 'hopelessness of the earthly condition' (2009: 81), in which tragic characters stood abandoned and alone, vulnerable to transience and devoid of anything beyond mere existence.

And yet as much as Benjamin utilizes the creaturely to name a negative condition or affliction of immediate, animalistic suffering in the secularizing age of capitalist modernity, he also asks how this deprived mode of life opens up new political possibilities. In his writing on surrealism, for instance, Benjamin praises the works of the dramatist Georg Büchner for developing a vision of 'anthropological materialism', a combination of 'political materialism and physical creatureliness' that situates human biological vulnerability within the project of 'dialectical justice' (2003: 217). The creaturely, standing now as 'the figure of modernity' (Nägele 2004: 161), thus refigures revolutionary politics as an expression of collective finitude rather than promethean energy carried by the winds of teleology.

Although Benjamin describes this creaturely politics as anthropological, it is by no means anthroponormative. When Benjamin turns to the creaturely, he often ends up interrogating the very borders and predominance of the human subject, calling for an ethical orientation towards animals in the process. As Beatrice Hanssen demonstrates in her exhaustive study, *Walter Benjamin's Other History*, Benjamin draws on the creaturely as part of an 'all-inclusive turn towards nature', developing 'a renewed attention to what traditionally was considered to be less than human', thereby breaking 'the confines of the merely human' (1998: 106–7). Physical creatureliness, then, signals that the human is a creature among other creatures, bound by earthly limitations. We can locate Benjamin's thinking on human–animal relations in fragments like 'Gloves', one of sixty aphorisms included in *One-Way Street*, his kaleidoscopic reflection on modernity, urbanization and Weimar-era economic misery:

> In an aversion to animals the predominant feeling is fear of being recognized by them through contact. The horror that stirs deep in man is an obscure awareness that in him something lives to akin to the animal that it might be recognized... He may not deny his bestial affinity with the creature [*bestialische Verwandtschaft mit der Kreatur*], the invocation of which revolts him: he must make himself its master [*Herrn*].
>
> (1928: 14; 1997: 50–1)

For Benjamin, the modern figure of 'man' is so repulsed by his latent affinities with nature that he abjects and disavows the animal. Through the metaphor of gloves, Benjamin describes how man refuses contact with the animal, thus sustaining the fantasy of exceptionalism, obscuring any awareness of kinship and authorizing his mastery over other species.

While Benjamin's *One-Way Street* bears witness to the ways in which 'man' separates himself from nature, his 1934 essay on Franz Kafka's literary project points more towards a reconciliation through the notion of *attentiveness*. 'Even if Kafka did not pray', Benjamin writes, 'he still possessed in the highest degree what Malebranche calls "the natural prayer of the soul": attentiveness [*Aufmerksamkeit*]. And in this attentiveness he included all creatures, as saints include them in their prayers' (2005: 810). Benjamin reads Kafka's work as developing a literary attentiveness towards creaturely life, arguing that his writing incorporates nonhuman animals in a substantive and generous way, like a form of prayer. In fact, Benjamin writes, 'of all Kafka's creatures, the animals have the greatest opportunity for reflection' (810). Perhaps Benjamin has Red Peter in mind, Kafka's melancholy ape from *A Report to an Academy*, whose performance of an acquired humanness ultimately calls into question the ostensibly fixity of human identity as such. In Coetzee's *The Lives of Animals*, which I will discuss in Chapter 3, Elizabeth Costello describes Red Peter as a hybrid creature whose capacity for reflection is shaped by his awareness of being a 'branded, marked, wounded animal' (2001: 26).

Benjamin also writes of Kafka's animals as being 'receptacles of the forgotten' (2005: 810). With this deceptive formulation, Benjamin wants to capture how Kafka's animals act as receivers, keepers and guardians of what modernity forgets, namely the relation between humans and other animals. Kafka's texts, by staging Red Peter's melancholia and Josefine's faltering singing voice, offer readers an opportunity to glimpse this forgotten knowledge, and to consequently remember and reimagine forms of relationality, within and across species, that are constantly obstructed by the war against animals. Across Benjamin's work, then, the creaturely represents a fracturing of anthroponormativity, as it signifies a being marked by an 'indeterminacy that puts the borders between particular life forms in question. The creature thus becomes a being that dwells in the gaps between species, a threat to the very system of classification' (Abbot 2008: 86). The creaturely invokes a dethroning of the human as the pinnacle of an evolutionary hierarchy and a consequent recuperation of a lost relationality between humans and other animals.[15]

Today, as academic discourses increasingly foreground the question of life, the creaturely has resurfaced as a paradigmatic yet volatile concept, caught up in an ongoing debate between humanists and pro-animal thinkers. Eric Santner, for instance, invokes the creaturely as a uniquely human biopolitical exposure to modern sovereignty and governmentality. For him, human subjectivity is so materially and psychologically beholden to the sovereign decision that humans are '*more creaturely* than other creatures' (2006: 26). Creaturely life hence names an 'ontological vulnerability… that permeates human being' (2011: 5–6), a form of 'biopolitical animation that distinguishes the human from the animal' (2006: 39). In contrast, Anat Pick's *Creaturely Poetics* contends that creaturely life is a shared condition of vulnerability that transcends species difference. Creatureliness is not specific to human subjectivity, Pick contends, but rather a biologically continuous category which signifies what it means to be 'first and foremost a living body – material, temporal, and vulnerable' (2011: 5–6). Santner and Pick are both indebted to Benjamin's work on the creaturely. They both share a similar critical vocabulary. They also ask the same fundamental question: whose lives, whose bodies and minds, are exposed to the machinations of political power? But they nevertheless reach antithetical conclusions. For Santner, the creaturely signifies the uniqueness of human subjectivity. For Pick, it connotes an interspecies ethics founded on vulnerability. Adopting a distinctly theological register, Pick crafts a vision of creaturely ethics founded on the idea that animals are saintly figures. Her study can therefore be read as an articulation of what Mari Ruti calls the 'posthumanist quest for the universal' (2015: 193), a critical theory that wishes to build an ethical universalism without the purported trappings of metaphysical humanism.

Both of these positions contain their problems. Santner's critique of sovereign power clearly relies on its own sovereign claim of human exceptionalism, while Pick's emphasis on animal vulnerability risks a purely negative universalism that misses out on how desires, wants and demands might ally humans and nonhumans together. But if there is one form which can build a bridge between these oppositional accounts of creaturely life, or at least stage them as antinomies, it is literature. For within literature, readers can be granted access to worlds which attest to the irreducibly distinctive perspective of human characters while also imagining a cross-species ethics that disabuses human exceptionalism and exceeds human community. As we will see in Chapters 3 and 4, texts like Coetzee's *Disgrace* and Mahasweta's *Pterodactyl* are narrated from specifically human positions which affirm the psychological complexity and ontological vulnerability of human life. But at the same time their wider formal mechanisms of plotting, characterization and metaphorics also draw attention to the relationship between humans and other forms of life. Novels and stories like these simultaneously point to the differences *and* connections between species, imagining forms of human subjectivity which are different but not superior, distinct but not exceptional. This is, ultimately, what separates *Creaturely Forms in Contemporary Literature* from the work of Santner and Pick. Although I share Pick's impulse to forge new nonviolent relations between humans and other animals, in this book I am primarily concerned with the question of what literature can do to construct these new modes of creaturely relation.

The more I have conducted research into the creaturely, the more I have found it generative to return to the thinking of the first generation of the Frankfurt School who, as Fredric Jameson once pointed out, 'can be counted among the philosophical ancestors of the ecology movement [and] animal rights' (2007: 96). In the years surrounding the Second World War, Theodor W. Adorno and Max Horkheimer embraced the concept of the creaturely in order to reflect on modernity's twinned domination of human and nonhuman life. Retaining Benjamin's focus on mastery, exposure and relationality, but also thinking through how modernity's escalating catastrophes are conjoined with the mastery of animals, Adorno and Horkheimer articulate an idea of the creaturely as being paradoxically constitutive of both violent domination and peaceful reconciliation. The Frankfurt School's writing requires attention not just because it registers modernity's war against animals, not just because it builds on previous theorizations of the creaturely, but because its articulation of sympathy for animals develops – indeed hopes for – a future reconciliation between human and nonhuman life, between society and nature.

This is most consistently demonstrated in *Dialectic of Enlightenment*, a project which they frame as wanting to 'gain greater understanding of the intertwinement of rationality and social reality, as well as of the intertwinement, inseparable from the former, of nature and the mastery of nature' (2002: xviii). Across this foundational work of critical theory, Adorno and Horkheimer conceive of modernity as being predicated on a perpetual disarticulation of humanity from nature, an alienating 'denial of nature in human being' (43) which enables a form of domination that it disguises as rationality. They write polemically of the 'perfected exploitation of the animal world today' (204), noting how 'we owe the serum which the doctor administers to the sick child to the attack on defenceless creatures' (185), and deploring the military pilot who, with access to toxic chemicals, could 'cleanse the last continents of the last free animals' (185) in just a few short flights.

Modernity's denial of (its own) nature also creates the conditions for a 'systematic domination' (185) of other human beings. In fact, Adorno and Horkheimer suggest that the domination of other human beings *derives from* this domination of nature: 'What human beings seek to learn from nature is how to use it to dominate wholly both it and human beings' (2). Adorno explores this notion further in 'Man and Animal', a draft essay which argues that modernity fuses biological hierarchies to essentializing projections of gender and race. In the patriarchal division of labour, women are cast as 'an embodiment of biological function, an image of nature' (206). And the 'caricature of the Jew' mobilized by Nazism relies on the same logic of 'biological inferiority', a stigma and weakness that 'invites violence' (206). It is the 'fascist colossus' (210) who, for Adorno and Horkheimer, most dramatically emblematizes this logic in their pity for innocent animals and hatred of other human beings. The fascist's performed 'love of animals, nature, and children is the lust of the hunter. The idle stroking of the children's hair and animal pelts signifies: this hand can destroy' (210).

Although Adorno and Horkheimer describe modernity as a 'quagmire', they still hold out for a 'solidarity with creaturely life' (208).[16] More specifically, indeed more dialectically, they call for forms of interspecies compassion and solidarity – *Mitleid*, meaning literally to suffer-with – which, by recovering 'the infinite patience, the tender, never-extinguished impulse of creaturely life toward expression and light' (187), might defeat the domination of others. They wish, then, to master modernity's mastery of nature:

> By conquering the sickness of the mind which flourishes on the rich soil of self-assertion unhampered by reflection, humanity would cease to be the universal antirace and become the species which, as nature, is more than mere nature, in that it is aware of its own image. The individual and social emancipation from domination is the countermovement to false projection, and no longer would Jews seek, by resembling it, to appease the evil senselessly visited on them as on all the persecuted, whether animals or human beings.
>
> (165)

Adorno and Horkheimer's 'hope for better conditions' (187) is contained within the reflection, or remembrance, of humanity as being a part of nature, what Adorno elsewhere terms *Naturhaftigkeit*, or our 'naturalness' (cited in Rose 2014: 103). Only by recovering its place *within* nature will humanity reconstitute its differences *to* nature, transforming its relationship from false projection and persecution towards emancipation. In *Minima Moralia*, Adorno describes this emancipation as 'the possibility of reconciliation' (2005: 116) between species, one which depends on a concomitant understanding of immanence and difference, one which even loves 'what is alien and different' (1973: 172), as Adorno suggests in *Negative Dialectics*.[17] Alfred Schmidt, a student of Adorno's whose scholarship elaborated the role of nature in Marxism, would later conclude that 'There remains at best the vague hope, that men, having been reconciled with each other… will learn to a far greater degree to practice solidarity with the oppressed animal world, and that in the true society the protection of animals will no longer be regarded as a kind of private fad' (2014: 156). The point being: a reconciliation, or truce, will bring to an end the war against *the* animal.

The creaturely, then, gives a name to forms of life, human and nonhuman, that are identified within modernity as being more biological than social, more animal than human, more natural than historical, those subjects who, perceived as objects, are subsequently rendered abject, killable, ungrievable, bare or dehumanized. But the creaturely, as a critical term, also articulates a reconciliatory horizon, a hope for a day of emancipation in which all life stands peacefully as a part of a differentiated nature. Returning to Benjamin's and the Frankfurt School's early articulations of the creaturely allows us to recapture this doubled understanding of an attentiveness towards other forms of life and a repudiation of modernity's colonial mastery over other beings. These two senses of the creaturely will be crucial for this book's reading of contemporary literature. Throughout *Creaturely Forms*, I analyse how writers represent and formalize the creaturely. More than any other recent authors I know, W. G. Sebald, J. M. Coetzee and Mahasweta Devi use their literary forms to bear witness to the war against animals and imagine future possibilities of human–animal reconciliation.

Notes

1. What role do animals play in both Marx's writing and Marxism more generally? Some critics have mobilized Marx's own concepts in order to critique his work's 'fundamental opposition between human and animal nature' (Benton 1993: 23). Others have argued that Marx's humanism actually 'seeks a harmony between humanity and nature, in which "nature" comprises both human and non-human nature' (Wilde 2000: 38; see also Gunderson 2011). Still others have suggested that, whatever Marx's views of human–animal relations, his analysis can be productively applied and extended to, as well as reimagined for, the impacts that capitalism has on animal life (see Painter 2016: 331). These debates continue today, especially so in the exchanges between John Bellamy Foster and Brett Clark (2018), Christian Stache (2018) and Ted Benton (2019) in *Monthly Review*. Yet it must also be noted that such debates about Marxism and human–animal relations have been far less present within animal studies itself, excepting important work by Nicole Shukin (2009) and Dinesh Wadiwel (2015).
2. The meat and dairy industry has lobbied, often successfully, for the proliferation of anti-whistle-blower 'ag-gag' laws in the United States and Canada, which make it illegal to conduct undercover reporting of the living and dying conditions of farmed animals. See Fiber-Ostrow and Lovell (2016).
3. For more on fisheries, see important contributions from Longo et al. (2015), McCormack (2017) and Telesca (2020).

4   See also Quammen (2012).
5   The legal and illegal exotic wildlife trade, another major contributor to species extinctions (Collard 2020: 4), also increases the possibility of zoonotic disease transmission, as writers like Felbab-Brown (2017: 72) have shown.
6   See Smil (2013: 66).
7   See Kingsford et al. (2009), Barnosky et al. (2011) and Kolbert (2014).
8   For Gary Steiner, anthropocentrism is the name for a 'long and complex historical turn against the notion of natural continuity' (2005: 52). The veterinary doctor and philosopher Roberto Marchesini notes that there is 'no single form of anthropocentrism nor a homogeneity and solidity/coherence of the paradigm' (2016: 180).
9   I am grateful to Tom Tyler for sparking my thinking on anthroponormativity.
10 Soper also remains sceptical of anthropocentrism as a concept because it elides material conditions: 'The problem of the destruction of nature has to be located at the level of specific relations of production and consumption and cannot be attributed to some generalized set of human attributes or attitudes' (1995: 13). Andreas Malm takes up Soper's critique in order to argue for a necessary anthropocentrism: because humans are the only forms of life that can work collectively to prevent further environmental degradation, '*any* call for a more environmentally beneficial practice by necessity puts humans front and centre' (2018: 116–17). See also Soper (2012). The question, then, is whether we can acknowledge and be responsible for this necessary anthropocentrism without also reproducing anthroponormativity.
11 Agamben's biopolitical project has received forceful criticisms for its Eurocentrism (Weheliye 2014: 38). Yet I think we ought to complicate, rather than simply abandon, Agamben's thought.
12 This list included works of literary studies such as Vermeulen (2015), Herman (2016), Menely (2015), Anderton (2016), Thompson (2018) and Kreilkamp (2018); theological texts like Moore (2014), Deane-Drummond and Clough (2009); and the magazine *POLLEN*'s second issue, 'Creaturely Life' (Gell et al. 2016). See also Christine M. Korsgaard's *Fellow Creatures*, a tightly argued book that utilizes Kantian ethics in order to persuasively outline our obligation to other sentient animals as ends in themselves.
13 Although I am focusing here on a trajectory that connects Buber to Benjamin to the Frankfurt School, the concept of the creaturely also appears in the writing of Franz Rosenzweig, Karl Kraus, Bertolt Brecht and Paul Celan. For more on this, see Nägele (2004: 161) and Celan (2011).
14 For more on the journal *Die Kreatur*, see Petuchowsk (1995).
15 Benjamin was not the only thinker to write about the literary valences of the creaturely. As Vermeulen and Richter point out (2015: 4), Erich Auerbach's

monumental work of criticism *Mimesis* wagered that literary realism pertains to 'man's subjection to suffering and transitoriness' (Auerbach 1991: 249). For Auerbach, creatureliness signifies a 'radical theory of the equality of all men, not in an active and political sense but as a direct devaluation of life which affects every man individually' (250). Another foundational critic, György Lukács, understands the *Kreatur* as connoting 'organic limitations' (1971: 122). In his writing on the differences between Greek and modern tragedy, Lukács turns to the creaturely in order to grasp the changing function of solitude: although loneliness is present in Greek tragedy, he writes, in modern tragedies solitude becomes a problem unto itself. Modern tragic drama depicts 'the torment of a creature condemned to solitude and devoured by a longing for community' (45).

16 I developed my thinking on this issue by reading Dorahy (2014).
17 In *Negative Dialectics*, Adorno argues that the imperialist subject rages against and devours the other. A non-imperialistic subject, he suggests, would refuse 'the philosophical imperialism of annexing the alien. Instead, its happiness would in the fact that the alien, in the proximity it is granted, remains what is distant and different' (1973: 191).

2

W. G. Sebald's creaturely melancholia

After nature, melancholic connection

Right across his literary project, from his essays to his fiction, W. G. Sebald's distinctive prose style is driven by a single thematic and formal motif: connection. In Sebald's texts, everything appears to be contingent and interconnected. The unnamed narrators of *Vertigo* and *The Emigrants* constantly draw attention to what they call the 'connections between events that lay far apart but which seemed… to be of the same order' (2002c: 94). In *Austerlitz*, his final work, Sebald invents a protagonist who speaks in 'perfectly balanced sentences', connecting ideas together 'in a kind of historical metaphysic, bringing remembered events back to life' (2002a: 14). And in interviews, Sebald frames his work as developing an 'aesthetic sense' of 'making in prose a decent pattern out of what comes your way' (Sebald and Turner 2006: 24). He writes: 'I have slowly learned to grasp how everything is connected across space and time… dates of birth with dates of death, happiness with misfortune, natural history with the history of our industries, that of *Heimat* with that of exile' (2014: 149). Sebald's multimodal literary form, his combination of a digressive prose style with grainy black-and-white images, can thus be read as an exercise in connection. Both the content and the form of his works, the *what* and the *how*, are shaped by a connective vision.

Over two decades of scholarship, critics have recognized the signal importance of this poetics of connection. They have argued that it is the 'guiding principle' of his literary project (McCulloh 2003: 63), the 'underlying force of Sebald's fictional and in part scholarly writing' (Wolff 2014: 81). The 'question of connection, the problem of connection', Timothy Bewes writes, 'might be said to be the central preoccupation' (2014: 3) of Sebald's project.[1] However, there has been surprisingly little said about how Sebald's connective form relates to his works' underlying ecological concerns. Sebald's texts, narrated from within an environmentally damaged late-twentieth-century world, often bear witness to modernity's natural history of destruction: the dualistic severing of humanity from nature, the storing and encaging of animals in zoological and natural history institutions, deforestation and the burning of trees, the over-fishing of pelagic species and more. Sebald's narrators often find themselves encountering animals, facing them and exchanging gazes with them. In these moments, his characters come to not just mourn but identify with these lost creatures, as if his narrators, too, feel trapped within the anthropological machine of modernity. Through his texts' many acknowledgements of a shared human and animal suffering, Sebald's work might be said to cultivate a creaturely awareness.

What bearing, then, does Sebald's literary form have on this awareness of creaturely life? How might we read his first-person narration, natural-historical style, ambiguously indexical in-text images and hypotactic style as attempts to narrate the war against animals? These are the questions that I asked myself when I began making detailed notes on the many animals that populate Sebald's writing: cormorants, sea-cows, raccoons, hares, polar bears, moths, deer, beetles and sand martins. In so doing I found that Sebald's works are not simply biodiverse in content but that his figuration of animals plays a crucial role in his works' wider thematics, poetics and metaphorics. What's more, Sebald's portrayal of animals was predominantly pessimistic or melancholic, and hence strongly related to his texts' wider critique of modernity's impacts upon all forms of life. Across Sebald's works, individual animals and their wider species families are depicted as being in decline, on the wane; and yet, at the same time, Sebald shows how some animals' disappearance from nature is coeval with their increased appearance within human culture, in zoological gardens and in natural history cabinets.

It seemed to me, then, that Sebald's writing was to some extent preoccupied with animals. This hunch was lent more credence when I learnt that Sebald had lived as a vegetarian for ethical reasons.[2] Yet still I wanted to think more deeply about how his works thematically and formally dramatize human–animal relations. Beyond noting his texts' representational biodiversity, as other critics have done, I wanted to interrogate the formal politics of Sebald's writing of nature and animal life, as well as how this relates to his critical reception as a writer of historical trauma.

This chapter is an outcome of this thinking. Focusing on *The Rings of Saturn* and *Austerlitz*, I seek to develop a critical understanding of the opportunities and risks of what I will be calling Sebald's creaturely poetics of connection. Under my reading, Sebald's writing reconnects the human to the animal. It stages, through its connective form, a remembrance, or *re-membering*, of a shared creatureliness that has been forgotten, or broken, by modernity. To lay the foundations for this argument I will need to unpack three key propositions. First, that Sebald conceives of his writing as an attempt at restitution; he imagines his fiction as an ethico-aesthetic form of restitution which remembers the forgotten and re-members lost connections. Second, that we must locate Sebald's texts as taking place in a world after nature. The present tense scenarios of Sebald's texts, as well as the various historical pasts over which his narrators ruminate, are depicted as being contained within an epoch of modernity that severs and remakes the social ties between humans and animals. Third, that Sebald develops a form of *creaturely melancholia* which colours his drive to re-member. Folding these three propositions together enables us to interpret Sebald's poetics of connection as a kind of memorialization of damaged life in modernity, and as a melancholic struggle against the forces of anthroponormativity. The question that arises from this interpretation, then, is whether this ethico-aesthetic struggle, this melancholic poetics of connection, ultimately offers anything more than a consolatory registration, or memorialization, of a deteriorating nature. I will return to this question later.

I begin with 'Scattered Memories' ['*Zerstreute Reminiszenzen*'], a public address Sebald delivered at the opening of the *Literaturhaus Stuttgart* just a few weeks before his sudden death in the winter of 2001.[3] Often interpreted as a quiet manifesto of his literary philosophy, the speech sees Sebald confront a single question: 'what is literature good for?' (2006: 215). He answers, tentatively, by suggesting that the literary is an instantiation of remembrance and restitution: 'Perhaps only to help us remember', he says, before adding that 'there are many forms of writing; only in literature, however, can there be an attempt at restitution [*ein Versuch der Restitution*]' (215). Preoccupied with the question of 'what the function, value or responsibility of literature might be at the dawn of a millennium haunted by the catastrophic legacy of the recent past' (Baxter et al. 2013: 1), Sebald privileges the work of literature as an ethical undertaking, one in which the writer, by piecing together 'the invisible connections that determine our lives' (2006: 210), offers forms of solace and remembrance. And it is Sebald's own 'method of procedure' (215) that, he says, structures this remembrance: by 'linking together apparently disparate things' (215) with 'an exact historical perspective' (210), Sebald seeks to connect the scattered memories together. In *Austerlitz*, published in the same year as this speech, Sebald describes this kind of memory-work with the neologism '*Erinnerungsfähigkeit*' (2001a: 404), a recollective faculty which is eroding under the conditions of modernity.

But what does Sebald mean when he says that his writing marks 'an attempt at restitution' (2006: 215)? Who does Sebald interpellate when he speaks of 'those to whom the greatest injustice was done' (215)? Here, Sebald is, of course, gesturing towards the victims of the Holocaust, with the word 'restitution' invoking the repayments, reparations and return of goods. By deploying this term, then, Sebald continues a wider tendency in his work, engaging with the topic of the Holocaust but doing so only 'obliquely, tangentially, by reference rather than by direct confrontation' (Sebald quoted in Silverblatt 2007: 80). And yet at the same time Sebald situates this notion of restitution within a wider historical period, reflecting on contemporary conflicts, occupations and displacements in Sudan, Kosovo, Eritrea and Afghanistan while also describing Enlightenment modernity as having released an entire 'epoch of violence' (2006: 212). Sebald thus frames his project as pushing against this tide, addressing a community of the vanquished that includes but extends beyond the Holocaust.

I want to also argue that Sebald situates his texts in a period after nature, within a modernity that instrumentalizes and thus separates itself from the natural world. In this I follow the work of J. J. Long, who argues that the principal motifs of Sebald's work – including the Holocaust, trauma and memory, melancholia, photography, travel and *flânerie*, intertextuality and *Heimat* – are 'epiphenomena of a much wider "meta-problem"… That is the problem of modernity' (2007: 1). Defining modernity as 'the seismic social, economic, political and cultural transformations that took place in European societies from the eighteenth-century onwards' (1), Long suggests that Sebald's writing poses a distinct literary response to modernity. Although Long overlooks Sebald's *longue durée* perspective, which stretches back to the early modern period, his argument nonetheless has significant implications for how we interpret Sebald's writing, which still tends to be framed as a melancholic reflection on 'what it means to be human after the Holocaust' (Cosgrove 2011: 200). The implicit humanism of this argument encourages a narrow reading of Sebald's work. It neglects the ways in which Sebald connects the Holocaust to modernity, and it neglects too how Sebald connects modernity to the war against animals. For Sebald, the Holocaust is not an aberration but a culmination of modernity. It 'tests' the claims of modernity, as Zygmunt Bauman once put it (1989: 6), and is thus thought of as the extreme 'endpoint of a long history of oppression tied to the rise of capitalism and the modern European bourgeoisie' (Martin 2013: 124). Sebald derives the force of this position from Theodor W. Adorno and Max Horkheimer, who, as we saw in the previous chapter, considered fascism as something immanent to modernity and its domination of creaturely life. Sebald spoke openly of his debt to Adorno and the Frankfurt School's 'alternative perspective' on modernity (2014: 8). 'From thematic preoccupations to stylistic idiosyncrasies', Ben Hutchinson writes, Sebald's work is 'permeated by the thought-forms of Adorno' (2011: 268). It is from this basis that Sebald's texts articulate connections between genocide and ecocide, between the fascist organization and extermination of human life and the commodified production and slaughter of nonhuman life.

Considering the need, then, to give a fuller interpretation of Sebald's writing of nature and modernity, it is apposite to turn to his first literary work. *Nach der Natur: Ein Elementargedicht* is a triptych prose poem that spans five centuries. Through its focus on the lives of three men – the Renaissance painter Matthias Grünewald, the Enlightenment-era naturalist Georg Wilhelm Steller and an autobiographical 'I' born in the years immediately following the Second World War – the text explores the shifting relationship between humanity and nature in modernity. The massacre of peasants, the felling of forests and the forced enclosures of the commons in the sixteenth century; the taxonomic, anatomical and cartographic logics of the Enlightenment, and its attendant colonial projects; the systematic destruction of cities during the Second World War – Sebald's narrative poem connects all of these together into one history, a 'silent catastrophe' (2003: 87) of material and symbolic ruptures between the human and nature. Indeed for much of the poem Sebald mobilizes naturalistic motifs of entropy in order to depict how the 'progress of history' (96) hastens nature's unnatural deterioration into 'a state | of pure dementia' (50); 'life diminishes, | everything declines' (63). Steller's life's work, for example, a study and 'endless inventory' (74) of marine species, also includes charts for hunters and notes on the counting of pelts. This document of zoological knowledge is also a document of anthropogenic extinction. Progress thus *produces* decline. In witnessing this history, one of poem's principal effects is to estrange human subjectivity. At one point, Sebald writes that 'An animal | is a human, in deep | mourning shrouded' [*Ein Tier | ist der Mensch, in tiefe | Trauer gehüllt*] (1995a: 48–9; my translation). As the human is defamiliarized, becoming the object rather than the subject of the sentence, the animal is depicted as a mournful human.

While Michael Hamburger's English-language translation renders the poem's title as *After Nature*, the layered meanings of the original German title are more redolent. This is because '*nach der*' is contranymic, concomitantly signifying *after*, *from* and *drawn from* (as in 'representing'). The phrase *Nach der Natur* therefore expresses how modernity arises 'from', comes 'after' and is nevertheless 'drawn from' nature. Modernity breaks away from nature ideologically at the very moment at which it begins irrevocably altering nature materially. I wish to argue, then, that Sebald's texts understand the progress of modernity, the supposed overcoming of nature, as actually cleaving humanity and nature in the full sense of the contronym: modernity is predicated on a paradoxical separation and new entanglement with nature.

Finally, Sebald's connective work is written under the melancholic sign of Saturn. At one level, his prose echoes a classical sense of *acedia*, a mood of scholarly wisdom and astrological sadness without a cause, a feeling of seasonal imbalance and seasickness on the shore. At another, his writing engages with the Freudian theorization of melancholia as a pathological obsession with lost objects. Yet Sebald himself framed his melancholic gaze as pushing beyond the affect's inhibiting and repetitive despair. Rather than offering a purely nostalgic or hopeless perspective, Sebald argued, melancholia offers a 'form of resistance' to the violence of progress: 'In the description of the disaster lies the possibility of overcoming it' (Sebald and Turner 2006: 24). In this, Sebald's melancholia echoes Walter Benjamin's 'Theses on the Philosophy of History', in which Benjamin formulated a left-wing melancholia that, self-consciously fixating on the past, remembers the vanquished of yesterday in order to redeem today. This is why Susan Sontag described Sebald as a 'militant elegist' (2003: 89).

However, Sebald's melancholia appears to be notably weaker, more resigned and less dialectical that Benjamin's. In fact, Sebald's tendency to view history as one continual catastrophe risks reproducing the passive, discouraged and 'negativistic quiet' (Benjamin 2005: 425) that Benjamin himself once criticized in an essay on radical melancholia. Worse still, Sebald's consistent depiction of human history as a 'long account of calamities' (2002: 295), as he puts it in *The Rings of Saturn*, may well succumb to a fatalistic misanthropy. In fact, this is J. M. Coetzee's final interpretation of Sebald's narrators, whose lives, he says, tend to be 'defined by a hard-to-articulate sense that they do not belong in the world, that perhaps human beings in general do not belong here' (2007b: 145).

Sebald's melancholia is thus overdetermined: claimed as radical yet critiqued as antiquarian, formulated as a literary mode of historical resistance yet tending towards an ahistorical misanthropy. Sebald characterizes his narrators as Benjaminian figures, as critical historians of modernity. But his writing nonetheless expresses a pessimistic 'disappointment with the outcomes of quotidian post-enlightenment rationality in its social, cultural and political aspects' (Morgan 2005: 91). My view is that Sebald's literary writing exhibits what Nietzsche once called the critical *and* antiquarian standpoints (1997: 67). Sebald's work is, in other words, variously radical *and* conservationist, offering political judgement on and an archivist's preservation of the historical archive. In fact it is not simply that Sebald is gripped by a passion to remember, but rather an inability to forget: the past returns, reasserts itself and makes a claim on his narrators.[4] In this sense, Sebald's texts recall Benjamin's early writings on the 'contemplative impulse' (2009: 146) of creaturely melancholia in the German mourning play. Adopting Benjamin's words here, we could say that Sebald, with his 'downward gaze… immerse[d] in the life of creaturely things' (152), 'embraces dead objects… in order to redeem them' (157). Or, to adopt Sebald's own words, let us say that his writing attempts to 'rescue something out of that stream of history that keeps rushing past' (Sebald and Turner 2006: 24), to hold on to what might otherwise be lost to the 'storm' of progress (Benjamin 2006: 394).

If Sebald conceives of his literary project as a rescue mission, then who or what is he trying to save? Who or what returns from the past to haunt the present? This chapter argues that Sebald's literary project develops a melancholic poetics of connection in order to redeem creatures from the acceleration of modernity. Sebald's work not only exhibits a kind of multispecies gloom for the ways in which industrial modernity destroys nature but, by doing so, wishes to rescue nonhuman life from this destruction. In making this argument, I wish to build on a handful of critical essays which address, albeit briefly, how Sebald's writing 'does not privilege the human being above all other forms of life' (Wolff 2014: 5). Anne Fuchs proposes that Sebald's fiction develops 'a distinctly ecological perspective which highlights the historical acceleration of the destruction of nature' (2006: 173), thus contesting the 'disastrously anthropocentric worldview of the modern era' (2007: 122). Elsewhere, Hans-Walter Schmidt-Hannisa posits that Sebald 'aims to correct a concept of history which completely neglects the fate of animals' (2007: 33).

But where these essays articulate a *thematic* argument about Sebald's inclusion of animals, I wish to go one step further by introducing a *formal* analysis. In this chapter I will analyse how Sebald's mediated first-person narration, his dialectical natural-historical prose style, his incorporation of images, his long sentences, his texts' deliberately slow temporality, and his use of lists, hypotaxis and parataxis, all work to slow down or pause the anthropological machine of modernity. In fact, I will argue towards the end of this chapter that Sebald's writing can be read as an interruption of the novel form as an anthropological machine. This is why my sense of Sebald's creaturely form differs so strongly from Eric Santner's as he develops it in *On Creaturely Life*. Against Santner's claim that only humans are creatures, I contend that Sebald's work positions humanity *within* nature even as modernity defines itself against the nonhuman. Put simply, Sebald's poetics of connection articulates an ethics of the more-than-human.

I will work primarily with the English-language translation of Sebald's work. But I will also turn to the original German, when appropriate, in order to tease out important nuances in Sebald's language and syntax. It is well documented that Sebald worked closely with his translators, regularly altering, rewriting and questioning their choices. This is especially true for Michael Hulse's translation of *The Rings of Saturn* and Anthea Bell's translation of *Austerlitz*, the latter of which was published simultaneously in both German and English. Owing to this closeness between Sebald and his English translators, Rebecca Walkowitz argues that texts like *Austerlitz* are 'born translated' (2015: 3). The English-language translations of Sebald's books are not simply incidental or secondary, Walkowitz contends, but rather built into their very production. Nevertheless it would be unwise to lose sight of Sebald's recourse to specialized vocabulary, compound nouns and subordinate clauses which are not fully replicated by his texts' translations. This chapter's close readings therefore suggest that we can deepen our understanding of Sebald's poetics – as well as his writing of human–animal relations – through comparative analysis.

The Rings of Saturn: *Unglück*, accident, exposure

As a writer known for his haunting portrayal of historical devastation, there are only a few moments throughout Sebald's literary project in which his protagonists look proleptically towards the future. One such moment is dramatized in *The Rings of Saturn* (henceforth, *Rings*). Subtitled in the original German-language edition *An English Pilgrimage* [*Eine englische Wallfahrt*], *The Rings of Saturn* is a mosaic of fiction, memoir, essay and travelogue, revolving around an anonymous narrator's analeptic recollections of a walking tour along the Suffolk coastline in August of 1992. For much of the book, Sebald's narrator conveys how East Anglia was fundamental to Britain's modernization and imperial history. But the book's melancholic tone detects entropy within the apparent work of progress, as Sebald foregrounds the ways in which Suffolk's modernization also occasions its dilapidation, deindustrialization and deforestation. Thus the pilgrimage of *Rings*'s original subtitle thus connotes a secular and orbiting psychogeographic journey through the landscapes of a country – and perhaps even a planet – locked in a spiral of decline, in which the narrator figure becomes keenly aware of the 'traces of destruction, reaching far back into the past' (2002b: 3).

Having made his way from Brundall to Lowestoft to Dunwich, Sebald's narrator arrives at the Orford Ness peninsula, a shingle-formation and former

Anglo-American weapons-testing site that now lies abandoned. Ferried across by boat, the narrator notices the overgrown yellowing grass, the stillness of the air and the heaps of scrap metal and defunct machinery scattered around him.

> It was as if I were passing through an undiscovered country. I had not a single thought in my head. With each step that I took, the emptiness within and the emptiness without grew ever greater and the silence more profound... The closer I came to these ruins, the more any notion of a mysterious isle of the dead receded, and the more I imagined myself amidst the remains of our own civilisation after its extinction in some future catastrophe.
> (2002b: 234–7)

Alluding here to Hamlet's soliloquy on the 'undiscovered country' of death, the narrator is struck by the stillness and emptiness of this abandoned island of military debris; he is propelled into momentarily leaving behind the past, this 'isle of the dead'. With the formulation 'as if', Sebald pitches his narrator anachronically into a time-space that goes well beyond the point of writing, and even beyond writing as human activity, to an imagined time *after* the extinction of the human species: 'Where and in what time I truly was that day at Orfordness I cannot say' (237). Walking around amidst the archival deposits of human history, *Rings*'s narrator surveys the *awfulness* (a near-homonym of the here-contracted 'Orfordness') of history's wreckage after a future disaster.

For this reason, scholars have argued that *Rings* anticipates the discourses of the Anthropocene.[5] And Sebald is thought to achieve this through the work of vertiginous narration, a style which observes reality as if from afar, spatially and temporally. At one point, Sebald's narrator measures humanity's 'spread over the earth was fuelled by reducing the higher species of vegetation to charcoal, by incessantly burning whatever would burn... Human civilization', the narrator remarks, 'has been no more than a strange luminescence growing more intense by the hour' (2002b: 170). Adopting a deep and long perspective, Sebald describes the human species as a geological actor whose advancement depends on the burning of the world. Nevertheless, Sebald's texts are also suspicious about this particular narration of history and its species-level vantage point: 'It requires a falsification of perspective', he writes. 'We, the survivors, see everything from above, see everything at once, and still we do not know how it was' (2002b: 125). Sebald's narrative form thus embraces a vertiginous narration – an art or poetics of levitation, as analysed by Ben Hutchinson (2009b: 146) – that it also undercuts, redirecting attention towards experience and the here and now. We can see this in the scene on Orford Ness, when the narrator's last man fantasy is interrupted by a startled hare that rushes out from among the weeds:

> I was frightened almost to death when a hare that had been hiding in the tufts of grass by the wayside started up, right at my feet, and shot off down the rough track before darting sideways, this way, then that, into the field. It must have been cowering there as I approached, heart pounding as it waited, until it was almost too late to get away with its life. In that very fraction of a second when its paralyzed state turned into panic and flight, its fear cut through me.
>
> (234)

Composed out of clauses that rhythmically mimic the 'this way, then that' of the hare's darting movement, Sebald's description returns us to the present moment and, with this, to an encounter between two species. The narrator is at a distance from the hare – reinforced here by the repeated insistence on sight, not touch – but he nevertheless feels its fear. The hare's terror is so palpable, in fact, that the narrator absorbs it until, paradoxically, he begins to view himself from the hare's own eyes:

> I still see what occurred in that one tremulous instant with an undiminished clarity. I see the edge of the grey tarmac and every individual blade of grass, I see the hare leaping out of its hiding-place, with its ears laid back and a curiously human expression on its face that was rigid with terror and strangely divided; and in its eyes, turning to look back as it fled and almost popping out of its head with fright, I see myself, become one with it.
>
> (234–5)

As the hare's face transforms into a human shape, the narrator metamorphoses, momentarily becoming 'one' with this creature. The undergirding theme of these passages is *exposure*. Rather than observing from a panoramic distance, Sebald's narrator becomes caught up in this cross-species encounter. In fact, both the narrator and the hare are depicted as being *mutually exposed*, both vulnerable in their own ways to the very environment that also sustains them, even frightened by one another.

It is precisely through this thematics of mutual exposure that Sebald articulates a provisional form of recognition, even solidarity, between his narrator and other species. Indeed, Sebald extends this theme of vulnerability throughout *Rings*. At one point, pummelled by sandstorms, his narrator is left breathless and covered in dust: 'A deathly silence prevailed. There was not a breath, not a birdsong to be heard, not a rustle, nothing' (229). Narrator and bird are together stunned into silence as the world comes to a sudden stop. For the rest of this section, then, I will foreground the ways in which *Rings*'s narration brings humans and nonhumans together, and those ways in which Sebald focuses on the body as a site of shared animality. I will suggest that Sebald positions his first-person narrator as a vulnerable creature who articulates himself through a sympathetic connection to other creatures.

Sebald's narrative form is well known for its dialectical movement between 'modernist polyphony on the one hand' and 'assertive monologism on the other' (Sheppard 2005: 428), its oscillation 'between affective immersion or embeddedness and distanced visual mastery' (Kilbourn 2018: 53–4). His texts develop a 'subtle art of transition' (Gray 2009: 54) in which digression, associative thinking, free indirect discourse and double- or triple-mediated prose – the periscopic style that Sebald partly gleaned from Thomas Bernhard – flexibly transitions the narrative between different voices, times and spaces.[6] In *Rings* especially, the narrator assumes the position of a 'metonymic-I', that is, and 'I' formed 'at the point of connection' (Clingman 2009: 184). The narrator is the connecting force of the text, a contradictorily all-controlling yet self-eliding and impersonal figure whose wanderings, both physical and psychological, determine, yet give way, to the many pathways that the work takes. As Bianca Theisen puts it, Sebald's narrator is a 'self, losing itself, becom[ing] an other' (2006: 573). Sebald thus places immense significance on his narrator's encounters and conversations (the vast majority of which are with men, as women remain notably minor, spectral or absent from Sebald's wider project), which serve as catalysts for the narrator's own comments and the narrative's digressive, essayistic and free-associative drives. It will be my contention here that this narrative form, as a poetics of connection, embeds its narrator within the world as a creature among other creatures, making room for connections that extend across species difference.

Rings establishes a sense of creaturely vulnerability in its very first pages by developing an astronomical outlook which foregrounds contingency, destruction and creation. The book's epigraph quotes the *Brockhaus Encyclopaedia*, which hypothesizes that Saturn's rings are fragments of a former moon, a satellite that was destroyed after it travelled too close to the planet; the planet's gravitational force thus overpowers the moon's, devouring it in the process, but thereby creating the conditions for the suspended accumulation of matter in distinctive orbital ring formations. This, then, becomes the book's governing symbol. It invokes natural laws of entropy and equilibrium that remain uncontrollable while also metaphorically alluding to the debris of history. But it also tells us something important about *Rings*'s form, a text that in its structure embodies 'a nether-state between de-composition and re-amalgamation, between disorder and order, collapse and coalescence' (Gray 2010: 42). *Rings* is a collection of lost particles, held together by the force of Sebald's narration.

Sebald presents his narration precariously, as if his narrator is burdened simultaneously by cosmic planetary shifts and sudden psycho-physiological ruptures. In the novel's long opening paragraph he writes that the book's existence and its plot are prompted by an accident, 'a fissure that has since riven my life' (2002b: 18). In the August of 1992, the narrator states, just as the fever, lethargy and bad luck of the dog days were drawing to an end, he embarked on a long walk around the county of Suffolk, hoping to dispel a feeling of emptiness that begins to take hold after completing a long project. However, his ambling brought little release and relaxation, only 'paralyzing horror' (3). 'Perhaps it was because of this that, a year to the day after I began my tour, I was taken into hospital in Norwich in a state of almost total immobility. It was then that I began in my thoughts to write these pages' (3–4). The text that we hold in our hands is thus occasioned by this accident. It is a frame narrative written from the perspective of a subject whose own subjectivity has been uprooted.

'Accident', or *Unglück*, is a keyword of Sebald's project. *Unglück* suggests a range of negative affects and afflictions: back luck, accident, melancholia and catastrophe.[7] In Sebald's texts, bad luck and accidents are often imagined *as* catastrophes. Yet they also propel the narrative forward, testifying to the happenstance and digressive pathways of the prose we read. This is precisely what happens in *Rings* when, in his hospital bed, the narrator becomes 'aware again' of his body (18). He discovers in his own accident a heightened sensitivity towards his own animality. The boundaries between what is human and animal begin to slip away. The two nurses who visit his bedside are heard making a peculiar 'fluting sound', a 'kind of warbling such as comes from the throats of birds' (18). And the narrator no longer thinks of himself as properly human, but more as a creature, something like 'poor Gregor Samsa' in Franz Kafka's short story 'The Metamorphosis'. Like Kafka's indeterminate inhuman figure (described only as a bug, or *Ungeziefer*), *Rings*'s narrator assumes 'the tortured position of a creature that has raised itself erect for the first time' (5). Sebald's intertextual characterizations thus portray his narrator as an embodied creature, appropriating the discourses of species degeneration in order to ironically invert the evolutionary ascent of hominization.

In her work on the ontology of the accident, Catherine Malabou writes that sudden accidental events can fracture one's subjectivity: 'as a result of serious trauma, or somethings for no reason at all, the path splits and a new unprecedented persona comes to live with the former person, and eventually takes up all the room' (2012: 1). Accidents can produce a bifurcation of subjectivity in which a new 'I' emerges, non-identical to its former self. Something similar is at work in *Rings*, in which the reader encounters a new self who, aware again of his own body, comes to feel like a creature. Speaking, then, from this creaturely perspective, old certainties about the human begin to disappear. A few pages on from the scene in the hospital, Sebald's narrator reflects on the Scientific Revolution, the 'undaunted investigative zeal of the new sciences' (2002b: 12), and the ceremonial spectacle of dissection in the seventeenth-century anatomy theatre. By railing against 'the archaic ritual of dismembering a corpse' (12), *Rings* deploys a critical manoeuver that has become foundational to the critique of anthroponormativity, namely a rejection of René Descartes's mechanistic philosophy, which ushered in what Silvia Federici calls 'an ontological divide between a purely mental and a purely physical domain' (2004: 138). Cartesianism and its attendant discourses of European civic humanism reified a new concept of the human being, no longer a human animal but a human machine. Sebald's narrator casts Cartesian philosophy as an emblem of a distinctly modern *Unglück*, 'one of the principal chapters of the history of subjection' (2002b: 13), which de-animates and instrumentalizes the human body.

Against what he calls 'Cartesian rigidity' (17), Sebald's narrator introduces Rembrandt's *The Anatomy Lesson of Dr Nicolaes Tulp* as a work which exemplifies an aesthetic critique of the anatomy theatre's instrumentalization of the body. The painting depicts a group of surgeons staring intently at an anatomical atlas, ignoring the lifeless body that lies in front of them. What they miss is precisely what the painting's viewers are drawn to: the corpse itself has a 'grotesquely out of proportion' hand, 'anatomically the wrong way round' (16). Sebald incorporates a cropped section of the painting within the text itself, stating that this erroneous hand is not an unfortunate error but a deliberate misrepresentation: Rembrandt's 'unshapely hand' signifies all of 'the violence that has been done to Aris Kindt' (17). Sebald's narrator thus sees Cartesianism as a thoroughgoing instrumentalization of life.

Although *Rings*'s anti-Cartesian tendencies have already garnered considerable scholarly attention, existing analyses often limit their focus to the human body. By concentrating solely on how Sebald textually reanimates the de-animated human, critics have overlooked how *Rings* also rebuffs Cartesianism's repudiation of animality. Think, for example, of the Orford Ness hare described above. The frightened hare bears little resemblance to the Cartesian understanding of the animals as a *bête machine*, and is anthropomorphically identified with the narrator as they become one. Think too of the narrator's description of sand martins 'darting to and fro over the sea' (67), whose flightpaths are imagined to hold together the world, or indeed the moment in which Sebald's narrator climbs into a field of dozing pigs, and softly tickles a pig behind the ear:

> I climbed over the wire and approached one of the ponderous, immobile, sleeping animals. As I bent towards it, it opened a small eye fringed with light lashes and gave me an enquiring look. I ran my hand across its dusty back, and it trembled at this unwonted touch [*unter der ungewohnten Berührung erschauernden Rücken*]; I stroked its snout and face, and chucked it in the hollow behind one ear, till at length it sighed like one enduring endless suffering. When I stood up, it closed its eye once more with an expression of profound submissiveness.
>
> (2002b: 66; 1995b: 87)

Sebald's literary project is well known for its reliance on seeing rather than touching. His melancholic narrators look at, but rarely touch, the objects they describe. Indeed, there are moments in which Sebald recoils from proximity and contact, associating touch with a kind of animalistic excess. When stumbling upon a couple making love on a Suffolk beach, *Rings*'s narrator retreats from their combined bodies, which appear to him 'like some great mollusc washed ashore' (68). This simile is soon dropped as the couple shapeshift into a 'many limbed two-headed monsters… the last of a prodigious species' (68). These instances of looking and repulsion make Sebald's seemingly innocuous human-swine encounter all the more striking, however minor and short it may be. For here, Sebald's narrator momentarily reconnects with a different species. Michael Hulse's translation of *ungewohnten* as 'unwonted' serves as a neat inversion of its English homonym, unwanted, implying an unfamiliar but by no means unwelcome contact. If Cartesian mechanical philosophy deadens animal vitality, then here Sebald presents nonhuman animals as being alive to the touch of human others.

The above passage ends with Sebald's narrator recalling the biblical teachings of his youth, in particular the Gospel of Mark and the healing of the Gadarene Demoniac. When Jesus exorcises a man of his impure spirits, the spirits parasitically occupy a herd of pigs: 'And the swine, some two thousand according to the evangelist, plunged down a steep slope and drowned in the sea' (67). The narrator ponders whether this parable was invented to 'explain the supposed uncleanliness of swine; which would imply that human reasoning, diseased as it is, needs to seize on some other kind that it can take to be inferior and thus deserving of annihilation?' (67). Instrumental reason is, for Sebald's narrator, a key component of the war against animals. So too is the disarticulation of animality from human subjectivity, which results in the hierarchizing impulses of the parable. At stake in Cartesianism's disregard for the flesh is an abandonment of the animality that is immanent to humanity. *Rings* suggests that this forgetting of animality is a historical catastrophe, not only because it creates the conditions for the ready 'annihilation' of animals but also because it conjures a new kind of human who can be put to work in factories, and whose dead body can later be dissected without thought.

Towards the end of the book, Sebald traces five centuries of sericulture, remarking on how the silkworm once lived 'open, left to its own devices, until man, having discovered its usefulness, was prompted to foster it' (276). He follows this fostering all the way forward to the twentieth century and the 'entire killing business' (294) of Nazi sericulture techniques, commenting along the way on how the development of capital, through industrialization, relied on the simultaneous exploitation of silkworms and human labourers. He laments how 'a great number of people... spent their lives with their wretched bodies strapped to looms made of wooden frames and rails, hung with weights, and reminiscent of instruments of torture or cages' (282). In *Rings*, then, one gets the sense that modernity's specific instrumentalizations of animal life are intertwined with that of human life. Both animals' and humans' bodies are put to work. Against this backdrop, Sebald's fleeting encounters with hares and pigs become fugitive moments of connection against the gravitational pull of anthroponormativity.

From natural history to natural-history

Writing in 1982 on Alexander Kluge and the horror of total war, Sebald asks whether 'the catastrophes which develop, so to speak, in our hands and seem to break out suddenly are a kind of experiment, anticipating the point at which we shall drop out of what we have thought for so long to be our autonomous history and back down into the history nature?' (2004: 66). For Sebald, humanity's supposed autonomy is merely 'what we have thought', an ideological mystification that precipitates the very catastrophes which now threaten it with destruction. Titled *Zwischen Geschichte und Naturgeschichte*, this essay conjures an image of humanity as being curiously situated *between* history and natural history, with modernity's practices of mastery and progress collapsing in on themselves and threatening the entire species. Sebald further develops this form of catastrophic thinking in texts like *Luftkrieg und Literatur*, published in English as *On the Natural History of Destruction*, as well as in interviews. When asked, for example, about the methodological and thematic concerns behind *Rings*, Sebald frames the book as an extended description of the 'aberration of a species' [*Aberration einer Species*] (2001c: 16):

> One can... go outward in concentric circles, and the inner circles always determine the outer ones. That means: one can contemplate one's own mental health, how this is determined by one's own family history, how this is in turn determined by the history of the petit bourgeoisie in twenties and thirties Germany, how this is defined by the economic conditions of these years, how these economic conditions have evolved out of the history of industrialization in Germany and Europe – and so on until the circles of natural history and the history of the human species collide [*wo die Naturgeschichte und die Geschichte der menschlichen Species ineinander changieren*].
>
> (2001c: 16; my translation)

In this connected world, stylistically rendered by determining clauses, where individual temperament is ultimately interlinked with world-historical processes of industrialization, in which class analysis goes hand-in-hand with an ecological perspective, Sebald asserts that human history and natural history are contingent on one another. Thus, despite his invocation of two specific concepts – natural history and human history – Sebald positions them both as deeply interconnected, as a dialectic.

Sebald's writing pays great attention to this convergence of human and natural history. Throughout *Rings*, Sebald explores how the history of nature – deforestation, storms, coastal erosion and extinction – interlinks with the history of modernity. And it is a seven-page passage in particular that most explicitly navigates this understanding of human-nature relations. Described in *Rings*'s contents page simply as 'the natural history of the herring' (2002b: n.p.), this section sees the narrator expound on the history of herring fishing in the North Sea. In this narrative Sebald echoes, yet also challenges, natural history in its classical forms as an antiquarian and later Enlightenment regime of knowledge. Foregrounding the long-term consequences of industrialized fishing practices on both coastal communities and commodified herring, Sebald develops a more *critical* natural history of over-fishing, oceanic acidification and ecosystem collapse.

Following the writing of Theodor W. Adorno, I want to claim that *Rings* develops a *natural-historical style*, that is a form of narration that destabilizes the binary between human and nature. In his 1932 essay 'The Idea of Natural-History' [*Die Idee der Naturgeschichte*], Adorno proposed to 'dialectically overcome the usual antithesis of Nature and History' (2006: 252). For Adorno, the hyphenated concept of natural-history is 'not concerned with natural history in the traditional pre-scientific sense of the history of nature, nor with the history of nature where nature is the object of natural science' (253). Rather, by reappropriating the concept of natural history into a more critical historico-philosophical frame, Adorno develops the hypothesis that nature and history are in a mutual tension, a 'concrete unity' (259). The essay therefore historicizes nature and naturalizes humanity, harnessing these categories as two 'mutually determining' concepts that are intertwined with one another, as Susan Buck-Morss explains: 'each provided the key for the demythification of the other' (1977: 54). In *Negative Dialectics*, Adorno later writes that 'it would be up to thought to see all nature, and whatever would install itself as such, as history, and all history as nature' (1973: 359). In other words, bringing nature and history together ultimately disputes the mythical aura of both, as it demands 'a reciprocal defamiliarization of the two incommensurable poles of the dualism of Nature and History', a 'perpetual process in which neither term ever comes to rest, any more than any ultimate synthesis emerges' (Jameson 2007: 99).

This explicitly dialectical formulation therefore seeks to 'comprehend an object as natural where it appears most historical and as historical where it appears most natural' (Hullot-Kentor 2006: 239). Yet, crucially, this does not result in the ecological hybridism of, say, Latourian actor network theory or new materialism, in which ontological differences become flattened or indistinct. Rather, Adorno's rhetorical chiasmus 'history is nature, nature is history' is intended to reveal the structural relationship *between* the two apparently binary poles. As Gillian Rose explains, while the concepts of history and nature may 'appear immutable and ahistorical, they are in fact historically determined' (2014: 152). Natural-history thus pushes beyond both a simple binary separation of humanity against nature without flattening humanity ontologically as mere nature.

Let us return to *Rings*. After touring Somerleyton Hall, Sebald's narrator arrives in Lowestoft, a town described as having transformed from 'one of the foremost fishing ports in the United Kingdom' into a place of 'insidious decay' (2002b: 45). 'It seemed incomprehensible to me', Sebald writes, 'that in such a relatively short period of time the place could have become so run down' (41). Despite weathering the storm of a long downturn throughout the late twentieth century, Lowestoft crumbled under the weight of Prime Minister Margaret Thatcher's 'hardline capitalist years' (41) [*realen Kapitalismus verschriebenen Ära* (1995b: 56)]. The narrator thus characterizes Lowestoft as suffering the consequences of the end of empire and the later neoliberalization of the British political economy. This context frames the narrator's arrival and check-in at the aptly named Albion Hotel, as if a metonym of the country itself. That evening, Sebald's narrator orders a plate of fish and chips:

> I was the sole guest in the huge dining room, and it was the same startled person who took my order and shortly afterwards brought me a fish that had doubtless lain entombed [*vergrabenen*] in the deep-freeze for years. The breadcrumb armour-plating had been partly singed by the grill, and the prongs of my fork bent on it. Indeed it was so difficult to penetrate what eventually proved to be nothing but an empty shell that my plate was a hideous mess once the operation was over. The tartare sauce was turned grey by the sooty breadcrumbs, and the fish itself, or what feigned to be fish [*was ihn vorstellen sollte*], lay a sorry wreck [*Hälfte zerstört*] among the grass green peas and the remains of soggy chips that gleamed with fat.
> (2002b: 43; 1995b: 58)

Sebald's telescopic and hyperbolic description neatly captures this scene of joyless and tasteless British pub food. With emphasis placed on the messy and soggy contents of the plate, as well as the frozen then burnt then empty then half-destroyed fish, it is understandable that this entire scene has been read as 'probably the funniest episode in Sebald's work' (Long 2007: 35), as if straight out of Fawlty Towers. The scene's comedy lies, James Wood writes, 'in the paradox of painstaking exaggeration (as if the diner were trying to crack a safe, or solve a philosophical conundrum), enforced by Sebald's calm control of apparently ponderous diction' (2017: n.p.).

But Sebald's punchline is also linked to what came before, namely his historical description of Lowestoft's decline. Once situated within its wider emplotment, this scene, in fact, derives its comedy from the tragic industrial and natural deterioration of Lowestoft itself. A metonymic signifier of the disinvestment, deindustrialization and deprivation of English seaside towns, the amour-plated fish is fundamentally *hollowed out*. Moreover, this scene of fish-eating deconstructs itself before our eyes. For in the end, this is an instance of non-consumption in which the narrator realizes that the fish itself, or what it merely 'signified' [*vorstellen*], was nothing but an empty shell. Read in isolation, this heightens the comedic irony of the passage. However, there is also an important relation between this non-fish and *Rings*'s following pages, in which Sebald discusses the natural history of the herring species. The non-fish becomes something of a catalyst for a natural-historical narration of the North Sea fishing industries. Leaving the Albion Hotel the following morning, Sebald's narrator begins simultaneously *historicizing* herring while *naturalizing* humanity. On the one hand, Sebald demonstrates how herring fishing is a historical process which necessarily changes nature, and on the other, Sebald shows how humanity is not autonomous but reliant on and subject to nature. Neither nature nor humanity is static here; the actions of both reciprocally affect one another.

Let us start with the latter: that Sebald naturalizes humanity. He does this, first, in his attention to urban decline, which characterizes Lowestoft as being trapped in a chain reaction of 'encroaching misery' (2002b: 42): neoliberalism takes hold, Lowestoft's wharves and factories close down, unemployment soars, personal debt increases, suicides escalate and education levels plummet. This sense of 'organic' decline – human morbidity, clinical depression, and educational lack – is presented as a repercussion of political choices: systematic disinvestment and de-industrialization. This becomes even more acute when Sebald's narrator, walking south of Lowestoft, notices 'dozens of decommissioned and unemployed trawlers' on the coast (44). He contemplates how 'the boats in which the fishermen once put out from the shore have vanished, now that fishing no longer affords a living, and the fishermen themselves are dying out' (52–3). Sebald's original German has it that the fishermen – just like the herring they fish – are becoming extinct [*selber ausgestorben* (1995b: 71)]. Indeed by the time of *Rings*'s construction in the mid-1990s, thirty vessels fishing out of two Scottish ports 'were catching most of the national allocation for pelagic fish, and caught even more out-of-quota fish illegally. This policy of going for bulk virtually put an end to hundreds of smaller boats and fishers for herring that has supported many communities on the east coast of the United Kingdom' (Couper et al. 2015: 58).

At the same time, Sebald depicts humans as being impacted by nonhuman actions. Throughout Britain's history, Sebald writes, 'there were repeated occasions when the herring avoided their usual grounds and whole stretches of the coastline were impoverished as a result' (2002b: 55). This is not a banal claim of cause and effect, but rather reveals how the herring's changing migration patterns directly affect the human population which relies on fishing in a yearly food cycle. Coastal communities are thus particularly vulnerable to natural changes. And *Rings* continues this theme in its later description of the erosion of the Dunwich coast, the 'catastrophic incursions of the sea into the land' as coastal erosion 'continued to take its natural course' (158).

Sebald also *historicizes nature*, unsettling the apparent separation of humanity from nature through his writing on over-fishing, heavy industrialization and what his narrator deems the Enlightenment's wider 'thirst for knowledge' (55). This is first shown in Sebald's attention to over-fishing, in particular the exhausted herring stocks, which connects human precarity to the nonhuman precarity of the herring. 'Out on the high seas the fishing continues, at least for the present', Sebald writes, 'though even there the catches are growing smaller', and 'the fish that are landed are often useless for anything but fish-meal' (53). Sebald implies a logic of diminishing returns in which 'ecological cycles have become subject to the dictates of economic cycles' (Longo et al. 2015: 100). Just as the battered fish and Lowestoft are both represented as hollow spaces, so too does *Rings* connect these to a longer-term hollowing out of the fish stocks in the North Sea.

Sebald's narrator invokes here a classical or antiquarian tradition of natural history, the very tradition from which Adorno snatched his concept. This heterogeneous tradition cultivated an encyclopaedic and taxonomical perspective which, while classifying nature into species hierarchies, also understood nature as an infinitely renewable resource. According to Michel Foucault, antiquarian natural history is an episteme that is synonymous with 'the nomination of the visible' (2002: 141). Reformulated in the words of Mary Louise Pratt, the project of natural history is a 'European knowledge-building enterprise of unprecedented scale' (2008: 25), consolidated in the nineteenth century and implicated in imperial expansion. Sebald's narrator describes how this tradition utilized herring ideologically as evidence of the purportedly self-regulating plenitude of life, a 'popular didactic model' of 'the indestructibility of Nature' (2002b: 53). Remembering from his childhood an educational film about fishing practices (which he later realizes is part of a series of Nazi educational films about nature which 'promised the best and cleanest of all possible worlds' (292)), the narrator recollects how herring fishing was regarded as a 'supreme example of mankind's struggle with the power of Nature' (54). In the English-language translation, Michael Hulse registers this tradition with his single capitalization of 'Nature', which reifies and essentializes the concept as humanity's other.

Yet it is clear that Sebald's narrator critiques rather than espouses these dominant traditions. This is demonstrated most clearly in the narrator's comments on the Enlightenment, which he sees as having instrumentalized and exploited herring in the name of human progress. The development of aggressive fishing practices saw an increase in the use of nets 'that could take almost a quarter of a million fish' (55). The fish would 'swim up against [the net] in desperation until at length their gills catch in the mesh; they are then throttled during the near-eight hour process of hauling up and winding in the nets'. Because of this, Sebald's narrator states, eighteenth- and nineteenth-century naturalists would 'suppose that herring die the instant they are removed from the water'. In a passage that recalls the book's earlier discussion of human dissection, Sebald writes about how countless experiments were performed on herring in order to ascertain the truth of this supposition:

> Noel de Marinière... investigate[d] more closely the fishes' capacity to survive, which he did by cutting off their fins and mutilating them in other ways. This process, inspired by our thirst for knowledge, might be described as the most extreme of the sufferings undergone by a species always threatened by disaster... [T]he natural historians sought consolation in the idea that humanity was responsible for only a fraction of the endless destruction wrought in the cycle of life, and moreover in the assumption that the peculiar physiology of the fish left them free of the fear and pains that rack the bodies and souls of higher animals in their death throes. But the truth is that we do not know what the herring feels [*Doch in Wahrheit wissen wir nichts von den Gefühlen des Herings*].
> (2002b: 56–7; 1995b: 77)

Pivoting on this 'but', Sebald's narrator refutes the earlier tradition of natural history. Rather than perceiving nature as a timeless abundance, he highlights the co-implication of the human and the nonhuman, and even draws the reader's attention to the limits of human knowledge. This appeal to non-knowledge is an ethically attuned corrective that cuts across the Enlightenment's rapaciousness. Against the notion that only the 'higher animals' feel pain and fear, Sebald's narrator articulates how such ideologies authorize intensive over-fishing and its attendant threats to the species. *Rings* thus conjures an ethical obligation to other creatures: not knowing is not enough to inflict pain.

Sebald's natural-history narration also highlights the toxicity, mutation and death among North Sea species affected by deposited pollutants. The narrator notes that the UK's rivers 'bear thousands of tons of mercury, cadmium and lead, and mountains of fertilizer and pesticides, out into the North Sea' (53). Owing to this industrial pollution, 'toxic substances sink into the waters of the Dogger Bank, where a third of the fish are now born with strange deformities and excrescences', and some fish develop male sexual organs: 'the ritual patterns of courtship are now no more than a dance of death, the exact opposite of the notion of the wondrous increase and perpetuation of life with which we grew up' (53). Against the tradition of natural history 'with which we grew up', Sebald's narrator documents how natural cycles are impacted socially under the conditions of modernity. Acidification causes catastrophic repetitions of ruination, pushing pelagic species to extinction.

When Adorno conceptualized his idiosyncratic reconstruction of natural-history in the 1930s, he wrote about it as a critical mode of analysis which would 'open up an alternative form of re-enchantment that remains socially critical' (Stone 2006: 249). I therefore want to stress the importance of Sebald's natural history of the herring as a narrative act, as an attempt to give literary form to the war against animals. Looked at this way, Sebald's natural-history becomes more than a standpoint. It is a creaturely form which grants nature its history in light of its ongoing relations with human history. Natural-history is critique and re-enchantment simultaneously, as it bears witness to modernity's impacts while re-membering forms of connection that tie the fate of humanity to the fate of animals.

Sebald's images: dreaded comparisons?

In-text images are one of the hallmarks of Sebald's writing, perhaps the 'most conspicuous surface feature of [his] texts' (Long 2007: 46). Pictures of animals are scattered throughout his works: taxonomic illustrations of moths, men on horseback and cropped photos of birds and marsupials. But until now I have not spoken about how these reproduced images contribute to Sebald's creaturely form. In fact, readers familiar with Sebald's work may well wonder whether my interpretations of his natural-historical narration are confirmed or rather contested by his incorporation of images. This will be my concern now, as I conclude my reading of *Rings* by focusing on three images that Sebald uses to supplement his natural-history of the herring. There are, of course, other images I might have focused on in this section: the many instances of silkworm moths, or the image of a quail in a deserted aviary, which makes the reader want to reach into the text and scoop it out. But I think that these three images are worth close analysis, not just because they reveal important aspects of Sebald's textual-photographic practice but because they also illuminate how his project articulates and visualizes relations between humans and animals.

In *Rings*, as elsewhere, Sebald juxtaposes his written prose with inserted pictorial clippings. At first, these images may seem to contribute to the work's reality effect. They create a documentary aesthetic that imbues the text with authenticity and 'opens up vistas into an unsuspected and yet strangely immediate past' (Sebald 1973: 286). And yet Sebald's black-and-white photographs, postcards, reproductions of paintings, architectural blueprints, incidental objects, landscapes and video stills do not, as a rule, straightforwardly represent the corresponding passage's content. Indeed, these grainy pictures often stand in curious comparison to, or even conflict with, the words on the page. Take, for example, Sebald's insertion of a zoological sketch of a fish (Figure 1) just a few lines down from his warning that 'we do not know what the herring feels' (2002b: 57). Sebald has spent this passage foregrounding the rapid decline of herring populations in the twentieth century, pinning this species' extinction crisis on the combined consequences of over-fishing and oceanic acidification. His narration links this contemporary crisis to centuries of exploitation, in which northern European societies have utilized the lives of herring in order to develop human societies. Readers may justifiably assume, then, that this is a drawing of a herring, a fish whose 'internal structure is extremely intricate and consists of more than two hundred different bones and cartilages' (57). Yet this is actually a representation of cod.

Sebald's images, so deadly serious on first look, are often opportunities for little tricks and jokes.[8] It is well known that Sebald would take an image and deliberately degrade it by feeding it through a photocopier until it broke down and blurred into a distinctive 'leaden grain' (Sebald quoted in Bigsby 2001: 155). Sebald's compositional practice, then, is a process of pictorial stylization and fabrication which attenuates the allure of the supposedly true, supposedly original and authentic historical document. His is a manufactured nostalgia, an achieved authenticity laced with the irony of the inauthentic. Indeed this manufactured nostalgia is enhanced by the absence of narrative framing. By withholding any rhetorical explanation or annotations, Sebald provides no map for readers to arrive at a final understanding of these untitled, uncaptioned images. Here, the reader encounters a symbol of a fish that, despite possessing the 'aura of

Figure 1 A red herring? © W. G. Sebald, *The Rings of Saturn*, 1998. Reproduced with the permission of the Wylie Agency and the W. G. Sebald Estate.

indexicality' (Hirsch 2008: 122), ultimately misrepresents its supposed linguistic referent. The cod is a red herring.

Yet it is precisely within this ambiguity of meaning, this momentary formal elision of the differences between herring and cod, that Sebald crafts a more-than-human ethics. On the one hand, this elision testifies to how modernity's specific articulations of species difference – symbolized here by the reifying and colonizing disciplinary knowledges of natural history – are concomitant with disarticulations of humanity from nature. Not knowing that the image refers to cod is not, then, an individual failing on the part of the reader but a symptom of modernity's wider instrumentalization and disregard for animal others. On the other, Sebald's intentional confusion of the signifier and the signified *connects* the pictured cod to the described herring. Both of these fishes are, he suggests, captured by modernity. And this recalls the scene at the Albion Hotel. The non-fish that Sebald's narrator fails to eat would have 'signified' (1995b: 58) cod, the traditional species of choice for fish and chips. Thus Sebald's red herring links the fate of the herring to that of the cod: two species over-fished, pushed to the brink of extinction.

In all of this it is clear that these images are unstable and open to interpretation. Sebald writes with images not to establish veracity but to unsettle the logic of representation itself. There is, then, something fundamentally ambiguous that lies at the heart of Sebald's multimodal formal practice, an ambiguity that permits his images to become spaces of projection, for readers and critics alike. Deployed to corroborate, decorate and yet also contradict his prose, Sebald's images call for competing readings. They invite readers to interact with them, that is, to make their own connections between the text's long sentences and the pictorially represented material. Nowhere has this been more apparent than in *Rings*'s apparent juxtaposition between two particular photographs. The first, a small postcard image, shows a Lowestoft fishing market from the early twentieth century, in which flat-capped men in wellington boots stand among thousands of dead fish (2002b: 54) (Figure 2). The second, some six pages later, is a double-page image that suspends the reading experience like no other in Sebald's *oeuvre*. Human bodies lie dead, strung out on the ground and covered with blankets (Figure 3). In both the German and English editions, this photograph immediately follows the words 'Bergen Belsen on the 14th of April 1945' (59).

How we read these images depends on whether we think that Sebald is *comparing* or *connecting* them. Critics have mostly taken the former path, suggesting that Sebald conflates animal slaughter and Jewish genocide. He therefore risks a *dreaded comparison* between human and animal suffering, as it has come to be known in animal studies discourses (Spiegel 1988). 'Is it tasteless to lump together such qualitatively different phenomena?', Mark McCulloh asks (2003: 65). Elsewhere, Richard Crownshaw writes that the contiguity

Figure 2 Connection or comparison? © W. G. Sebald, *The Rings of Saturn*, 1998. Reproduced with the permission of the Wylie Agency and the W. G. Sebald Estate.

Figure 3 Comparison or connection? © W. G. Sebald, *The Rings of Saturn*, 1998. Reproduced with the permission of the Wylie Agency and the W. G. Sebald Estate.

of these phenomena 'induces a reading of these images as visually rhyming' (2010: 54). Others put it more strongly, arguing that because Sebald offers no criteria for interpreting these images – no simile, no metaphor, no analogy – he confuses his own narrative's ethical commitment to the victims of history. For J. J. Long especially, Sebald's literary attempt at restitution 'begins to look like a meaningless gesture in a text that cannot differentiate between the murder of the Jews and industrial trawling for herring' (2007: 144). Sebald is thus said to flaunt this dreaded comparison while also abdicating the narrative responsibility for it, putting the burden of interpretation on the reader and equating human and animal mass killing. In other words, Sebald's ambiguous textual-photographic poetics falls into what Frédéric Neyrat has described in a more theoretical register as an 'ontological undifferentialism', a 'flat immanence where everything becomes equivalent with everything else' (Neyrat and Johnson 2014: n.p.). While Sebald's narrative of natural-history linguistically sustains its dialectic between nature and history, his non-linguistic photographic practice flattens out their differences, in turn reducing history and nature to equivalence, turning 'all human history into repetition as such' (Jameson 2007: 99). Difference, unevenness and scale are all lost as these photos come to resemble one another.

However, these images are fundamentally non-identical, not just in their content but in scale. In both the German and English-language editions of *Rings*, the postcard of the Lowestoft catch commands only half a page of print, while the photo of Bergen-Belsen takes up two full pages. Their differential arrangement in the text consequently indicates disparity, not similarity. The latter image's distinctiveness even accentuates its non-comparability. Reading these images as they are composed on the page thus unsettles the existing critique of equivalence. Yet still, their chiasmatic proximity still urges 'on us the thought that the slaughter of the herring and the Holocaust belong together', part of 'the same natural historical constellation' (Bernstein 2009: 51). How, then, to interpret them? Moving from comparative to connective thinking allows us to tease out the ethics of these images. In fact, seeing them as connected opens up a reading in which human and animal ethics are not conflicting but mutually reciprocal. If we think of Sebald's images as creating a logic of *relation without analogy*, that is, a relation without equivalence, then we appreciate simultaneously the distinctions and the links between these images. The relation between them is governed by modernity, a time after nature in which forms of life are measured against anthroponormative visions of community. Anne Fuchs, in her reading of these images, pushes in this direction when she writes that both scenes are connected by a 'cold and objectified biopolitics which disregards the value of life by means of a reductive interpretation of nature' (2007: 126).

What becomes unthinkable for Sebald's humanist critics, then, is that his works appear to discover a solidarity with slaughtered animals *through* their literary engagement with the historical trauma of the Holocaust. At stake in this relation is a literary-formal reconsideration of the cleaving – meant in the double sense of a connection and separation – of Jews and animals in modernity. In *Of Jews and Animals*, Andrew Benjamin details how dominant traditions of metaphysical thought drew on and constructed an image of the properly human against the figure of animality, emblematized by the purportedly inhuman Jew and the nonhuman animal. Under this schema of anthroponormativity, Benjamin argues, Jewish diasporas and nonhuman animals have been differently excluded from the realm of humanity. Thus any project of restitution and justice should begin not with an extension of the circle of humanity but rather a 'fundamentally different form of relationality' (Benjamin 2010: 16), one which incorporates human and nonhuman justice. Perhaps, then, these images seek to redeem this historically negative coupling of Jews and animality, just as we saw Adorno and Horkheimer articulate in *Dialectic of Enlightenment*. Relational but not analogical, these images invite us to consider a creaturely ethics. They compel us to connect, without equating together, the fascistic politics of genocide with the commodification, exploitation and eventual near-extinction of living beings.

The false world: *Austerlitz*'s zooscapes

From the very first pages of *Austerlitz*, the reader encounters another unnamed narrator who recognizes animals' distress under the conditions of modernity. *Austerlitz* begins with its narrator looking back over a period in the late 1960s during which he shuttled between England and Belgium, 'partly for study purposes, partly for other reasons which were never entirely clear to me' (2002a: 1). He recalls how, during one excursion to Antwerp in 1967, he suddenly became overwhelmed by anxiety. 'Plagued by a headache' and gripped by 'uneasy thoughts', the narrator remembers taking 'refuge' (1) in Antwerp's zoo. But far from rescuing him [*retten*] (2001a: 5), the zoo intensifies his maladies. Entering a Nocturama, he peers in at a number of bats, jerboas, owls and lemurs, each 'leading their sombrous lives' (2002a: 2). The narrator says that, as his eyesight acclimatized to the Nocturama's artificial dark, he focused his attention on a lone raccoon in the corner of the room:

> I watched it for a long time as it sat beside a little stream with a serious expression on its face, washing the same piece of apple over and over again, as if it hoped that all this washing, which went far beyond any reasonable thoroughness, would help it to escape the unreal world [*der falschen Welt*] in which it had arrived, so to speak, through no fault of it its own.
> (2002a: 2–3; 2001a: 5)

Throughout Sebald's work, the gaze of the animal carries both a palpable sadness and 'a kind of special knowledge' (Boxall 2011: 131). With their 'unwavering searching gazes' [*unverwandt forschenden Blick*], the Nocturama's animals are like 'painters and philosophers who seek to penetrate the darkness which surrounds us purely by means of looking and thinking' (2002a: 3). These animals' philosophies remain elusive to the narrator. All he and the reader can do is stare into their eyes, wondering what it is they wish to communicate.

Austerlitz's opening scene is significant, then, because it bears witness to and hence undermines the sovereign gaze of the zoological garden. Brian Massumi writes that the zoological garden 'is an exercise of human sovereignty vis-à-vis the animal', a modern space in which humans 'hold themselves at a distance in the role of unimplicated observer' (2014: 65, 68). Jacques Derrida calls this the 'autopsic gaze', a de-vitalizing objectification 'that precisely inspects, sees, looks at the aspect of a *zōon* the life and force of which has been neutralized either by death of by captivity' (2009: 296). For Sebald's narrator, the Nocturama is not a habitat but the simulacrum of one, an 'unreal' or 'false' world [*falsche Welt*]. This marks another moment in which Sebald nods to Adorno (2005: 39), who wrote in *Minima Moralia* that there is no right way to live in the false world. Adorno was writing, here, about human life, but in *Austerlitz* Sebald suggests that animals too are living in a false world. In this 'topsy-turvy miniature universe' that combines 'artificial dusk' with a 'pale moon' (2002a: 4), Sebald writes that animals live out their '*Dämmerleben*' (2001a: 5). While Anthea Bell translates the German *Dämmerleben* as 'sombrous lives', Sebald's original compound noun suggests 'twilight lives', at once a technical description of nocturnal life and a judgement on these animals' decline. Imprisoned within this stifling simulated environment, the raccoon incessantly cleans an apple as a kind of embodied response, its behavioural ticks constituting a form of psychopathological zoochosis. Denatured and exposed, the raccoon has degenerated into exhibiting a purely reactive twitch. Almost paradoxically, the narrator hints that the raccoon's twitching is an appropriate response – perhaps the only response – to the 'unreal world' of the Nocturama. Only by descending into madness will the raccoon discover a form of escape.

Austerlitz's opening scene shapes the way the rest of the novel is read, alerting the reader to the significance of animal figures, the spectacle of the zoo as a site of modernity's relationship with nature and to the thematics of imprisonment and madness which perpetuate throughout the text. *Austerlitz* even imagines the logic of the zoo as underpinning modern social relations. The zoo is constitutive of the 'architectural style of the capitalist era' (44). Throughout the novel, the narrator writes that 'lawcourts and penal institutions, railway stations and stock exchanges, opera houses and lunatic asylums' (44) are in their own way carceral spaces that stymy rather than encourage collective freedom. This impacts upon animal life. Towards the end of the novel, for example, Sebald's narrator notes how the rebuilt Bibliothèque Nationale de France, with its governing 'Cartesian' structure, leads numerous birds to strike the glass windows and fall 'lifeless to the ground' (392). But it also impacts upon human life. Sebald's narrator reveals that his memories of the Nocturama 'have become confused in my mind with my memories of the *Salle des pas perdus*', the waiting room – or, literally, hall of the lost – in Antwerp station. Human and nonhuman worlds slide into one another. The railway passengers 'seemed to me somehow miniaturized' like the 'large number of dwarf species' in the zoo. 'If I try to conjure up a picture of that waiting-room today I immediately see the Nocturama, and if I think of the Nocturama the waiting-room springs to my mind' (4). Sebald's rhetorical chiasmus creates a continuity between human and nonhuman. The train station becomes 'another Nocturama', the railway passengers 'creatures in the Nocturama' (5–6). The spaces of modernity are, for Sebald, zooscapes.

The narrator then draws a more specific connection between the raccoon and one of the people waiting in the waiting room, namely the novel's titular character, Jacques Austerlitz. Over the course of the novel, the narrator's chance encounters with Austerlitz spark the momentum of plot, which is then sustained by Austerlitz's meditative monologues about his complicated biography. *Austerlitz* is narrated from a present-tense position of the 1990s, but it traces episodically the conversations between its two protagonists over the years from the 1960s to the present, as Austerlitz slowly unravels his life story: born in Czechoslovakia during the rise of Nazism, Austerlitz is sent on the *Kindertransport* to the United Kingdom. Arriving in Wales as a Jewish refugee, the young Austerlitz is adopted by a Calvinist household who rename him Dafydd Elias. Brought up as Dafydd, Austerlitz remains unaware of his personal and family history until his adulthood when, working as an architectural historian, his memories burst out from repression into cognition. His resulting personal crisis precipitates a determination to uncover his family's history, and it is this ongoing search for memory that is slowly articulated, forming the content of the book. During Austerlitz's first conversation with the narrator in Antwerp Centraal, his ruminations on oppressive architectural styles lead him to convey how deeply he feels the 'marks of pain which… trace countless fine lines through history' (16). On first look, then, *Austerlitz*'s plot has little to do with animals. Yet as the narrator presents it, Austerlitz's lifelong quest for humanization, his obsessive search for an escape route of trauma, resembles the raccoon's own unceasing hopes for liberation; both Austerlitz and the raccoon are trapped in false worlds, living lives that are not their own. Indeed, all the travellers in Antwerp station are described as exhibiting the same 'sorrowful expressions as the creatures in the zoo'. The narrator admits that this passing thought, although 'nonsensical in itself', led him to think of the station's travellers as 'last members of a diminutive race which had perished or had been expelled from its homeland' (6). Within *Austerlitz*'s zooscape, human and animal characters are imagined as both being enclosed, exiled, even on the brink of extinction.

The Nocturama therefore doubles up as a metaphor for the captivity of humans in the social world of train stations, fortresses, prisons and concentration camps. When pointing this out, though, Sebald's critics tend to leave behind the Nocturama, subordinating it as mere allegory for the novel's more sustained inquiries into human experience.[9] To be sure the Nocturama is a metaphor for both the narrator's and Austerlitz's psychologies, for their own sense of imprisonment as they feel, like the raccoon, out of time and out of place. But in *Austerlitz* the practices of animal enclosure, exemplified by the Nocturama, are never far from the narrator's mind. In fact, the book's frame narrative suggests that it is only after entering the Nocturama, only after fixing his attention on the raccoon, that Sebald's narrator looks at the modern world differently, as if every space around him is also a site of imprisonment and simulation.

We might say, then, that Sebald's *Austerlitz* develops a metaphorics of the zoo. The 'false world' of the Nocturama informs the book's representation of lived space, as it imagined the spaces of modernity negatively as oppressive and melancholic. In other words, Sebald imagines the zoo *and* modernity as false worlds that structure, control and simulate the relations between creatures. The unreadability of the zoo animal's gaze is not, therefore, a confirmation of some essential ontological species barrier. Rather, *Austerlitz* thematizes the incomprehensible gaze of the animal as a symptom of modernity. The false world of the Nocturama has ruptured the raccoon's species-being, rendering its gaze all but impenetrable to an onlooker. Thus the zoo, invented as a technology of spectacle and encounter across species lines, is imagined in *Austerlitz* as destroying the opportunity for a real meeting point between human and animal.

In *Minima Moralia*, the same book in which he wrote of the false world, Adorno also spoke of the modern zoological gardens as representing the 'inescapability of imprisonment. It is a consequence of history. The zoological gardens in their authentic form are products of nineteenth-century imperialism. They flourished since the opening-up of wild regions of Africa and Central Asia, which paid symbolic tribute in the shape of animals' (2005: 116). 'The more purely nature is preserved and transplanted by civilization, the more implacably it is dominated' (115), Adorno writes in his paradigmatic dialectical syntax. In the menageries of early modernity, zoo animals first stood as fetishized signifiers for exotic otherness, used to confirm the supposed progress and power of particular civilizations. The menagerie became the zoological garden during the same period in which European imperialism began its colonization of life. As wild populations declined, zoo animals came to stand as lost objects of and representatives for their dying species, 'allegories of the specimen or the pair who defy the disaster that befalls the species *qua* species' (115). For Adorno, then, zoos testify to a concomitant conservation and obliteration of nature. Zoo animals are preserved remnants of a nature that is increasingly eradicated. The modern zoo has 'abolished the exotic' (116).

Sebald himself echoed this critique of the zoo in his 1997 Zürich lectures on aerial warfare and literature, in which he wrote that zoos 'owe their existence to a desire to demonstrate princely or imperial power' (2004: 92). Like Adorno, Sebald considered the zoological garden to be a space of hierarchy and colonization that, persisting and transforming in modernity, reaffirms forms of human sovereignty over animal life and hence perpetuates a war against animals. In *Austerlitz*, Sebald interweaves this critique of imperial sovereignty and imprisonment through his descriptions of human and nonhuman characters, as well as through his narrator's pronouncements on Belgium's colonial history, the riches of which built Antwerp train station itself. Because Antwerp Centraal was 'constructed under the patronage of King Leopold II', Sebald writes, it cannot be understood as serving a 'purely utilitarian function' of democratizing continental travel. The station's façade houses 'a monument to the world of animals and native peoples of the African continent' (2002a: 4–5), an image of human and nonhuman exploitation. That the patronage of the Belgian royal family is implicated in this history is further borne out by the fact that King Leopold II's father, Leopold I, inaugurated the Antwerp Zoo in 1844, and that the 1885 and 1894 World's

Fairs saw over one hundred indigenous Africans brought to Antwerp to live temporarily in so-called 'Negro villages'.[10] *Austerlitz* thus connects Antwerp Centraal and Antwerp Zoo. The train station and the zoological garden are spaces that materially develop out of and symbolically monumentalize imperial conquest. When Jacques Austerlitz begins speaking, taking over the narrative voice, he describes the station as a 'cathedral consecrated to international traffic and trade' (12).

In academic writing on zoos it has become a commonplace to turn to John Berger's 1977 essay 'Why Look at Animals?'. A foundational yet disputed text within the emergent animal studies canon, 'Why Look at Animals' argues that public zoos 'came into existence at the beginning of the period which was to see the disappearance of animals from daily life. The zoo to which people go to meet animals, to observe them, to see them, is, in fact, a monument to the impossibility of such encounters' (2009: 21). Focusing on the period of capitalist industrialization in the nineteenth century, Berger conceives of zoos, in similar terms to Adorno, as 'endorsements of modern colonial power', institutions which act as a 'demonstration' of capitalism's 'remorseless' commodification and marginalization of nature (26). The captured and displayed zoo animal is 'a symbolic representation of the conquest of all distant and exotic lands' (21). Thus Berger writes that zoo animals 'constitute the living monument to their own disappearance' (26): 'Everywhere animals disappear. In zoos they constitute the living monuments to their own disappearance' (24). 'However you look at these animals... you are looking at something that has been rendered absolutely marginal' (27). Moreover, Berger argues that the zoo's technologies of mediation foreclose the potentiality of an interspecies encounter, writing that 'nowhere in a zoo can a stranger encounter the look of an animal' (24). Despite the title of Berger's essay, then, he is also interested in the ways in which animals might look back at the human. The animals of pre-modernity, Berger writes, 'scrutinize[d the human] across a narrow abyss of non-comprehension' (5). The zoological garden has not narrowed this abyss, nor ruptured it totally, but *widened* it: 'At the most, the animal's gaze flickers and passes on. [...] They have been immunized to encounter' (24). *Austerlitz's* opening scene in the Nocturama therefore bears witness to such a thwarted cross-species encounter. The raccoon becomes, like the taxidermy polar bear in *Rings*, a 'ghost bowed by sorrows' (2002b: 36).

But more than being a useful reference point for interpreting *Austerlitz*, 'Why Look at Animals?' is in fact partly constitutive of the text itself. Later in the novel, Austerlitz recalls his visit to the Paris's *Jardin des Plantes* with his close friend, Marie de Vernueil. An 'old zoo' with a 'dreary terrain', the *Jardin* is a false world which now lies almost empty: 'large animals had once been put on display, said Austerlitz, elephants, giraffes, rhinoceroses, dromedaries and crocodiles, although most of the enclosures, decked out with pitiful remnants of natural objects – tree stumps, artificial rocks and pools of water – were now empty and deserted' (2002a: 368). Austerlitz remembers spotting a family of fallow deer who are all, as the inserted photo suggests (Figure 4), huddled together and vigilantly monitoring the spectator's actions. Hovering at the edge of their enclosure, the fallow deer do not confirm the 'autopsic gaze' but block it by offering back their own alert and guarded stares. Here, Sebald incorporates 'Why Look at Animals?' into the novel, disguising his intertextual engagement by translating Berger's arguments and formulations into Marie's French:

> I recollect that I myself saw a family of fallow deer gathered together by a manger of hay near the perimeter fence of a dusty enclosure where no grass grew, a living picture of mutual trust and harmony which also had about it an air of constant vigilance and alarm. Marie particularly asked me to take a photograph of this beautiful group, and as she did so, said Austerlitz, she said something which I have never forgotten, she said that captive animals and we ourselves, their human counterparts, view one another *à travers une brèche d'incompréhension*.
> (2002a: 368–9)

Sebald's critics have rarely noticed this. For those who have, they often relegate it to footnotes as if it were merely of interest to 'intertext hunters' (Long 2007: 45 fn 21). Nor have they attended to the fact that, as the passage continues, Sebald paraphrases Berger again through the mouths of disappointed children: 'On these walks', Austerlitz says, 'it was not unusual for us to hear one of the children whose adult companions still took them to the zoo calling out, in some exasperation: *Mais il est où? Pourquoi il se cache? Pourquoi il ne bouge pas? Est-ce qu'il est mort?* Sebald translates this directly from Berger's parenthetical questions: '(As frequently as the calls of animals in a zoo, are the cries of children demanding: Where is he? Why doesn't he move? Is he dead?)' (2002a: 369). For Berger, the children's demands equate to the following question: 'Why are these animals less than I believed?' (2009: 23). At the same time, Sebald's translation extends Berger's essay, radicalizing it anew. For Sebald, human spectators are the 'counterparts' of these captive animals. They too are imprisoned. Moreover, the formulation '*une brèche*' (2002a: 369) turns Berger's 'narrow abyss' into a breach, offering a more dramatic and indeed more polemical description of the zoo.

In *Austerlitz*, then, encounters with captive animals – and the always restricted cross-species meeting of humans and nonhumans – provide occasions for critical

Figure 4 Returning the gaze © W. G. Sebald, *The Rings of Saturn*, 1998. Reproduced with the permission of the Wylie Agency and the W. G. Sebald Estate.

reflection on both the diminishment of natural life in modernity and the sense that both humans and nonhumans find themselves enclosed. In this logic, zoo animals become mirrors for Sebald's characters, who interpret their loneliness as a reflection of their own alienation. Thus while the zoological garden testifies to a rupture in human–animal relations, it also creates an opportunity for a new, melancholic connection between human and nonhuman.

Archiving life

Sebald's literary project is often said to explore the feverish archival impulses of contemporary life. His poetics of connection formally collects and connects together assorted lost objects, redeeming them through narrative articulation.

One of my goals in this chapter has been to show that this archiving of life includes nonhuman animals, and that Sebald's particular formal repertoire bears witness to the fates of animals under modernity.

Now, by way of a conclusion, I wish to investigate the effects of Sebald's narrative style, focusing on how his texts' syntactic hallmarks – such as hypotaxis, parataxis and lists – convey connections between humans and other animals. When, for example, Austerlitz describes how moths become trapped in the curtains of houses, he says that he believes 'they know they have lost their way'. Ascribing agency and sentience to moths, and projecting a creaturely sympathy, he continues:

> Sometimes, seeing one of these moths that have met their end in my house, I wonder what kind of fear and pain they feel while they are lost. As Alphonso had told him, said Austerlitz, there is really no reason to suppose that lesser beings are devoid of sentient life. We are not alone in dreaming at night for, quite apart from dogs and other domestic creatures whose emotions have been bound up with ours for many thousands of years, the smaller mammals such as mice and moles also live in a world that exists only in their minds whilst they are asleep, as we can detect from their eye movements, and who knows, said Austerlitz, perhaps moths dream as well, perhaps a lettuce in the garden dreams as it looks up at the moon by night.
>
> (2002a: 133–4)

Similar in tone to *Rings*'s description of the dissected herring, here we encounter another occasion in which Sebald's narrators speculate on nonhuman sentience, unsettling the anthroponormative dogma that only humans have complex cognitive capacities. Imagining a multi-species dreamscape, Austerlitz negates the sense that animals are 'lesser beings'.

But what makes this passage flow is its use of hypotaxis. Hypotaxis and parataxis are syntactic devices of arrangement; they are the means by which prose travels, by which sentences are connected together. Derived from Greek rhetoric, hypotaxis and parataxis denote respectively the vertical (arranging under) and the horizontal (arranging side by side).[11] Hypotaxis, as I illustrate in this sentence, is a practice of syntactic subordination in which conjunctions, piling up on top of one another, form a narrative whole that leads the reader from one point to the next, continuously, or perhaps not continuously, as subclauses momentarily digress to discuss other matters entirely, returning only later to the point at hand, as the combination of dependent clauses and connectives builds up. Sebald states that his hypotactic style derives from a loose tradition of eighteenth- and nineteenth-century prose forms that have 'fallen into disrepair' (quoted in Silverblatt 2007: 77–8). From naturalists and essayists like Georg Wilhelm Steller and Adalbert Stifter, whose 'multiple subordinate clauses bolstered their observations with thick detail while outlining complex relationships within and among different phenomena' (Davis 2015: 226), Sebald develops an authoritative, elevated, antiquarian and essayistic hypotaxis, a patient and less plot-driven style that is driven – or better, held in suspension – by the author-persona. Yet from modernist and postmodernist authors such as Robert Walser, H. G. Adler, Peter Weiss, Thomas Bernhard and Marianne Fritz, Sebald conjures a hypotactic form which militates against the speaker's narrative mastery. Sebald's narration adopts the voice of others, who adopt the voice of others (said Alphonso, said Austerlitz, said the narrator), in order to draw sharper attention to the narrator's own position within the storytelling. It functions like a Russian doll, perhaps, or – to take a phrase from Austerlitz himself – 'nested egg cartons' ['*ineinander verschachtelten Eierkartons*'] (Sebald 2001a: 135–6). In *Austerlitz*, Sebald intensifies this hypotactic practice, composing sentences of such length that the reader, following the twists and turns of clauses, might momentarily forget who is speaking. The novel's leitmotif, 'said X', reminds readers whose voice is in play during this multi-storied hypotactic narrative.

Critics have argued that Sebald's hypotaxis subverts the hierarchical ordering of plotted narrative. Kasia Kaakinen writes that Sebald's style creates 'undetermined narrative and historical linkages across vast temporal and geographic distances' (2017: 176), while Lynn Wolff suggests that Sebald's sentences – especially in their original German – hasten readers 'to arrive at the subject or object of the sentence' while compelling them at the same time 'to return and reread passages' (2014: 64). But what has gone mostly unnoticed here is how Sebald's writing *horizontalizes* the verticality of hypotaxis. By this I mean that Sebald's habitual subordination of clauses does not privilege particular events, or particular living beings, over one another, but rather connects events and beings together, utilizing hypotactic forms through a side-by-side logic. The politics or ethics of this formal move is demonstrated by the passage above, in which each clause incrementally broadens the horizon of dreaming, extending outwards from the human to mice and moles, even to lettuces. As a result, Sebald's use of hypotaxis unsettles the hierarchy of species.

Parataxis, in contrast, connotes a discontinuous practice in which juxtaposing clauses are articulated without coordinating subordination. Paratactic formulations offer discrete syntactic elements with only minimal relation or causal explanation. As Eric Auerbach put it, parataxis is 'fraught with background' (1991: 12), implying some connection between sentences but only through their gaps or fissures. Sebald's narratives are predominantly hypotactic. Yet his writing has a tendency to paratactically pivot from one memory to another, often without any explication or framing beyond apparently free associations. Moreover, his hypotactic grammar sits in tandem, as well as in tension, with his in-text images, which might be described as a kind of non-linguistic parataxis: not only do they destabilize the accompanying linguistic content but there is also no guidance for the reader to determine how they might be read together. In sum, then, Sebald's prose combines hypotaxis and parataxis, the syntactic and the non-syntactic, the long sentence and the list, the passage and the image. Critics argue that this produces a 'complex kind of narrative time' (Lee 2012: n.p.), as Sebald's combination of hypotaxis and parataxis constructs a 'poetics of suspension' (Eshel 2003: 71) which, they argue, seeks to pause the onrushing force of modernity. But how does this relate to Sebald's writing of nature, and of other creatures?

It is through Sebald's characterization of Great-Uncle Alphonso, mentioned in the passage above, that the novel develops its most sustained – and often paratactic – articulation of the role of nature in modernity. Throughout the novel, Austerlitz talks at length about his childhood friend Gerald Fitzpatrick and his decadent family home, Andromeda Lodge. Austerlitz speaks of visiting the Lodge over consecutive school holidays, a peaceful idyll near the seaside town of Barmouth that made him feel like he was 'living in another world' (2002a: 115). For the young Austerlitz, the Lodge presented a window onto the exotic, its acreage offering Welsh mountains and estuaries in the background and giant rhubarb and New Zealand ferns in the foreground, as well as housing numerous rare or exotic species – dead and live – that he had never previously encountered. The Fitzpatrick family kept a working orangery, a collection of taxidermy parrots and a number of living cockatoos that were, Austerlitz says, 'very like human beings in many ways' (116), sighing, laughing, sneezing and yawning. While the cockatoos took kindly to the land-owning Fitzpatricks, they 'screeched at [the Welsh housekeeper] in the most obnoxious way' (116), as if they had absorbed the class interests of their owners. Andromeda Lodge therefore testifies to as well as ironizes the opulence of the landed class and their private empires of nature.

Sebald utilizes parataxis throughout his descriptions of the Lodge's collections of preserved nonhuman specimens. Austerlitz notes that 'there was some kind of cabinet of natural curiosities in almost every room at Andromeda Lodge', explaining that the collections began with Gerald's 'great-grandfather or great-great-grandfather from his circumnavigation of the globe' (117). The Lodge began transforming into a private natural history gallery in the late nineteenth century, after Gerald's 'parrot-collecting ancestor made the acquaintance of Charles Darwin'. Austerlitz remembers the thousands of specimens, collected across generations of Fitzpatricks, that he saw displayed in cases and cabinets throughout the house:

> cases with multiple drawers, some of them glass-fronted, where the roundish eggs of parrots were arranged in their hundreds; collections of shells, minerals, beetles and butterflies; slowworms, adders and lizards preserved in formaldehyde; snail shells and sea urchins, crabs and shrimps, and large herbaria containing leaves, flowers and grasses.
>
> (118–19)

Sebald's lists, catalogues, classifications and inventories have received much critical discussion. The central question of such critical commentary is whether Sebald's lists merely re-present their objects and materials. On the one hand, there is a formal symmetry between Sebald's prose style and the collections he describes. By using the list form to describe what is preserved and contained, telescoping in on the name and characteristics of each specimen, Sebald's prose risks becoming a linguistic counterpart to Alphonso's taxidermic practices, preserving in language what Alphonso preserves in formaldehyde, hence reinforcing a sense of human sovereignty over nature. Sebald's lists, which help construct the often-observed *Wunderkammer* feel to his books, might therefore be said to formally replicate the logic of natural history as form of classificatory objectivization.

Yet Sebald constructs these lists in order to reflect critically on naturalism's legacies in the mid-twentieth century. Sebald's sentences, I think, adopt the archival impulse against itself, bearing witness to the sheer scale of British imperialism's expropriation of nonhuman nature while also parodying these practices of imperial antiquarianism. There is a sense of unsustainable excess here that spills over into decay. Indeed, Sebald folds the history of the Lodge into the novel's larger thematic focus on decline. By the time of Austerlitz's adulthood, and his meetings with the novel's narrator, Alphonso will have passed away and the Lodge will have been auctioned off. Andromeda Lodge, as a bountiful space of preserved nature, with its allusion to an entire galaxy, is thus presented metonymically. Like the British Empire, the Lodge is a 'fading world' (2002a: 158). Sebald's paratactic list form, in its sheer accumulation of life forms, presents the excess at the heart of the imperialist and naturalist project, typified by the opulence and decline of the British country house.

This complicated interrelation between Sebald's lists and the world of imperialism is exemplified by Great-Uncle Alphonso himself. On the one hand, Alphonso's passion for the natural sciences renders him acutely aware of nature's importance. As a naturalist he is well positioned to mourn modernity's increasing 'disturbances and disruptions' of nonhuman life (127). But on the other, Sebald characterizes Alphonso as exhibiting what he described in *Rings* as the 'thirst for knowledge', the desire for mastery. Austerlitz recalls, for instance, how Alphonso would speak nostalgically of the chalk cliffs of Devon and Cornwall from his childhood, 'where hollows and basins have been carved and cut out of the rock by the breakers over millions of years'. Alphonso recalls 'admiring the endless diversity of the semi-sentient marvels oscillating between the vegetable, animal and mineral kingdoms, the zooids and corallines, sea anemones, sea fans and sea feathers'. But all this will soon change when his 'passion for collecting' is met by its consequence, namely biodiversity loss and extinction:

> At that time the whole south-west coast of the island was surrounded by a colourful fringe ebbing and flowing with the tides, and now, said Uncle Alphonso, barely half a century later, those glories had been almost entirely destroyed by our passion for collecting and by other imponderable disturbances and disruptions.
>
> (126–7)

Sebald also juxtaposes Alphonso's melancholic attachment to the British coast's depleting biomass with his failure to mourn the unseen damage his natural collections have caused elsewhere in the world. The existence of the Fitzpatricks' estate is, in fact, made possible by British imperialism; it is a beacon of 'domestic imperialistic culture' built on the materials of conquest, as Edward Said (1994: 95) once suggested of Jane Austen's *Mansfield Park*. It is not unimportant that Alphonso's taxidermy parrot is an African Grey Parrot from 'the Congo' (117). This situates Alphonso within a history of colonialism, turning the taxidermy parrot into an emblem of empire's colonization of the wild. In sum, then, Alphonso acts out empire's conquest *and* preservation of nature. And Austerlitz's recollections of the Lodge therefore demonstrate an ambivalent, rather than celebratory, relationship between the human collector and the nonhuman collection.

Sebald's lists represent and formalize humanity's mastery of nature. They also develop a formal modulation of narrative temporality which contributes to his texts' creaturely form. For Sebald, the list is an important feature of his non-syntactic or more-than-syntactic repertoire, which encompasses his use of photographic images, tables, signatures, diagrams, maps, and stamps. What is the relationship, then, between Sebald's syntactic composition of narrative temporality – his disruption of hypotactic hierachizing – and his texts' representation of animals? Famously, Sebald refused to describe his works as novels, preferring to call them 'prose fictions'. Even *Austerlitz*, Sebald's most novelistic work, is for him more of a 'prose book of an indeterminate kind [*unbestimmter Art*]' (quoted in Doerry and Hage 2001: 228). Sebald even went so far as to rebuke the stylistic tendencies of the popular and dominant novel form. In two interviews conducted late in his life, Sebald criticized the contemporary novel for its mechanical function: he pushes back against the 'mechanisms of the novel' (quoted in Silverblatt 2007: 77–8), describing the writer's formal desire to 'get to the next phase of the plot' as being akin to 'wheels… grinding and going on' (Lubow 2007: 169).

These pronouncements on the novel form, however brief they may be, communicate an important feature of Sebald's literary project. *Rings* and *Austerlitz* are not interested in oiling the novel form's grindingly mechanical pursuit of plot. Instead, Sebald's essayistic prose pauses the novel's steady linearity of progression, which he associates with the destruction and marginalization of other forms of life. *Austerlitz* contains no chapters and no paragraphs (in the German edition at least) and ends ambiguously, without closure. *Rings* has its own orbiting narrative logic which ultimately circles back to where it began. Thus for all that is said of Sebald's ambulatory narratives, his texts ultimately perform a kind of stasis. His literary form, with 'its own insurgent tendency to kick against plot', develops what David James calls a kind of 'critical solace' (2016: 484) which refuses the plots of modernity, suspending the novel's rearticulation of modernity's dominant temporality and providing symbolic compensation to the victims of anthropocentric modernity.

While the novel form can function as an anthropological machine, a machine that crafts a vision of the human subject as sovereign, Sebald's indeterminate fictions attend to and connect together those forms of life and literary forms that have 'fallen into disrepair'. Whether zoo animals, over-fished herring or even essayistic hypotaxis, Sebald re-members these forms and, in doing so, suspends the onward rush of plot, pausing the associated narratives of progress which ideologically sanction modernity's war against animals. This formal gesture may ultimately stand as a limited, even hopeless tactic for contesting the war against animals, merely witnessing and hence memorializing the lives of species as they decline. But still, Sebald's creaturely melancholia relates human and animal, history and nature, genocide and ecocide in such a way that softens the anthroponormativity of literature. Compellingly, his writing suggests that the progress of modernity and the progress of plot are imbricated with the loss of culture and loss of nature. Against this progress, Sebald offers his slow form of remembrance.

Notes

1   There are, it must be said, crucial differences between these accounts. McCulloh and Wolff suggest that Sebald's work is governed by a secret order, while Bewes argues that connections are yearned for yet ultimately impossible for Sebald. At stake in this dissensus is the question of how Sebald's writing develops its literary ethics: one side says that Sebald creates a totalizing perspective, informed by the unifying principle that history is one long catastrophe; the other says that Sebald in fact suspends totalization, forestalls exemplarity and hence treats connection as something fundamentally uncertain. We will see both of these notions played out across this chapter.
2   To my knowledge, Uwe Schütte – a former graduate student of Sebald's at the University of East Anglia – is the only other critic whose work acknowledges Sebald's vegetarianism (2011: 200; 2020: 28). In private email correspondence, Schütte confirmed to me that Sebald's vegetarianism was an intentionally ethical position.
3   The speech was first published in *Stuttgarter Zeiting* (Sebald 2001b).
4   I take this idea from Ben Hutchinson (2009a: 326).
5   Rosanne Kennedy argues that Sebald's texts construct a posthumanist perspective which 'decentres the human by gesturing towards a species view that imagines the human, like other species, as facing possible extinction' (2012: 172). Jason Groves similarly writes that Sebald 'explores a postnatural world of anthropogenic climate change, biological invasion, and mass extinction' (2017: 277).
6   On Sebald's debt to Bernhard, see Doerry and Hage (2001: 233).
7   Sebald elaborates on the word *Unglück* in his essay collection on Austrian literature, *Die Beschreibung des Unglücks* (1994).
8   For more on Sebald as trickster, see Sheppard (2005: 441).
9   Silverblatt is one such critic who falls into this trap (2007: 77).
10 On the history of displayed peoples and zoos, see Couttenier (2014: 107), Blanchard et al. (2008) and Qureshi (2011).
11 See Greene et al. (2012: 650).

3

J. M. Coetzee's creaturely trouble

Deforming the novel, transforming personhood

When J. M. Coetzee was awarded the Jerusalem Prize for literature in 1987, he used his acceptance speech to express how colonialism and apartheid had deformed South Africa. Speaking at the height of the nationwide state of emergency, a time in which internal resistance to and international sanctions against the apartheid regime had intensified the country's political crisis, Coetzee described how not just social relations but also the very writing of social relations had become distorted by the 'unfreedom' of colonial domination:

> The deformed and stunted relations between human beings that were created under colonialism and exacerbated under what is loosely called apartheid have their psychic representation in a deformed and stunted inner life. All expressions of that inner life, no matter how intense, no matter how pierced with exultation or despair, suffer from the same stuntedness and deformity. I make this observation with due deliberation, and in the fullest awareness that it applies to myself and my own writing as much as to anyone else.
>
> (1992: 98)

Coetzee's speech hopes for a day in which South African literature will be able to 'take up residence in a world where a living play of feelings and ideas is possible'. But until that day comes, he suggests, it will remain a 'literature in bondage', 'exactly the kind of literature you would expect people to write from a prison'. It is, in fact, a 'less than fully human literature'.

Coetzee's account of South African letters is also an act of self-description. Despite wishing for his writing to reach 'the vast and complex human world that lies beyond', Coetzee concedes that his texts are trapped within, even *articulated through*, these stunted and deformed relations. Indeed, it might be said that Coetzee makes this 'less than fully human' condition the very content or object of his fiction.

For him, I think, it is ethically impossible for literature to prematurely transcend colonial domination. Instead, if writing is to remain responsive to its specific historical conjuncture it must retain, explore and work through the deformities of society itself. Coetzee's novels, by continuously interrogating the impacts of domination, take on the ethical challenge of shouldering its very distortions.

In doing this, Coetzee's fiction stages a dual deformation. His writing bends and reshapes the formal and generic conventions of the novel form, and in turn transforms the characteristic senses and individuating tendencies of personhood, subjectivity and humanity which typically lie at the heart of literature. On the one side, Coetzee has developed a deep engagement with novelistic forms, whether the nineteenth-century epistolary novel of sensibility, the Russian novel of ideas or the South African farm novel, the *plaasroman*. From *Dusklands* to *The Schooldays of Jesus*, as well as throughout his public lectures, works of criticism, published correspondences and private notebooks, his writing is built on an 'abiding concern with the origins, history, and ongoing cultural legacy of the form of the novel' (Hayes 2010: 1–2). Coetzee once wrote that the crucial question of the novel has always been 'what next?' (1992: 37). And by posing this question within his fiction, Coetzee has constantly reworked novelistic forms, in effect building his own 'countergenres' (Hayes 2010: 134) that strive to 'defy, reform, and to some degree reinvent the realist novel' (Ogden 2010: 466), to 'remake or even unmake the novel' (Zimbler 2014: 199). In his foundational study of Coetzee's first six works, David Attwell explains how Coetzee developed a form of 'situational metafiction' (1993: 20), a mode of postmodern novel-writing positioned against colonial discourses. This style has, to a greater or lesser extent, persisted until today. In the autofictional novel *Summertime*, for instance, Coetzee has his characters reflect on the career of a writer, coded as a fictional rendering of Coetzee himself, whose work has tried to 'deform his medium' (2010: 242). To put this in the words of Gayatri Chakravorty Spivak, Coetzee's literary project can be said to 'ab-use' (2012: 395) the novel form: he uses it otherwise; he finds another use for it.

Just as Coetzee ab-uses the novel, so too does he ab-use the human person, or character, whose experience structures and propels the given work's plot. Coetzee's novels worry away at the ostensibly stable selfhood of their characters. He repeatedly throws his protagonists into narrative situations of alienation, ambivalence, vulnerability and fragmentation in which their previously established ways of life break down and recalibrate, are de- and reformed, through an encounter with the Other. Coetzee's characters, whether they are administrators of colonial regimes, as in the unnamed Magistrate from

Waiting for the Barbarians, active participants in US post-war imperialism, as in *Dusklands*'s Eugene Dawn, or supposedly passive bourgeois beneficiaries of South African apartheid, like Elizabeth Curren in *Age of Iron*, have been and continue to be stunted and deformed by the social sedimentation of hierarchies of domination. The result is a literary thematization of negative transcendence that, as Sam Durrant puts it, 'brings the self into an abject, bodily relation with itself' (2004: 48), thereby hastening the 'breakup of the dominating rationalist subject of colonialism' (Attwell 1993: 1–2). Coetzee's characters are continually made to give things up, to let things go. His literary project thus offers us what Regina Janes describes as 'the recurrence of loss' (1997: 105). In the words of the Magistrate from *Waiting for the Barbarians*: 'I lose myself' (2004c: 28). And this loss implicates the very 'humanity' of Coetzee's characters, as they enter forms of 'minimal humanity' (Wiegandt 2019: 60), of bare and vulnerable life, in which the apparent protections of the social world give way.

It will be my contention throughout this chapter that Coetzee's twinned deformation of the novel and the person is inextricable from, even intensified by, his writing of human–animal relations. Coetzee's dramatization of human and nonhuman life, underpinned by his desire for a more socially just relationship between humans and other species, necessarily troubles the form, genres and characters of his texts. In other words, when Coetzee writes animals, writes *about* animals, his literature's 'less than fully human' form takes on an ethical stance, disputing both the authority of the novel form and the autonomy and rectitude of the protagonist. I take the term 'rectitude' from Adriana Cavarero, who critiques the Enlightenment discourse of rectitude – of being simultaneously upright, erect, correct, autonomous – for constructing a figure of 'Man' as the exceptional endpoint of the evolutionary chain. Against the ascendency of rectitude, which imposes patriarchal, racial and ontological hierarchies, Cavarero suggests that we cultivate a sense of *inclination*. To deliberately incline ourselves towards others – to lean down towards those lives that are construed as lower or lesser – reveals that we too are 'creatures who are materially vulnerable and… consigned to one another' (2016: 13). Inclination is thus an ethical project of interrelation set against what we might call the anthropological machine of uprightness. In Coetzee's writing, an inclination towards animal life constitutes a challenge to anthroponormative subjectivity.

Coetzee's critics have been keen to point out that his works' preoccupation with negative transcendence, of deformation and inclination towards the other, has often involved the figure of the animal. Jacqueline Rose, for example, observes that because Coetzee's worlds do not allow for transcendence, his characters often find themselves travelling the other way, plummeting 'down the great chain of being towards animals' (2013: 155). (It must be said, though, that Coetzee's articulation of this slide towards animality actually deconstructs the hierarchy of this great chain of being; as we will see later on in this chapter, texts like *Disgrace* suggest that encountering the embodiment and vulnerability of human animality promises its own forms of psychic and ethical emancipation.) Others have appraised Coetzee's entire oeuvre as being concerned with how to write this figure of the animal into the terrain of literature: 'from his earliest to his most recent work', Louis Tremaine writes, Coetzee builds 'a pattern of incorporating animals as narrative elements associated with suffering and death' (2003: 595).

Coetzee has even become the most written-about author in the burgeoning canon of literary animal studies. In fact, I cannot think of a single monograph on contemporary literature and animals that is not, in one way or another, underpinned by Coetzee's writing on animals – this book included. *The Lives of Animals* has been especially foundational here, not least because of its literary engagement with major debates in animal ethics, its notably metafictional style and its distinctly academic purview. As I will discuss later, *The Lives of Animals* stands as both a kind of campus fiction and a text produced for scholarly reflection, originally delivered to an academic audience and later published with footnotes and follow-up essays. It is perhaps unsurprising, then, that Coetzee's work has been taken up by literary animal studies, its proponents confessing how haunted they have been by his portrayal of human–animal relations, and arguing that his works point towards a posthumanist ethics.[1]

Despite all of this, many of Coetzee's foremost critics still consider animals, or *the animal* in its more conceptual form, as a secondary concern of his writing. David Attwell, for instance, writing in his archival study of Coetzee's career, claims that documents in the University of Texas at Austin's Harry Ransom Center reveal Coetzee to be a writer whose engagement with human cruelty towards animals is better read as a mere 'touchstone for debates about cruelty in general' (Attwell 2015: 219).

Yet this appeal to a conveniently abstract idea of 'cruelty in general' obscures Coetzee's development of a real public, intellectual and literary concern with the lives of animals: with animal liberation, rights and welfare. Coetzee became a vegetarian as early as 1974. He has long been a critical reader of the major works in animal ethics. And he began public-facing pro-animal advocacy in the lead-up to his emigration to Australia in 2002.[2] In 2007, Coetzee delivered the opening remarks at an exhibition by the Australian animal rights charity, Voiceless, speaking of the manifold 'ways in which our relationship with animals is wrong'; 'there is', he writes, 'something deeply, cosmically wrong with regarding and treating fellow beings as mere units of any kind' (2007a: 17). Indeed the Coetzee archive in Austin, opened in 2013, contains numerous examples of correspondence between the author and advocacy groups such as Animals Australia, the Humane Society of the United States, People for the Ethical Treatment of Animals and the Royal Society for the Prevention of Cruelty to Animals.[3]

But beyond these public and private expressions of commitment towards other creatures, I want to argue that Coetzee's concern with animal ethics has had real effects on shaping and reshaping his literary style. In the 1990s especially, the period I will focus on in this chapter, Coetzee embarked on what we might call an *animal turn*. Pivoting within the pages of his fiction towards the lives and deaths of unwanted dogs and slaughterhouse cattle, creatures that are produced, killed and reproduced by human society for its own needs, Coetzee wrote a cluster of works that not only expressed anger about the treatment of individual animal lives but also conceived of modernity as having ushered in a perpetual war against animal life. In *The Lives of Animals*, *Disgrace* and *Elizabeth Costello*, three texts that were conceived, researched and drafted in tandem around the turn of the millennium, Coetzee foregrounds the pain inflicted on animals at a local and global level, emphasizing how society is organized in such a way that expands *and* hides the organized death of animals. At the same time, Coetzee emphasizes that this human characters are animals too; his works thus attest that there is a 'life we share with animals', as *Disgrace's* Lucy Lurie puts it (2000: 74). Coetzee's fiction articulates a shared animality that raises the question of our obligation to other creatures.

I will argue in this chapter that Coetzee's preoccupation with animals has had a major impact not just on the politics and ethics of his novels but also on the very forms of his texts. By inclining his writing towards animal life, Coetzee repeatedly confronts literature's tendency towards anthroponormativity. His texts, then, are the end products of an encounter between literary traditions and animal ethics, between the humanistic disposition of Literature and the anti- or posthumanist impulse of solidarity with nonhuman life.

Coetzee first announced his growing inclination towards animals in a sensitive and now much-quoted passage from *Doubling the Point*, a book comprised of interviews and reflections on his career up to the early 1990s:

(Let me add, *entirely* parenthetically, that I, as a person, as a personality, am overwhelmed, that my thinking is thrown into confusion and helplessness, by the fact of suffering the world, and not only human suffering. These fictional constructions of mine are paltry, ludicrous defences against that being-overwhelmed, and, to me, transparently so.)

(1992: 248)

It is easy to underestimate the complexity of this short reflection, as well as the significance of Coetzee's adjacent subordinate clause, *and not only human suffering*, which becomes all the more central precisely due to Coetzee's insistence that it is parenthetical. Derek Attridge reminds us that Coetzee is meticulous and deliberate, a writer who pays painstaking attention to his 'shaping of language, the phrasing of syntax, the resonating of syllables' (2004: 48). In the passage above, Coetzee layers the speaking voice, his first-person 'I', as a dialogic combination of private self (the I), subjectivity and personhood (the person) and public-facing author (the personality). While the authorial personality, the writer, creates fictional worlds that might protect its other selves from the reality of suffering, the defences of literary form do not hold. Each of Coetzee's selves is overwhelmed by human and nonhuman suffering. And his literary style is a poor barricade, articulating rather than defending against this state of 'being-overwhelmed'.

Critics have often posited that Coetzee's fiction stakes out an ethical position because it remains inconsolable before the pain of others. Because Coetzee's work is 'speechless before apartheid' (2004: 23), Sam Durrant writes, it bears witness to the violence of colonialism without prematurely realizing forms of reconciliation. But as Coetzee's qualifying clause *and not only...* suggests, his work also remains speechless before the war against animals. In texts like *The Lives of Animals* and *Disgrace*, Coetzee works to enunciate or stage an entire ethics beyond humanism. Yet at the same time I wish to argue that his writing becomes overwhelmed by the very animal pain he seeks to portray, by the difficulty of realizing an animal ethics within literary form. Despite his characters' many attempts to put animal suffering into words, Coetzee's texts attest, above all, to the difficulty of comprehending the scale of modernity's exploitation and killing of other species. At the start of her speech on philosophy and animals, Elizabeth Costello states that 'the horrors I here omit are nevertheless at the centre of this lecture' (2004a: 63). It is as if narrating the war against animals is, somehow, beyond the scope of rhetorical force. Yet if Coetzee deems the excesses of organized animal suffering to exceed narration, then it is precisely by voicing this resistance to narratability that his writing captures the horror of living in social worlds that rely on the slaughter of other creatures.

Focusing in turn on *Disgrace* and then *Elizabeth Costello*, I wish to argue here that Coetzee is striving to craft literary forms that can express a creaturely affinity with other animals. In these texts Coetzee is testing out, at a sentence-by-sentence level, the capacities and affordances of differing genres and styles to accommodate this creaturely perspective and ethic. To what extent, then, can literary forms articulate a challenge to anthroponormativity? How does *Disgrace*'s inhabitation of literary realism dramatize interspecies care? And how, in comparison, do the more overtly metafictional tendencies of *The Lives of Animals* and *Elizabeth Costello* help differently contest the war against animals? Why does Coetzee turn to what he calls 'dull realism' (cited in Attwell 2015: 187) in order to write *Disgrace*, and why does he then utilize a metafictional 'anti-illusionism' (1992: 27) for *Elizabeth Costello*, a form that Coetzee had previously depreciated as a passing phase in the history of the novel? What do both of these forms achieve? What are their limits? Put differently, I will be examining how literature and pro-animal thought mutually impact upon one another. Reading Coetzee's work allows us to ask: What happens to the ideas and commitments of animal ethics when they come up against plotted events that threaten the possibilities for cross-species care? And how does the formalization and figuration of literary style and character transform in its encounter with pro-animal thought?

Throughout this chapter I will conceive of Coetzee's animal turn as a kind of textual experiment, a multi-text investigation that attends simultaneously to the problem of writing fiction *about* animals and the problem of writing pro-animal thought *into fiction* as such. By using this term, 'textual experiment', I aim to invoke the notion of the thought-experiment, the act of philosophical or ethical problem-posing which provokes particular logics, modes and trains of thought. Carrol Clarkson has written that 'just as philosophers develop thought-experiments, Coetzee develops formal and literary ones' (2009: 13). Spivak puts it that the 'formal logic of Coetzee's fiction mimes ethical moves in an uncanny way' (2002: 25 fn. 10). Coetzee himself writes that storytelling is, for him, 'another, an other mode of thinking' (1998: 4). And yet Coetzee's articulation of ethical problems does not simply reproduce within fiction the prototypical thought-experiment as an expression of abstract moral reasoning. Instead, Coetzee's textual experiments work to unsettle this idea of a detached and cerebral experiment. They suggest instead a more embodied experiment that is guided by the internal logics of his fictional settings, the bodies of his characters and the emplotment of the novels themselves. This 'biologico-literary experiment', as Coetzee puts it in *Slow Man* (2005: 114), offers an experiment with literary form which troubles the anthroponormativity of literature and life.

But as with any experiment there is always the risk of encountering unexpected constraints and failures. Derek Attridge once argued that Coetzee's writing frequently stages vexing, intractable and open questions without ever resolving them (2004: xi). This continues in Coetzee's animal-centred works which, by staging this convergence between the motor of plot and the commitment to animal lives, end up proposing a number of aporetic questions that undermine the possibility for an idealistic conclusion: *Disgrace* seems to ask whether the euthanasia of dogs can be counted as an act of love, while *The Lives of Animals* and *Elizabeth Costello* jointly wonder whether it is truly possible for someone who has opened their eyes to animal suffering to break bread with those for whom the commonplace slaughter and eating of dead bodies is normal. This ambivalence at the heart of Coetzee's writing of animals – this refusal to transcend the unjust relations we humans have with animals – makes his work knotted and intractable. It creates its own trouble, a formal and ethical trouble which testifies to rather than escapes the profoundly unequal and deformed relations between humans and other animals. Indeed Coetzee's animal turn reaches such a formal impasse that, after the publication of *Elizabeth Costello*, nonhuman animals will largely fade out of Coetzee's writing altogether. Yet the underlying questions, the problem of our own animality and of what we owe to other creatures, nevertheless remain deeply embedded in his writing to this day.[4]

Closer to the ground: *Disgrace*, dogs and depersonalization

In 2002, Coetzee reviewed the posthumous publication of W. G. Sebald's debut literary work, *After Nature*. Reflecting on Sebald's rise to international literary recognition, as well as the scope and thematics of Sebald's wider writing, Coetzee describes Sebald's narrators as experiencing 'hallucinations of being in a high place looking down on the world… A spinning of the mind followed by mental collapse' (2007b: 148).[5] What Coetzee notices in Sebald's work is his preoccupation with the vertiginous, a deep and long perspective on the human species which – as I showed in my previous chapter – poses formal as well as ethical challenges for his writing. In contrast to the perspectival heights of Sebald's narrator, though, Coetzee's writing appears considerably *closer to the ground*. Where Sebald often crafts his creatureliness through a distant species-level narrative, Coetzee does so through an attention to characters who are firmly entrenched within their specific social situation, without any opportunity to rise above their historical conjuncture.

'Closer to the ground' is an important phrase in Coetzee's writing, one which he articulates word-for-word in some texts, thematically encodes into others and plots into almost every single one. *Closer to the ground* sometimes invokes a negative dehumanization; at other times, it signals a potentially (but never actualized) liberatory horizon out of social circumstance. Always, it is related to how regimes of domination produce deformed modes of living in and relating to the world.

In *Age of Iron*, for example, the phrase becomes associated with a rejection of a specific form of colonial subjectivity. Set during the escalating violence of the late apartheid years, *Age of Iron* is an epistolary novel in which a mother writes to her absent daughter. The novel revolves around a white, middle-class narrator, Elizabeth Curren, who is slowly dying of cancer, and black communities in the townships who suffer the systemic impoverishment and interpersonal oppression of the racial regime. As Curren confronts both her own mortality and the onto-political violence of apartheid – metaphorically braided together in the novel as two wounds, afflictions, illnesses – she begins to disavow her humanity in favour of a more creaturely existence. She starts associating herself with nonhuman figures such as crabs, whales, dogs, grubs and moths. In turn, she questions the very concept of 'Man'. After spending a night sleeping rough, Curren returns home to find her house ransacked: locks forced, windows smashed, 'nothing left untouched'. In shock, she swallows two pills and slides down onto her bedroom floor:

> Man, I thought: the only creature with part of his existence in the unknown, in the future, like a shadow cast before him. Trying continually to catch up with that moving shadow, to inhabit the image of his hope. But I, I cannot afford to be man. Must be something smaller, blinder, closer to the ground.
>
> (1991: 155)

Curren instantiates and then revokes the exceptionality of anthroponormativity. Catalysed by her recognition of two wounds, her confessional narrative effaces the personal pronoun 'I', suggesting a withdrawal from the self-consolidating event of first-person narration. Curren assumes a mode of living that is less than fully human. Abstaining from the sovereign-seeking logic of 'Man' she becomes, in her own words, a 'liminal creature' (127). Curren's invective overturns the evolutionary narrative of man's ascent, and with it denounces the associated domains of personhood, property and propriety. And this dehumanization is a response to apartheid, a kind of white 'deracination', according to Benita Parry (1996: 37), in which Coetzee plots out the dissolution of the late colonial subject. This construction of creaturely life is decidedly negative. The novel's figuration of animality promises Curren only a momentary release from the personal and political vortex. And there is no final answer as to whether Curren's letters, the words which make up the text we hold in our hands, will ever be read by her distant daughter.

Disgrace takes up Curren's challenge to live closer to the ground, but it does so in a different form and a different register, with a more deliberate inclination towards postcolonial futurity. *Disgrace*'s plot is by now well known. The novel is set in a fledgling post-apartheid South African in the years following the Truth and Reconciliation Commission. The novel is focalized through the figure of David Lurie, a twice-divorced and middle-aged adjunct professor of communications (formerly a professor of modern languages, with a specialism in European Romanticism, before management embarked on a period of institutional restructuring), who leaves his job at the Cape Technical University after raping a young female student, Melanie Isaacs, facing her charges for sexual harassment, and then refusing to issue an apology to the university's disciplinary tribunal. Lurie exiles himself from his home in Cape Town and moves in with his self-identified lesbian and feminist daughter, Lucy, at her smallholding farm in the Eastern Cape. Here they are both brutally assaulted: Lucy is gang-raped, and David is splashed with ethanol and set alight. Both survive this attack, but it dramatically changes their relationship to one another and with their daily existence in South Africa. Lucy, despite learning that she is pregnant, and despite also discovering that her Xhosa-speaking neighbour, Petrus, is related to one of her attackers, decides both to carry the baby and to accept Petrus' formal proposal of marriage as an offer of protection. David, shaken by his daughter's choices, commits to volunteering at a local animal welfare clinic, at which he assists in putting to sleep the shelter's many stray and unwanted dogs. 'Curious that a man as selfish as he should be offering himself to the service of dead dogs' (2000: 146). It is here that David warms to Bev Shaw, the clinic's owner. Although earlier on in the novel David had described Bev as a 'remarkably unattractive' (82) woman with a name that reminds him of cattle, they will later have sex on the clinic's operating floor, a moment which appears to further consolidate David's recognition of his own disgrace: 'And let him stop calling her poor Bev Shaw. If she is poor, he is bankrupt' (150).

Critical interpretations of *Disgrace* have often hinged on whether and to what ends the novel ought to be read as an arc that charts David's journey from personal bankruptcy to provisional salvation. The question is: can you teach an old dog new tricks? For Coetzee's humanist critics, David's recognition of his moral disgrace, his dawning sense that he has got himself in trouble, leads to his transformation from a 'monad divorced totally from other beings' into a more 'selfless' subject (Marais 2006: 76). According to Elleke Boehmer, it is David's communion with animals that engenders his 'surrender of self through empathy' (2002: 346). Willingly identifying himself as a 'dog-man' (Coetzee 2000: 146), David undergoes a creaturely transformation, a kind of becoming-animal; by relegating himself to the assumed shame and poverty of animality, approximating his existence to that of dogs, David becomes 'stupid, daft, wrongheaded' (146), and is thus paradoxically released from the shackles of his ingrained masculine self-interest (Herron 2005). For many animal studies critics, though, David's apparent redemption is fundamentally tainted because it relies on his sacrifice of nonhuman animals, a 'normative cleansing process' (Gal 2005: 250) that reestablishes the sovereignty of the human subject. Thus for all of the ways Coetzee's novel generatively dissolves the boundaries between human and nonhuman, they argue, *Disgrace* ultimately reinstalls the figure of the human protagonist over and above other canine lives.

Both of these readings are largely borne out by the novel, in which Coetzee utilizes the ambivalences and contradictions of David's arc in order to drive the narrative tension. David arrives in the Eastern Cape with no intentions to surrender to his disgrace. Instead his hope is to take stock, even fantasizing about returning 'triumphant to society as the author of an eccentric little opera' (214). Provisionally titled *Byron in Italy*, David first conceives of this chamber opera about eros as a mirror to his own story: early in the novel he tells his students that Byron did not die in Italy, but in Greece. 'He went to Italy to escape a scandal, and settled there' (15).[6] But for all of David's grandiose wishes to reclaim his former life, he soon becomes undone, sundered: 'If he came for anything, it was to gather himself, gather his forces. Here he is losing himself day by day' (121). This pattern of David 'losing himself', a leitmotif for almost all of Coetzee's protagonists, correlates with his growing attachment to voluntary labour at the animal shelter: 'He goes off to the Animal Welfare clinic as often as he can, offering himself for whatever jobs call for no skill' (142). David feeds, cleans, cares for *and* kills these dogs, before carefully feeding their stiff bodies into an incinerator. What is at stake here for David is his 'idea of the world, a world in which men do not use shovels to beat corpses into a more convenient shape for processing' (146).

It is inarguable that David develops an affinity with animal life. In one particularly illustrative scene, David climbs into a bulldog's cage and tickles her behind the ears, like Sebald's narrator does with the pigs in *The Rings of Saturn*: '"Abandoned are we?" he murmurs. He stretches out beside her on the bare concrete. Above is the pale blue sky. His limbs relax' (78). This image of intimacy and companionship stands in marked contrast to the novel's other scenes of relaxation, which invariably arrive after David has had sexual intercourse.

In a similar scene, David recognizes that a 'bond seems to have come into existence' (125) between himself and two sheep that are soon to be slaughtered. David's growing inclination towards animals catches him off guard: 'Sunday evening, driving home in Lucy's kombi, he actually has to stop at the roadside to recover himself. Tears flow down his face that he cannot stop; his hands shake. He does not understand what is happening to him' (142–3). Like Coetzee's Michael K, who wonders 'Is that how morals come, unbidden, in the course of events, when you least expect them?' (2004: 183), David experiences a sudden jolt of moral feeling. When he is served two mutton chops, he thinks: 'I am going to eat this and ask forgiveness afterwards' (131).

And yet David's increasing care for animal life does not necessarily guarantee his redemption. In fact, his relationship with other humans remains fraught. Early in the novel, David refers to his attackers as 'running-dogs' (131) and describes Lucy's rapists as animals who were 'mating' (199). A few pages before the book's end, when taking Katy the bulldog for a stroll, David discovers one of Lucy's attackers, Pollux, peering into their bathroom window. He lashes out, striking the boy in the face, yelling 'You filthy swine!' (206) before labelling him a 'jackal' (208). To the last, then, David continues to think within the logics of a metaphorical equivalency between racialization and animality, including animals within the orbit of moral concern while also relegating racialized others to the realms of the beastly. Coetzee therefore dramatizes how compassion towards animals can go hand-in-hand with racism towards other human beings. *Disgrace* suggests, in other words, that it might be easier for David to care for animals than his black neighbours. What then of his redemption?

But I do not wish to write yet another critique or recuperation of David Lurie. Doing so would not simply re-tread ground covered by others but it would also elide the ways in which *Disgrace* actively cautions its readers from dwelling too long on David. With *Disgrace*, Coetzee has written a novel that is suspicious about the very logics of realist protagonicity that it is formally wedded to. In *The One vs. the Many*, Alex Woloch writes that the novel form employs a 'distributional matrix' (2003: 13) that unevenly apportions characterization between narrators, focalizers and protagonists on the one side and marginal or minor characters on the other. *Disgrace* encourages a criticality about this typically asymmterical allocation of narrative space, even incorporating a suspicion of protagonicity into the novel's dialogue. At one point, Lucy criticizes her father for thinking of himself as the centre of the world:

> You behave as if everything I do is part of the story of your life. You are the main character, I am a minor character who doesn't make an appearance until halfway through. Well, contrary to what you think, people are not divided up into major and minor. I am not minor. I have a life of my own, just as important to me as yours is to you, and in my life I am the one who makes the decisions.
>
> (198)

Speaking in a language that her literary critic father might understand, Lucy strikes a Copernican blow as she implores David not to interpret his life as if it were a realist novel composed of a single protagonist's story. And with this Lucy interrupts the reader, too. Coetzee is alerting us to the fact that there is a world beyond David's focalization, beyond the distinct narrative voice and perspective that drives the novel forward. Indeed, Spivak argues that Coetzee deliberately constructs *Disgrace*'s narration through David's strict focalization so that it provokes readers into what she calls 'counterfocalization' (2002: 22). *Disgrace* has troubled many readers, Spivak says, because it appears on the surface level to act as a vehicle for the sympathetic portrayal of its protagonist. But 'if we, like Lurie, ignore the enigma of Lucy, the novel, being fully focalized precisely by Lurie, can be made to say every racist thing' (Spivak 2002: 24). Coetzee thus tasks his readers with counterfocalizing *with* Lucy *against* David, against the grain of the narrative voice and, by implication, against the residual colonial imagination that haunts the novel. This is most clearly demonstrated in Lucy's repeated insistence that her father keeps 'misreading' her (2000: 112).

Through its call for counterfocalization, *Disgrace* undermines its allocation of narrative space to David, thereby destabilizing its adherence to realist protagonicity. At stake in this gesture is a readerly recuperation of both Lucy's role in the novel and the novel's other, supposedly minor characters, *including* its animals, such as Katy the bulldog and *Driepoot*, who I will discuss below. Lucy's countervoice thus rejects David's racism while also contesting the story of human exceptionalism which novels habitually preserve:

> You think I ought to be painting still lives or teaching myself Russian. You don't approve of friends like Bev and Bill Shaw because they are not going to lead me to a higher life… They are not going to lead me to a higher life, and the reason is that there is no higher life. This is the only life there is. Which we share with animals. That's the example that people like Bev try to set. That's the example

> I try to follow. To share some of our human privilege with the beasts. I don't want to come back in another existence as a dog or a pig and have to live as dogs or pigs live under us.
>
> (74)

Lucy contends that the 'higher life' of humanistic aesthetics, advocated by her father and embodied in the novel we hold in our hands, contrasts with the lives of dogs and pigs who currently 'live under' human sovereignty. Although *Disgrace*'s plot dramatizes David's supposed descent into animality, it incorporates Lucy's interruptions in order to formally disabuse the hierarchical logic of this arc. For her, turning to animals does not mean plunging down an ontological order, for this ontological order is itself a social construction. At the same time, this does not mean abandoning the opportunities of 'human privilege', but rather redistributing them more justly between species. In this passage, Lucy crafts a mode of creatureliness that repudiates anthroponormativity while also recognizing the specific position of humans as ethical actors with a responsibility towards the lives of other beings.

I wish to argue, therefore, that Lucy's creatureliness is not a refutation of her humanity but a deconstruction of the kinds of colonial personhood which have colonized our sense of what humanity is. In an early review of *Disgrace*, Jane Taylor describes how Coetzee's novel 'considers the failure of a Western liberal tradition… a culture which contradictorily holds as sacred the absolute rights of the individual and the absolute value of private property' (1999: 25). Indeed, when David warns Lucy that she is humiliating herself by carrying the baby, she replies that 'perhaps that is a good point to start from again':

> To start at ground level. With nothing. Not with nothing but. With nothing. No cards, no weapons, no property, no rights, no dignity.
> Like a dog.
> 'Yes, like a dog.'
>
> (205)

Lucy embraces her putative likeness with dogs. However, in doing so she does not abandon humanity but rather rejects the liberal notion of personhood and its attendant paraphernalia of weapons, property and rights which are positioned against a degraded notion of bare animal life. From Roman law to Christian theology to secular modernity, personhood is an apparatus or mechanism that has organized predominantly Western formations of human subjectivity. For thinkers like Roberto Esposito, personhood is 'seen as the only semantic field that can overlap the two spheres of law and humanity' (2012: 3). Personification literally *masks* our notion of subjectification. It is an anthropological machine that aims to pull the human subject from a bare biology upwards into rights, duties, citizenship. But this process of personification has been historically uneven, unequal, claimed by the dominant in order to separate themselves from those gendered, racialized and animalized others who are forced to exist outside the bounds of proper humanity. Esposito argues that the problem of personhood is not resolved by making every being into a full person, nor by simply abandoning the binary between person and non-person, but by complicating it through the figuration of an impersonal 'third person' (15). Lucy is *Disgrace*'s third person, a character positioned at the margins of the novel's realist distribution of subjectivity, but whose very marginality – between characterization and depersonalization – troubles the apparent abyss between personhood and animality, between subject and object.

In fact, Lucy's articulation of a creaturely responsibility to animals arises out of an understanding of what it means to live 'in this place, at this time' (Coetzee 2000: 112), that is, as a descendent of settlers in post-apartheid South Africa. Lucy realizes that, within this new conjuncture, there is a complex recalibration of social relations under way – one which has implications for both human and animal lives. She notes that the 'watchdogs' on her smallholding farm – 'Dobermanns, German Shepherds, ridgebacks, bull terriers, Rottweilers' (61) – were previously trained as security for the functioning of the apartheid state: 'They are part of the furniture, part of the alarm system' (78). South Africa is a 'country where dogs are bread to snarl at the mere smell of black man' (110). Now, though, the dogs are only wanted for 'short contracts: two weeks, one week, sometimes just a weekend' (61). Lucy realizes that many of these dogs, coached in racist practices of property defence, are now undergoing a process of decommodification and obsolescence. 'There is no funding any longer', Lucy says. 'On the list of the nation's priorities, animals come nowhere' (73). 'The trouble is', Bev Shaw states, 'there are just too many of them'. 'Too many by our standards, not by theirs' (85). In post-apartheid South Africa, these dogs stand as a surplus population whose lives and deaths are in the hands of a retreating state infrastructure that places the burden of care on private human decisions. Lucy recognizes that Katy the bulldog is 'in mourning. No one wants her, and she knows it. The irony is, she must have offspring all over the district who would be happy to share their home with her. But it's not in their power to invite her' (78).

At the same time, Lucy rethinks notions of private property ownership and landholding. Gifting the land's title deeds to Petrus, Lucy develops a form of small-scale subsistence farming that Zoë Wicomb calls a 'translation from settler into something new' (2002: 220). Lucy transforms her material and epistemic relationship with this land, the former frontier of the Cape Colony, shrugging off the image of the colonial *boervrou*, or farm-wife, in favour of what her father fears is a life of peasantry as a *bywoner*. 'Stop calling it *the farm*, David. This is not a farm, it's just a piece of land where I grow things' (200). In contradistinction to Curren's being-towards-death and David's self-assumed evolutionary descent into a dog-man, Lucy enacts a form of personal postcolonial creatureliness that remaps the relations between humans and other animals. Lucy does not see land or dogs as property.

In its remapping of the interface between nature and culture in post-apartheid South Africa, *Disgrace* evokes two of its literary intertexts, two novelistic forebears which push at the limits of realism and disrupt the progressive telos of the *Bildungsroman* in their literary incorporation of creaturely life. In Thomas Hardy's *Jude the Obscure*, which imbricates Darwinian evolutionary thought into novelistic social setting, the protagonist Jude Fawley increasingly recognizes his own animality in the desires of farm animals – their hunger, their procreation, their mortality is not unlike his own. Yet as the novel progresses towards its bleak conclusions, Jude's child, Little Father Time, internalizes the darker side of evolutionary theory's universal laws of natural selection, extinction and population. Gripped by a Malthusian fever which identifies children as parasitic organisms, as blights on population, Little Father Time kills himself and his half-siblings. His suicide note reads 'Done because we are too menny' (Hardy 2002: 325). *Disgrace* thus translates this threatening excess of over-population back to nonhuman life, and it does so through its 'piece of land'.

Property is also a key motif in Olive Schreiner's *The Story of an African Farm*, a novel that Coetzee analyses in *White Writing* as a contribution to the *plaasroman* genre because it locates its Karoo farm as 'an unnatural and arbitrary imposition on a doggedly ahistorical landscape' (1988: 66), a site of everyday colonial life set against the backdrop of tensions between Dutch, German and Irish settlers and the indigenous peoples, who mostly serve as labourers. However *The Story of an African Farm*, like *Disgrace* after it, has a literary criticality about its own pastoralism, undermining the *plaasroman*'s dominant sentimental nostalgia for a return to the land through its attention to Cape landholding as a colonial encounter. Indeed, both *Jude the Obscure* and *Story of An African Farm* differently call into question literary realism as an anthropological machine. As Ivan Kreilkamp has shown, Hardy's and Schreiner's integration of animals into their fiction as minor characters 'questions fiction's role in humanizing and marking human/nonhuman distinctions' (2018: 3). *Disgrace* is thus a postcolonial contribution to a tradition of novelistic writing which wishes to test realism's capacity to include the lives of animals, to repair connections between human and nonhuman.

Coetzee pushes this home towards the end of the novel, when Bev Shaw points out to David that the time has come for him to 'let Lucy work out solutions for herself. Women are adaptable. Lucy is adaptable. And she is young. She lives closer to the ground than you' (2000: 210). While David is sceptical about Bev's claims, the novel positions her remarks as a fitting characterization of Lucy's determination to continue: to carry the child and to welcome a postcolonial future. This is doubtless an uncertain and unstable future. But its inbuilt insecurity is mitigated, to a degree, by the ways in which Lucy already lives 'closer to the ground'. By returning to this phrase that he first used in *Age of Iron*, now rearticulating it in a postcolonial context, Coetzee casts Lucy as a character who embodies a new way of living without personhood, and as a figure whose presence formally troubles the novel form's anthroponormative protagonicity.

The putting-to-death of *Driepoot*: tensions of tense in *Disgrace*

Sunday has come again. He and Bev Shaw are engaged in one of their sessions of Lösung. One by one he brings in the cats, then the dogs: the cold, the blind, the halt, the crippled, the maimed, but also the young, the sound – all those whose term has come.

(2000: 218)

Disgrace's closing scene is deceptive. If we were to read only the critical literature on the novel's ending, and not the ending itself, we would come away thinking that it concludes with an image of hesitant but caring euthanasia, a scene which depicts David killing his closest canine companion, a three-legged-dog, *Driepoot*. 'The novel ends on one of the killing Sundays', Derek Attridge writes. 'Lurie brings in a dog of whom he has grown particularly fond and gives him up to the waiting needle' (2004: 190). With this critical concentration on emplotment and narrative resolution, the major interpretations of *Disgrace*'s final pages have gravitated around the meanings and ethics of this culminating event of putting-to-sleep. Critics ask: Should David's work at the clinic be read as a sign of his rehabilitation (Attwell 2002: 339)? Or would it be a fundamental miscalculation to understand David's voluntary slaughter of surplus dogs as somehow redressing his transgressions that initiate the novel's plot (Attridge 2004: 188)? Is it possible for us to conceive of his slaughter of dogs as an act of cross-species care (Graham 2002: 9)? Or does David's self-proclaimed 'business of dog-killing' (Coetzee 2000: 161) represent little more than a continuation of a form of colonial domination, in which dogs function as expendable objects for David's – and hence the novel's own – narrative of redemption (Cornwell 2008: 136; Herrick 2016: 89)? In a scene whose imagery echoes at once the death and resurrection of the lamb of god and Abraham's sacrifice of the ram in the book of Genesis, what is the role of sacrifice here? What, really, is being given up, and what does this bring forth?

But, *Disgrace*'s ending is not quite as it appears. If we stick too closely to reading for the plot, we overlook one of the novel's most curious and formally inventive moments: a momentary glitch in the novel's overwhelmingly synchronic timeline, a rearrangement of narrative temporality right at the last. As we will see below, *Disgrace* is preoccupied by the uses and meanings of tenses. Throughout, it is a novel that stages a tension between the continual unfolding of the present simultaneous and the finality and closure of the perfective, with the final scene its formally climactic conclusion. How, then, are we to read Coetzee's novel in light of this formal reorganization of tense? What does it *do* to *Disgrace*'s writing of human–animal relations? And what does it tell us about the novel form?

Let us begin again. At the very start of the novel, Coetzee characterizes David as a self-interested figure whose primary relation to others is through an economy of desire and exchange. Each week David drives to Green Point, where he exchanges four hundred South African Rand for a session with a sex worker, Soraya. Come the end of the novel, though, David's world has changed – or, perhaps, the world has changed him. Now, his weekly routine involves visiting the Animal Welfare clinic. Engaging in unpaid labour with unwanted dogs, David gives up the economy of exchange for acts of gift-giving and care-taking. 'He and Bev do not speak. He has learned by now, from her, to concentrate all his attention on the animal they are killing, giving it what he longer has difficulty in calling by its proper name: love' (219). Learning from Bev, David cultivates a sense of concentration, attentiveness and care towards animals, both during their lives and after their deaths.

As this passage continues, though, another kind of economy enters the picture: sacrifice. With the novel's final sentences, David brings into the operating room a three-legged dog, a dog that 'he has come to feel a particular fondness for. It is a young male with a withered left hindquarter which it drags behind it' (214–15). Coetzee portrays the dog only marginally, only on the peripheries of description. But what he tells us is that David has made sure not to take ownership of the dog, knowing that, because no visitor has shown interest in adopting it, he may one day be responsible for its death: 'It is not "his" in any sense; he has been careful not to give it a name (though Bev Shaw refers to it as *Driepoot*)' (215). Yet it is the dog that has taken ownership of him. David admits that 'Arbitrarily, unconditionally, he has been adopted; the dog would die for him, he knows' (215). Just as David wonders whether he can incorporate the dog's howling into his opera, so too does Coetzee wonder here about how to incorporate the dog into realism. For only a moment, *Driepoot* becomes a minor character. He emerges out of the crowd of noisy animals as a figure, a personality, as the *one who*: 'He ties the last bag and takes it to the door. Twenty-three. There is only the young dog left, the one who likes music, the one who, given half a chance, would already have lolloped after his comrades into the clinic building' (219). Note here the change in pronoun, from it to he, as David affords *Driepoot* a form of humanizing subjectivity and sympathy.

Driepoot will not last long, however. Coetzee has David imagine the next steps, extrapolating from the present into an unavoidable future:

> He can save the young dog, if he wishes, for another week. But a time must come, it cannot be evaded, when he will have to bring him to Bev Shaw in her operating room (perhaps he will carry him in his arms, perhaps he will do that for him) and caress him and brush back the fur so that the needle can find the vein, and whisper to him and support him in the moment when, bewilderingly, his legs buckle: and then, when the soul is out, fold him up and pack him away in his bag, and the next day wheel the bag into the flames and see that it is burnt, burnt up. He will do all that for him when his time comes. It will be little enough, less than little: nothing.
> (219–20)

Coetzee is wrestling here with the apparent *inevitability* of this death. And he does so by adopting prolepsis, which looks forward to a predetermined conclusion: *Driepoot* 'will have to' die. In the novel form, prolepsis tends to function as a secularized and weak version of the epic's recourse to divine fate and justice. By jumping forwards in time and narrating future events – think here of the final chapter of George Eliot's *Middlemarch* – novelistic prolepsis instantiates a future distribution of justice that, Bruce Robbins writes, 'throws attention onto the boundaries and uncertainties of the community of fate' (2012: 199). In the novel form, prolepsis is often harnessed in order to decide, resolve or complicate the question of *who* is included in this community of the future.

Disgrace's use of the future tense is noticeably different to *Life and Times of Michael K*, the only other instance in which Coetzee ends a novel with recourse to prolepsis. After escaping an internment camp, Michael K daydreams about how might travel back to 'the farm, the grey thornbushes, the rocky soil' (2004b: 183). He imagines what would happen if an 'old man' accompanied him on his journey: 'They could share a bed tonight.' 'At first light, they could go out searching the back streets for an abandoned barrow.' Gripped by this hypothetical scenario – indicated by Coetzee's reflexive and parenthetical aside '(things were gathering pace now)' – K projects the thought even further into the future: What if K and the old man did make their way towards the veld? And what if, in need of water, they found a pump that had been destroyed by the civil war that rages around them? Writing now in the conditional tense, Coetzee grants K the possibility not just of imagining these problems but also of finding answers, however wishful they may be. Producing a teaspoon and roll of string, K

> would clear the rubble from the mouth of the shaft, he would bend the handle of the teaspoon in a loop and tie the string to it, he would lower it down the shaft deep into the earth, and when he brought it up there would be water in the bowl of the spoon; and in that way, he would say, one can live.
>
> (183–4)

Whether K's hope is misplaced or not, *Michael K*'s final lines at least contain an immanent if miniscule hope. Conversely, *Disgrace* turns the spoon into a needle, turns life into death, utilizing prolepsis in order to foreclose rather than open up narrative possibility. Here, Coetzee's deployment of an anachronic temporality articulates a train of thought in which the outcomes are predetermined, with the passage's opening future conditionals, *if* and *can*, quickly and surely replaced by the inescapability of *will* and *must*. Coetzee thus forecloses David and *Driepoot*'s story, presenting to us a kind of novelistic *telos* that undermines the subjunctive mode. While David can still determine the conditions of care and hospitality for *Driepoot*'s death – signalled by the parenthetical 'perhaps' of whether he will carry the dog in his arms – the narrative decision has already been made: the dog 'must' die.

Why is this so? One answer, encoded within the novel's plot, is that there are simply 'too menny' unwanted dogs (146). There are too many dogs and too few resources, an abundance of one thing and a scarcity of another. Another answer, hinted at in *Driepoot*'s characterization, the dog's adoption of David and Bev Shaw's act of naming him, is that he is one dog among a crowd. It is as if David is asking himself: why spare one dog when I am abandoning the rest? However, another way of reading the purported inevitability of *Driepoot*'s death is that it is *necessary* for the novel itself to come to an end. With the dog's death, *Disgrace* achieves a form of narrative closure, fulfilling its devotion to

David's story as he gives up his own ownership of other lives. The novel, as an anthropological machine, sacrifices the dog for its disgraced protagonist's redemption. But this need not mean that Coetzee or even the novel itself necessarily endorses this plotted story of rehabilitation. In fact, my contention is that Coetzee, by dramatizing this scene in this way, reveals and hence calls into question what we might call the sacrificial structure of the novel form, a structure which authorizes the 'noncriminal putting to death' (Derrida 1992: 278) of animals. And it is through the articulation of tense that this happens.

From his stylistic criticism of Kafka to his fiction's own consistent adoption of the present simultaneous tense, Coetzee has long been interested in what he terms the 'analytic intensity' of the narrative time (1992: 199).[7] In *Disgrace*, Coetzee repeatedly draws attention to the role and function of narrative tense, and in doing so imagines the grammar of tense as a political issue related to histories of domination. In the novel's very first sentence, David boasts about his weekly visits to Soraya: 'For a man of his age, fifty-two, divorced, he has, to his mind, solved the problem of sex rather well' (2000: 1). What makes the novel's opening sentence quite so perturbing, John Mullan says (2006: 71), is that the present perfect tense constructs sex as a problem to be solved. Indeed David's world, which is the focalized world of the novel, is presented as being solved, settled, final: 'His temperament is not going to change, he is too told for that. His temperament is fixed, set' (2). But because Coetzee positions David as a leftover of a now residual age, a stubborn and untimely 'hangover from the past' (4), he shifts the tense in order to initiate and plot David's disgrace, his transformation: '*Then* one Saturday morning everything changes' (6; my emphasis).

With the present simultaneous, Coetzee destabilizes David's 'fixed, set' position, setting in motion the novel's plot. The novel's perpetual now removes the distance between experience and telling, offering us a focalized figure who narrates events exactly as they happen. But David himself spends much of the novel trying to hold on to the perfective tense as a bulwark against his own deformation. In one of David's lectures on Romantic poetry, he teaches his class about the 'unusual verb forms' found in Wordsworth's reflections on Mont Blanc: '*usurp upon* means to intrude or encroach upon. *Usurp*, to take over entirely, is the perfective of *usurp upon*; usurping completes the act of usurping upon' (21). For David, the perfective tense unlocks how Wordsworth's real encounter with the real mountain eclipses his previously held *idea* of Mont Blanc. 'We don't have Alps in this country', David continues, 'but we have the Drakensberg, or on a smaller scale Table Mountain, which we climb in the wake of the poets, hoping for one of those revelatory, Wordsworthian moments' (23). As David later throws himself at his student, Melanie, the sublime of nature blends with the sublime of eros: 'He has given her no warning; she is too surprised to resist the intruder who thrust himself upon her' (24). Coetzee implies a relation, then, between the masculine conquests of tense, nature and women. Later on in the novel, now with Lucy in the Eastern Cape, David reflects on how just a fortnight ago he was 'explaining to the bored youth of the country the distinction between drink and drink up, burned and burnt. The perfective, signifying an action carried through to its conclusion. How far away it all seems! I live, I have lived, I lived' (71). The perfective's finality vies with the perpetual now of the present.

David reaches for the perfective again in the novel's final scene, when he imagines how he will euthanize *Driepoot* and 'pack him away in his bag, and the next day wheel the bag into the flames and see that it is *burnt, burnt up*' (219; my emphasis). David, then, is concerned with carrying this action through to its conclusion. But Coetzee ends the novel in a more indeterminate tense, a moment of suspension rather than resolution:

> He crosses the surgery. 'Was that the last?' asks Bev Shaw.
> 'One more.'
> He opens the cage door. 'Come,' he says, bends, opens his arms. The dog wags its crippled rear, sniffs his face, licks his cheeks, his lips, his ears. He does nothing to stop it. 'Come.'
> Bearing him in his arms like a lamb, he re-enters the surgery. 'I thought you would save him for another week,' says Bev Shaw. 'Are you giving him up?'
> 'Yes, I am giving him up.'
>
> (220)

Disgrace's closure hinges on the death of the dog. The question of the novel's resolution is inextricable from its sacrifice of the animal. There is, Coetzee suggests here, something of a sacrificial structure inherent to the narrative logic of novelistic plotting. It is as if Coetzee has written himself into a corner, found himself compelled to end the novel in this way, just as David is compelled to end *Driepoot*'s life. Both the novel and the dog are being given up. Yet David's closing speech act requires a second look. Delivered in the present continuous, it continues without ever completing its journey towards perfective finality. Because the progressive verb form never ends, so too does David's action. *Driepoot*'s death is thus set in motion but, crucially, remains necessarily incomplete. *Driepoot* is becoming-killed.[8]

In *Disgrace*, then, Coetzee finds himself bound to end the novel with David's sacrificial killing of the dog. But mindful of this gravitation towards sacrifice, Coetzee rearranges narrative time from the synchronic to the anachronic, thereby troubling his novel's ostensible anthroponormative resolution. Drawing on the narrative resources of tense, Coetzee deforms the text's temporality, grammatically rescheduling novelistic time so as to leave open the possibility of a non-violent solution to the novel. This not only leaves unresolved the question of David's so-called rehabilitation but also defers the animal's death. This is an ending, then, that acknowledges and rebuffs realism's demands for an animal offering as its syntax initiates but ultimately displaces *Driepoot*'s death, letting it escape beyond the novel's pages. With this formal move Coetzee dramatizes while also defying the novel form's ostensible anthroponormativity. Situating *Driepoot*'s death in this extra-textual future, Coetzee acknowledges its unavoidability within a world structured by the war against animals, but he also leaves open a narrative possibility for survival. Put simply, at precisely the same moment that David begins giving up the dog, Coetzee gives up *Disgrace* and with it a form of literary realism in which plot comes to demand animal death.

A belief in frogs, a distrust of realism: *Elizabeth Costello*

Where *Disgrace* ends with one dog, *Elizabeth Costello* ends with another. In the novel's final chapter, 'At the Gate', Coetzee constructs an elaborate but deliberately unconvincing set piece in which his eponymous protagonist – an ageing Australian novelist – struggles to negotiate her way through purgatory. Arriving at a simulacrum of an Austro-Italian border town, Costello pulls her suitcase across its cobbled streets and makes her way towards a gate. There she meets a gatekeeper who says that, for Costello to gain entry, she must write a 'statement of belief' for a panel of judges: 'For each of us there is something we believe. Write it down, what you believe. Put it in a statement' (2004a: 194). But what Costello scribbles down turns out to be more a statement of disbelief. As a writer, she says, 'It is not my profession to believe, just to write' (194). The judges are dismayed, and they send Costello away to reconsider her statement. So she tries again, this time professing a passionate belief in frogs, the frogs of the Dulgannon River, who every year erupt into a 'chorus of joyous belling' when the drought-ending rains pour down, ending their period of aestivation. Evoking Marianne Moore's meta-poem 'Poetry', Costello professes a belief in imaginary gardens with real toads in them: 'What do I believe? I believe in these little frogs…. They exist whether or not I tell you about them, whether or not I believe in them… It is because of their indifference to me that I believe in them' (217). But still the judges are unmoved: 'Is childhood on the Dulgannon another of your stories, Mrs Costello? Along with the frogs and the rain from heaven?' Costello pleads back that 'The river exists. The frogs exist. I exist. What more do you want?' (218).

Denied entry, Costello grows frustrated. She begins to imagine what might lie on the other side:

> She has a vision of the gate, the far side of the gate, the side she is denied. At the foot of the gate, blocking the way, lies stretched out a dog, an old dog, his lion-coloured hide scarred from innumerable manglings. His eyes are closed, he is resting, snoozing. Beyond him is nothing but a desert of sand and stone, to infinity. It is her first vision in a long while, and she does not trust it, does not trust in particular the anagram GOD-DOG. *Too literary*, she thinks again. A curse on literature!
>
> (224–5)

Both *Driepoot* and the GOD-DOG are mangled mongrels that put pressure on their respective literary texts. But while *Driepoot* is in a sense too real for *Disgrace*, enveloped within its plot as a living and breathing minor character, this dog is too allegorical, too metaphorical and too clichéd, impossible to integrate within the text's fictional world. In fact, when Costello scoffs at her own imagined figure of the GOD-DOG, putting a curse on the practice of literature in the process, she signals one of the overarching thematic and formal concerns of the work as a whole. Namely, *Elizabeth Costello* is a text at pains to call the reader's attention to the disintegration of its prose, the stumbling awkwardness of its figuration and the deformation of its style. Coetzee, turning away from the kinds of literary realism that he worked with in *Disgrace*, composes here an emphatically metafictional aesthetics, a mode of writing which generates a critical attitude towards realism itself. In this section, I will explore to what extent this change in register, from realism to metafiction, implicates Coetzee's writing of human–animal relations. Does metafiction open up new possibilities for thinking and writing the war against animals?

Much has been made of Coetzee's aesthetic shift towards a late style. In this 'third stage' (Atwell 2015: 233) of Coetzee's career, demarcated perhaps by his emigration from South Africa to Australia in 2002, his texts begin to more overtly foreground their fictionality, explore ideas over plots and flag up their own inadequate rendering of the real. Following Theodor W. Adorno's and Edward Said's foundational formulations of late style, critics argue that Coetzee's later works are marked by recalcitrance and decay. Coetzee's late style, Julian Murphet writes, enacts a 'progressive worrying away at the distinction between fiction and non-fiction, art and opinion, illusion and truth', thus retreating from 'the very comforts of novelistic form. Novels against the novel' (2011: 86). Less, however, has been said about how animals and animality lie at the heart of this formal fragmentation. Indeed, Coetzee's stylistic shift coincides with his animal turn. After *Disgrace*'s ambiguous dead-end, *Elizabeth Costello* inaugurates his late style, laying the thematic and formal groundwork that he will intensify in later works such as *Summertime* and the *Jesus* novels.

Although published in 2003, *Elizabeth Costello*'s origins stretch back to 1996, when Coetzee was invited to give the annual Ben Belitt lecture at Bennington College, Vermont. Rather than speaking earnestly as a postcolonial author navigating his positionality, as we saw him do a decade earlier in his Jerusalem Prize acceptance speech, Coetzee saw this as an opportunity to read new work. But this new work assimilating its conditions of production into its plot, troubling the conventions of the lecture form by telling the story of a novelist who, when invited to give a public speech, elects to speak 'not about herself and her fiction, as her sponsors would no doubt like, but about a hobbyhorse of hers, animals' (2004a: 60). By developing the character of Elizabeth Costello, Coetzee cleverly throws off the expectation of speaking directly to his audience, 'as a person, as a personality', opting instead to speak of and through Costello, who becomes something of a 'compromise and surrogate' (Attwell 2006: 33) for his own beliefs without ever directly rearticulating them. By the time of *Elizabeth Costello*'s eventual publication, seven of the book's nine chapters were already recited or published elsewhere, including two sections as the standalone text *The Lives of Animals*. For this reason, the novel's 'novelty' has been called into question, with critics such as Sarah Brouillette contending that the book stands less as a fully formed novel and more as a 'testament to the proliferating possibilities for subsidiary or auxiliary rights for what writers produce' (2007: 136).[9]

But I want to argue that Coetzee, knowing that *Elizabeth Costello* is a flimsy repackaging of previously aired and published work, consistently foregrounds the exhausted conventions of his storytelling. Indeed, Coetzee announces this metafictional approach with the novel's very first sentences:

> There is first of all the problem of the opening, namely, how to get us from where we are, which is, as yet, nowhere, to the far bank. It is a simple bridging problem, a problem of knocking together a bridge. People solve such problems every day. They solve them, and having solved them push on.
> Let us assume that, however it may have been done, it is done. Let us take it that the bridge is built and crossed, that we can put it out of our mind.
>
> (2004a: 1)

Building a bridge between 'nowhere' and the 'far bank' is precisely what fiction makes possible. But Coetzee's world-building metaphor expresses how arbitrary this process is, using the phrase 'it is done' as a kind of performative utterance which cheats its way into fictional believability. Coetzee invites his readers to participate in a metafictional game which disrupts the opening as form, in turn defamiliarizing the logics of fiction itself. With the 'bridging problem' complete, Coetzee introduces Costello: 'Elizabeth Costello is a writer, born in 1928, which makes her sixty-six years old, going on sixty-seven. She has written nine novels, two books of poems, a book on bird life, and a body of journalism. By birth she is Australian' (1). Coetzee's characterization is intentionally awkward. This, he knows, is a mere sketch of Costello: 'the blue costume, the grey hair, are details, signs of a moderate realism. Supply the particulars, allow the significations to emerge of themselves' (4). Signposting his characterization, implying and yet undermining the adage *show, don't tell*, Coetzee deploys a 'moderate realism' only so as to point out its grinding operation as an anthropological machine, a machine that produces human character.

Elizabeth Costello is assembled out of a tangle of literary forms. In a review of the book, the novelist David Lodge remarks that Coetzee 'mixes and transgresses generic conventions', building a book which 'begins like a cross between a campus novel and a Platonic dialogue, segues into introspective memoir and fanciful musing, an ends with a Kafkaesque bad dream of the afterlife' (2003: n.p.).[10] Yet Coetzee brings each of these forms and genres to an abrupt halt. Whether that is the short story form, metafiction and metanarrative, monologue and its attendant rhetorics of performance, academic symposium and debate, intertextual engagement and pastiche, or epistolary narrative, Coetzee cuts short each of his chapters and announces his writing's failures and enervation. Indeed the book's chapters are not called chapters at all but 'lessons', as if Coetzee and Costello alike are learning the inadequacies of different literary modes to articulate the real. In lesson five, for example, 'The Humanities in Africa', Coetzee points out to readers the story's potential endpoints: 'That would be another good place to end the story', he writes. 'As a story, a recital, it could end here... But in fact it goes on a little longer' (2004a: 153). In lesson six, 'The Problem of Evil', Coetzee ends by depicting Costello in a hotel, faced with a decision whether to retreat to her room or sneak into a conference auditorium. 'There ought to be a third alternative', Coetzee writes, 'some way of rounding off the morning and giving it shape and meaning'. But for Costello and the book's readers, the corridor, 'it seems, is empty' (182). *Elizabeth Costello* thus makes a point of telling its readers that it is struggling to make sense of reality, that the language and logics of literature are somehow lacking, that each of its stories is a dead-end.

This carries over into *Elizabeth Costello*'s foundational suspicion of realism itself. In the book's opening lesson, Coetzee focalizes the narrative through Costello's son, John, who she visits during an invitation to receive a literary prize. A few pages in, the narrative voice suddenly switches, becoming the author's voice, which asserts that:

> Realism has never been comfortable with ideas. It could not be otherwise: realism is premised on the idea that ideas have no autonomous existence, can exist only in things. So when it needs to debate ideas, as here, realism is driven to invent situations – walks in the countryside, conversations – in which characters give voice to contending ideas and thereby in a certain sense embody them. The notion of *embodying* turns out to be pivotal. In such debates ideas do not and indeed cannot float free: they are tied to the speakers by whom they are enounced.
>
> (9)

At one level, then, *Elizabeth Costello* strives to be a 'novel of pure ideas' (Herron 2005: 470), a text which criticizes realism's inability to communicate ideas except through invention and embodiment. This continues, as we have seen above, in the novel's final lesson, in which Coetzee constructs and then laments a rickey, 'excessively literary' world, 'a kind of literary theme park' (2004a: 208). The real becomes pastiche, as Costello herself notes when she says that 'The wall, the gate, the sentry, straight out of Kafka… Kafka reduced and flattened to a parody' (209). *Elizabeth Costello* creates a world, then, in which the gears of literary realism have rusted. Here, Coetzee foregrounds the tired workings of what Roland Barthes called literature's 'reality effect' (1989: 142). When Costello delivers a lecture on realism, she announces to her audience: 'There used to be a time when we knew. We used to believe that when the text said, "On the table stood a glass of water," there was indeed a table, and a glass of water on it… But all that has ended. The word-mirror is broken, irreparably, it seems' (2004a: 19). Suddenly it appears as if, with realism's undoing, so too does the distinction between humans animals give way: 'About what is really going on in the lecture hall your guess is as good as mine: men and men, men and apes, apes and men, apes and apes. The lecture hall itself may be nothing but a zoo' (19). Without realism, Costello implies, the species divide is no longer upheld; humans and animals become indistinguishable creatures.

Nevertheless, what Coetzee calls 'the notion of *embodying*' becomes integral for salvaging literature's articulation of ideas and its relationship with the animal.

Throughout the novel's eight lessons, Coetzee stages scenes in which Costello curses literature's clichéd figurations and interpretations of animals. She rallies against fables for their abstract representation of animals, and for their formal instrumentalization of animals as mere figures which 'stand for human qualities: the lion for courage, the owl for wisdom, and so forth' (95). She speaks of her mistrust of primitivist writing for its nostalgic and 'deeply masculine, masculinist' (97) pursuit of an authentic oneness with nature. She cautions against one reader who has scribbled the word 'Anthropomorphism!' (74) in the margins of a book by Wolfgang Köhler, the German psychologist who conducted problem-solving experiments with apes in the Canary Islands. Yet still Costello is sceptical of Köhler's own methods, reproaching him for pushing his simian test subjects towards 'practical, instrumental reason' (73). She further worries that 'when we divert the current of feeling that flows between ourself and the animal into words, we abstract it forever from the animal' (96). Human language, Costello says, exemplified by literature, is a poor substitute for the experience of meeting the animal. *Elizabeth Costello*'s metafiction thus self-consciously interrogates literature's uses of animals for human ends.

Although *Elizabeth Costello* distrusts literature's utilization of animals as 'vessels of revelation' (229), as semiotic signs rather than living bodies, the novel also calls for different kinds of literary encounters with animals; it reaches for modes of writing that encapsulate the embodied animal. In Costello's seminar on poetry, for instance, she explores the extent to which there could be a form of literature 'that does not try to find an idea in the animal, that is not about the animal, but is instead the record of an engagement with' the animal (96). Poetry about animals, that *registers* animal life, is not *for animals*, she says: 'the poem is not a gift to its object, as the love poem is. It falls within an entirely human economy in which the animal has no share' (96). Yet, because it is for humans, the poem might yet disclose something crucial about our relationship with animals. Costello urges her audience to 'read the poets who return the living, electric being [of animals] to language' (111). Even so, she remains wary of poetry's own involuntary abstraction of the animal being. 'There remains something Platonic' (98), she says, about how poets write about individual animals but nevertheless imply the abstract, socially constructed notion of species. Although Costello reads Ted Hughes's 'The Jaguar' as the record of an engagement with a particular jaguar, it ultimately ends up being a poem about '*the* jaguar, about jaguarness' (98). This metaphoricity and universality of the signified 'jaguar' is a problem for Costello because she thinks that this process of abstraction sanctions an abdication of ethical responsibility. If each animal is simply a reproduced object of its species, preprogrammed and without agency of its own, then that licenses humanity to claim a sovereign function as 'managers of the ecology' (99). Costello's reading of literature therefore ends in gridlock, as she doubts whether there ever can be literary forms that escape this abstraction from *this* animal to *the idea* of the animal.

Faced with this impasse, Costello says to her audience that 'If I do not convince you, that is because my words, here, lack the power to bring home to you the wholeness, unabstracted, unintellectual nature, of that animal being... And if the poets do not move you, I urge you to walk, flank to flank, beside the beast that is prodded down the chute to his executioner' (111). Yet it must be underscored here that the fundamental irony of *Elizabeth Costello* is that the novel itself appears to rarely provide a 'record of an engagement' with nonhuman animals. In contradistinction to *Disgrace*, *Elizabeth Costello* shifts the emphasis from plot and character to the *question* of plot and the *question* of character. In other words, when Costello rallies against literary abstraction, she does so within a text in which Coetzee routinely utilizes the abstraction of metafiction. The corollary here is that the nonhuman animals of *Elizabeth Costello* are by and large spoken about, contemplated, even vouched for, but rarely lived with, rarely written into the text as minor characters, as they are in *Disgrace*. By discussing animals as ideas, *Elizabeth Costello* seemingly excludes them as living beings.

And yet, this apparent diminishment or marginalization of animals from characters to ideas is, paradoxically, exactly where Coetzee develops a new kind of engagement with animality. By no longer including nonhumans as characters, Coetzee does not plot out their sacrificial deaths for human development or narrative resolution. Indeed Costello seems well aware of this in the book's final chapter, first in her musings on the life cycle of the Dulgannon frogs, which 'may sound allegorical, but to the frogs themselves it is no allegory' (217), but also in her haunted recollection on an episode from Homer's *Odyssey*. Shivers shoot down her spine when she recalls Tiresias instructing Odysseus to 'cut the throat of his favourite ram', to 'let its blood flow into the furrow' (211). This scene evokes *Disgrace*'s conclusion: both Odysseys and David Lurie are tasked with sacrificing their favourite animal in order to meet the demands of the narrative. But here, Costello's focalized narration diverts attention away from the heroic human decision and towards the haunting violence of the cut itself, as well as to the body of the dying ram as it oozes its 'sticky, dark, almost black' blood: 'She believes, most unquestionably, in the ram, dragged by its master down to this terrible place. The ram is not just an idea, the ram is alive though right now it is dying... treated in the end as a mere bag of blood' (211). Costello does not wish to use this story to pass through the gate. Instead, the ram's death reminds Costello of her own animality: 'She could do the same, here and now: turn herself into a bag, cut her veins and let herself pour on to the pavement, into the gutter. For that, finally, is all is means to be alive: to be able to die' (211). Costello would rather sacrifice herself than kill an animal; perhaps Coetzee would rather sacrifice his book than write another animal death.

Costello herself thus becomes the central 'animal' of the text, a human character whose animality is constantly being foregrounded for the reader. Coetzee depicts her as feeling as 'unpleasantly heavy, unpleasantly corporeal' (215) as the animals she speaks so passionately about. Costello herself is preoccupied with her own embodiment: 'For the moment, all she hears is the slow thud of blood in her ears, just as all she feels is the soft touch of the sun on her skin.' Reflecting on what it means to be a body, she thinks:

> That at least she does not have to invent: this dumb, faithful body that has accompanied her every step of the way, this gentle lumbering monster that has been given to her to look after, this shadow turned to flesh that stands on two feet like a bear and laves itself continually from the inside with blood. Not only is she *in* this body, this thing which not in a thousand years could she have dreamed up, so far beyond her powers would it be, she somehow *is* this body.
> (210)

Coetzee develops this across the entire book. In 'The Novel in Africa', for example, Costello is invited to appear as a guest speaker on a cruise ship circling the Antarctic. She accepts, hoping to experience 'what it is like to be a living, breathing creature in spaces of inhuman cold' (35). Embarking on a short excursion to Macquarie Island in the Southern Ocean, Costello feels like 'an old old woman' as she is helped ashore. 'Suddenly, unexpectedly', she spots an albatross and its chick: 'She recognizes the long, dipping beak, the huge sternum' (55–6). The albatross 'regards her steadily' and its fledgling lets out a 'long, soundless cry of warning'. In this moment, Costello does not call attention to the literary symbolism of the albatross. The albatross does not become a metaphor to be hung around Costello's neck, as in Coleridge's mariner, but merely stands, warily scrutinizing this human intruder. 'An albatross', she says to a Russian traveller. 'That is the English word. I don't know what they call themselves' (56). While on Macquarie Island, Costello considers the commercial exploitation of Antarctic nature which began in the nineteenth century. 'It was the hub of the penguin industry. Hundreds of thousands of penguins were clubbed to death here and flung into cast-iron steam boilers to be broken down into useful oils and useless residue' (55). Adopting a mode of description reminiscent of Sebald's narrators and their natural-historical accounts of the exploitation of nonhuman life, Coetzee narrates how the expansion of modern industry destabilized ecologies at the very corners of the globe.

We could argue, then, that while *Elizabeth Costello* appears to largely exclude real, embodied animals from its purview, its portrayal of Costello as an animal among other animals crafts a form of characterization that ultimately undermines the novel's reproduction of anthroponormativity. Costello shares a 'flesh', an experience, with the Dulgannon frogs, the ram, the albatrosses, even if these animals remain different and indifferent to her. But at stake in this gesture is, of course, Coetzee's own sacrifice of Costello. In each and every lesson, Coetzee stages a miniature sacrifice of Costello, a trial of some sort in which Costello ends up further alienated from her family, from strangers, from the human species. In place of animals, then, Costello becomes the text's beast of burden.

Vegetarian killjoy

In 1997, Coetzee was invited to give the Tanner Lectures on Human Values at Princeton University. Typically philosophical in format, habitually humanist in content, the Tanner Lectures invite figures from across the poles of public life – from Judith Butler to the likes of Antonin Scalia – to reflect on aspects of the human condition in essayistic argumentation.[11] Coetzee's contribution turned out to be two works of fiction, read aloud, which stage Elizabeth Costello's own delivery of lectures during an invited visit to a prestigious college. Republished as *The Lives of Animals* in 1999 with authorial footnotes and scholarly essays by Marjorie Garber, Peter Singer, Wendy Doniger and Barbara Smuts, and then later incorporated into the novel *Elizabeth Costello* (this time without the footnotes and scholarship), Coetzee's lecture-stories follow Costello's struggles as she wishes to reveal 'what is being done to animals at this moment in production facilities..., in abattoirs, in trawlers, in laboratories, all over the world' (2004a: 63). 'The Lives of Animals' thus gives us a character whose express intention is to narrate the war against animals: 'We had a war once against the animals… That war went on for millions of years. We won it definitively only a few hundred years ago, when we invented guns.' Now, she says, many animals function as prisoners of war, 'slave populations [whose] work is to breed for us' (104).

Coetzee's text unsettles the Tanner format. Formally, his delivery of fiction rather than lectures contorts the assumed relationship between speaker, speech and audience. And this formal turn, which lets Coetzee speak as someone else, produces a thematic, even ethical intervention: as Costello implies that human values are founded on the 'industrialization of animal lives and the commodification of animal flesh' (107), Coetzee's fiction addresses 'human' values in order to rebuke them. Costello argues that by valuing animals primarily as mere commodities for consumption we have profoundly corrupted our own human values; by measuring animal intelligence by 'human standards', we have arrived at the 'profoundly anthropocentric' conclusion that 'animals are imbeciles' (108). In 1996, a Tanner Lecture series claimed to demonstrate 'Why Animals Don't have Language' (Cheney and Seyfarth 1997). A year later, perhaps not unintentionally, Coetzee writes that the death cry of a slaughtered hen affected Albert Camus so powerfully that he was inspired to write a polemic against capital punishment. 'Who is to say', Coetzee writes, 'that the hen did not speak?' (108).

A wealth of critical discussion has already been devoted to exploring 'The Lives of Animals' as performed lecture-narratives that critique anthropocentric philosophical discourses, as metafictional stories to be read as fiction, not as lectures, and as integrated episodes or lessons within the culminating novel that is *Elizabeth Costello*. Robert McKay argues that Coetzee's dramatization of Costello's conflicting obligations to human community and justice towards animals marks out 'The Lives of Animals' as 'the most profound attempt in contemporary writing to answer the challenge of animal ethics' (2010: 67). Cora Diamond puts it that Coetzee explores the 'difficulty of reality' (2009: 45), the knottiness of a social life founded on others' pain. Costello exhibits 'a kind of woundedness or hauntedness, a terrible rawness of nerves. What wounds this woman, what haunts her mind, is what we do to animals' (Diamond 2009: 47). Coetzee thus brings to the foreground the suffering of animals not through the philosophical precision of the lecture but through the attention to Costello's wounded body, an animal body that is offered as the site of argumentation, as an embodied appeal to reckon with our own creaturely relations with other beings. In this final section of Chapter 3 I wish to deepen these analyses by thinking of Costello as a vegetarian killjoy, a character whose rhetorical invectives against the consumption of animal flesh are so sharp, so uncompromising, that rather than winning people over Costello generates bad affects: 'acrimony, hostility, bitterness' (2004a: 112). I will argue here that Costello's vegetarianism turns out to be troublesome, as its troubling of anthroponormativity causes trouble for her own relationships with other human beings, while also creating problems for the text itself. This creaturely trouble – of calling into question the war against animals, but at a cost – is ultimately where Coetzee leaves us, both in this text and in his wider literary experiment with the lives of animals.

Recently, Sara Ahmed's writing on the figure of the 'killjoy' has become key for articulating how feminist struggle is perceived by the very institutions and epistemologies it counters. Developed across Ahmed's writing since 2010, the feminist killjoy is someone who punctures the putatively happy facades of communities undergirded by inequalities. Take the family table, Ahmed says, a table host to 'polite conversations, where only certain things can be brought up' (2010: n.p.). Here, even a surreptitious eye-roll at sexist comments can result in the eye-roller, not the sexist, being ostracized from the table: 'To be willing to go against a social order, which is protected as a moral order, a happiness order, is to be willing to cause unhappiness, even if unhappiness is not your cause' (n.p.). A killjoy, then, is the subject who 'gets in the way of other people's happiness', who by speaking up upsets a social balance that is founded on imbalance. 'That you have described what was said by another person as a problem means you have created a problem. You become the problem you create' (n.p.). For Ahmed, feminist killjoys are 'willful subjects', subjects who actively assert their own will against the dominant order, who risk becoming 'affect aliens': 'to be unwilling to participate is not only assumed to kill the joy of participation but it is read as motivated by the desire to kill joy' (2014: 160). In *Living a Feminist Life*, Ahmed adds that the killjoy is 'the one who puts others off their food… Another dinner ruined. So many dinners ruined' (2017: 39).

Elizabeth Costello is constantly ruining dinners. Whether in a restaurant or at a family home, one of Costello's primary effects as a character is to put others off their food. But Costello does not do so out of an explicitly feminist response to patriarchal norms, even if we might argue, as Laura Wright does (2006: 199), that her stance is largely consonant with a vegetarian-feminist ethics. Rather, in 'The Lives of Animals' Coetzee dramatizes how the relations between the table's guests is inextricably from what is on the table itself. Costello, then, is not so much a feminist killjoy as a vegetarian killjoy. Those characters who know Costello are acutely aware of her capacity to ruin dinners. Norma, Costello's daughter-in-law, grumbles to her husband, John, that she resents the way Costello tries to 'get people, particularly the children, to change their eating habits. And now these public lectures! She is trying to extend her inhibiting power over the whole community!' (2004a: 113). Costello's vegetarianism poses a threat. When Costello and John arrive for a celebratory meal with the university faculty of Appleton College, John is already anticipating the 'damage' that his mother will wreak. I quote this passage in full because its combination of visceral imagery and dry comedy exemplifies just how much Costello's vegetarianism has gotten under her son's skin:

> What he dreads is that during a lull in conversation someone will come up with what he calls The Question – 'What led you, Mrs Costello, to become a vegetarian?' – and that she will then get on her high horse and produce what he and Norma call the Plutarch Response. After that it will be up to him and him alone to repair the damage.
>
> The response in question comes from Plutarch's moral essay. His mother has it by heart; he can reproduce it only imperfectly. 'You ask me why I refuse to eat flesh. I, for my part, am astonished that you do not find it nasty to chew hacked flesh and swallow the juices of death wounds.' Plutarch is a real conversation-stopper: it is the word *juices* that does it. Producing Plutarch is like throwing down a gauntlet; after that, there is no knowing what will happen.
>
> (83)

Contemporary meat production relies on processes of abstraction and obscurity. Industrialized farming happens out of sight, on the margins of the city; its production methods sanitize animal flesh so that the product appears as de-animalized pre-packaged goods; its attendant systems of advertising never depict the slaughterhouse, instead showing either living animals, happily bred, or no animals at all. As Carol J. Adams once put it, the system of factory farming works by turning real animals into 'absent referents' (2010: 13), a cleaving of signification in which the slaughter of living animals is hidden so that their bodies can be symbolically and literally reproduced as meat. Costello's Plutarch response is a gauntlet, then, because she identifies meat as animal flesh. Costello re-animalizes meat, returning the life of the dead animal to the table and hence repairing the gap between the product and its referent: 'fragments of corpses that they have bought for money' (2004a: 114).

This is, as John says, a conversation-stopper. By pointing out the killing of animals, Costello kills the joy of the dinner table. Indeed, Costello grows increasingly alienated from her hosts because of her appeals on behalf of animals. Come the end of her visit to Appleton, Costello feels like trip has been nothing short of a disaster. She sobs in the car as John drives her to the airport: 'I seem to move around perfectly easily among people, to have perfectly normal relations with them. Is it possible, I ask myself, that all of them are participating in a crime of stupefying proportions?' (2004a: 114–15). Prefiguring the moment in *Disgrace* in which David stops at the roadside, tears flowing down his face, Coetzee dramatizes here the stakes of opening one's eyes to the lives of animals.

Everyone else can come to terms with this state of reality, it seems, except for her. Costello's alienation from the human community is upsetting, confusing, even destructive.

For Coetzee and the text itself, though, this alienation is surely strategic, political, as it throws into relief the ways in which the 'normal relations' of human community rest on the unacknowledged slaughter of animals. Yet Costello is not simply a shell who vocalizes Coetzee's own beliefs, dropped into invented scenarios in order to persuade other characters, and hence the reader, of the virtues of vegetarianism. Coetzee's texts, from *Dusklands* on, regularly adopt 'a position they deliberately devalue' (Janes 1997: 111). And here, too, Coetzee appears to depict Costello's vegetarianism as singular, idiosyncratic and tactless. She is a weak authority, and thus the text itself cautions against any instrumental reading: 'The Lives of Animals' turns out to be both an endorsement *and* a critique of vegetarianism.

The patience and hospitality of Costello's audience breaks down not just because her vegetarianism goes against the dominant dietary order but because she uses her lecture to make dreaded comparisons between industrialized animal slaughter and the Holocaust, a trope used by Peter Singer and Isaac Bashevis Singer before her and since popularized, and made even more controversial, by People for the Ethical Treatment of Animals. Costello states that for daily life to continue in the west, 'We need factories of death; we need factory animals. Chicago showed us the way; it was from the Chicago stockyards that the Nazis learned how to process bodies' (Coetzee 2004a: 97). Put more directly: 'Each day a fresh holocaust' (80). Costello asks her audience to pardon the 'tastelessness' (66) of her rhetoric, and concedes this analogy is a 'cheap point' (66), but she continues with it throughout her talk. This leads one of the university's staff members, the poet Abraham Stern, to refuse to break bread with her at the post-lecture meal. In a private letter, Stern accuses Costello of wilfully abusing the simile as rhetorical device: 'The Jews died like cattle, therefore the cattle die like Jews, you say. That is a trick with words which I will not accept. You misunderstand the nature of likenesses… The inversion insults the memory of the dead' (94). For Coetzee's audience at the Tanner Lectures, Stern's letter might be said to function as a way for the author to pre-empt and hence mitigate against the offence of his own fictional alter-ego. Like Sebald's use of non-indexical images in *The Rings of Saturn*, then, one gets the sense that both authors are inventing formal means for relating human genocide to organized animal death without ever approaching this comparison directly. It is ultimately Costello, not Coetzee, who says, 'Let me say it openly: we are surrounded by an enterprise of degradation, cruelty, and killing which rivals anything the third Reich was capable of, even dwarfs it, in that ours is an enterprise without end, self-regenerating bringing rabbits, rats, poultry, livestock ceaselessly into the world for the purpose of killing them' (65).

But once reproduced as text in the *The Lives of Animals* and *Elizabeth Costello*, Stern's criticism offers an opportunity for readers to reflect more closely on Costello's language and the specific kinds of trouble it sparks. For Stern, the Holocaust can never be 'like' anything else. Thus Costello insults the memory of the dead by speaking of factory farming and Jewish genocide in the same breath. Costello, however, is reaching for the kinds of horrifying imagery that would be immediately comprehensible to a humanist audience. She is attempting, by invoking the Holocaust as touchstone, to shock her audience out of their 'willed ignorance' (64) into a recognition of the war against animals, of abattoirs, trawlers and laboratories. But because this is ultimately unsuccessful, even deleterious to Costello's own cause, Coetzee's analogy becomes less a comparison to be logically thought through and more of a testament to the paucity of human language for articulating the reality of this war against animals. If historical analogy breaks down here, it is because the war against animals is unprecedented.

Coetzee further complicates Costello's vegetarianism by having her refuse to accept any sort of purity or virtuousness. Although John and Norma characterize her as a killjoy engaged in a power game, Costello finds no consolation by adopting a vegetarian ethos. When the College's president asks her whether her vegetarianism comes out of a moral conviction or not, she replies that 'It comes out a desire to save my soul.' When the president diplomatically says that he respects her way of life, Costello pushes further: 'I'm wearing leather shoes… I'm carrying a leather purse. I wouldn't have overmuch respect if I were you' (89). Costello presents her own vegetarianism not as morally righteous but as a minimal ethics, a compromised and complicit position. Jacques Derrida once wrote that while vegetarians seek to escape the literal consumption of animals, they still participate in the symbolic sacrifice of animals.[12] For Costello too, vegetarianism offers no escape from animal suffering, only fewer 'degrees of obscenity' (89).

By devaluing Costello's vegetarianism, Coetzee turns away from moral reasoning and towards affect. At the end of the celebratory meal, Costello chides philosophy's recourse to the adverb 'therefore'. Because animals are thought to possess 'no consciousness that we would recognize as consciousness', philosophy inserts a therefore: 'Therefore what? Therefore we are free to use them for our own ends?' (90). For Costello, 'therefore' is exemplary of a kind of language that produces and sustains species hierarchies, the 'great Western discourse of man versus beast, of reason versus unreason' (69). Costello knows this discourse well, even beginning her lecture by appealing to 'a way of speaking to fellow human beings that will be cool rather than heated, philosophical rather than polemical' (69), a language indebted to thinkers from Aristotle to Mary Midgley. Yet she jettisons this discursive register of rationalist speech, presenting what Derek Attridge calls 'less a reasoned case than an expression of intense response' (2004: 203): 'if you had wanted someone to come here and discriminate for you between moral and immortal souls... you would have called a philosopher, not a person whose sole claim to your attention is to have written stories about made-up people' (Coetzee 2004a: 66).

Thus there is an underlying tension between Coetzee's text on the one side, which worries away at the possibilities for fiction, and his protagonist on the other, a fellow author who privileges the ability to imagine, to feel, as a way of releasing oneself from the grip of anthroponormativity. Costello turns against 'instrumental reason' (73), invoking instead what she terms the 'sympathetic imagination', our faculty to 'think ourselves into the being of another' (80). For Costello, this momentary inhabitation of other minds, other bodies, is transformative. By becoming others, 'any being with whom I share the substrate of life' (80), we open our hearts. There is something both metaphorical and material about this way of thinking. When Costello compels her audience to 'listen to your hearts', she offers this as both a metaphorical plea of sentiment and as something more literal: listen to the 'slow thud' (210) of blood pumping around your body, the substrate which is shared across the species barrier. In the end, though, Costello is not interested in asking whether we 'have something in common' (79) with animals, but rather why do we not think ourselves into their place. Is this what 'The Lives of Animals' really is, underneath it all: a stage on which one human character is symbolically sacrificed in the place of the animal? In place of *Driepoot*, in place of Red Peter, in place of Thomas Nagel's bat, Costello is offered – offers herself, even – in order to fleetingly, perhaps failingly, break the willed ignorance of her audience and call attention to the war against animals.

Yet Costello insists that she *is* an animal, a 'branded, marked, wounded animal' (70–1). Thus in Coetzee's hands the logic of sacrifice that is immanent to fiction will continue. What is read by some as a complicated appeal to vegetarianism is, at the very same time, a text which uncovers the deep structures of symbolic sacrifice that obtain within literary fiction itself. In other words, *Elizabeth Costello*'s metafictional pursuits reproduce, with a difference, the very logics that they seek to escape. Is this a capitulation to the novel form as an anthropological machine? Or is this limitation of form, this threshold of animal ethics, presented as an opportunity to acknowledge the anthroponormativity of literature? What is certain is that, in both the dull realism of *Disgrace* and the late style of *Elizabeth Costello*, Coetzee foregrounds above all else the very intractability and uncertainty of the positions taken up by his texts and characters. 'A way out?', Costello remarks. 'It's not for me to offer you a way out' (50). Coetzee's creaturely form does not propose a route out of anthroponormativity. But it nevertheless inclines towards a form of defiance: 'I don't know what I want to do. I just don't want to sit silent' (104).

Notes

1. See, for example, Weil (2012: xviii), Ciobanu (2012), McKay (2010).
2. On this, see Kannemeyer (2012: 154, 588).
3. See the Harry Ransom Center's website for more. The full list of the Coetzee archive can be found at https://norman.hrc.utexas.edu/fasearch/findingAid.cfm?eadid=00717 (accessed 1 April 2021).
4. Although Coetzee's more recent novels have gravitated away from the debates of animal ethics, he has continued to write and publish stories about his vegetarian protagonist, Elizabeth Costello. Coetzee has collected these stories in the manuscript *Moral Tales*, which remains unpublished in English despite its appearance in Spanish, French and Italian.
5. Coetzee also discusses Sebald's work with Arabella Kurtz in *The Good Story* (2015: 182–90).
6. For more on David Lurie's operatic pursuits, see Easton (2007).
7. Coetzee has 'probably had the greatest influence on the contemporary popularity of present-tense narration', speculates Irmtraub Huber (2016: 45).
8. Mark Sanders (2002: 368), Chris Danta (2007: 735) and Jan Wilm (2016: 192) are, to my knowledge, the only other critics who have analysed how the novel's transformation of tense relates to its closing scene's depiction of *Driepoot's* death.
9. Gareth Cornwell writes that *Elizabeth Costello* is only 'a kind of novel', 'patently a product of authorial entrepreneurship rather than artistic design' (2011: 248). An anonymous Booker Prize judge reportedly described it as 'a deplorable book, a dishonest book' (Taylor 2003: n.p.).
10. In private correspondence with Coetzee, the critic Wayne C. Booth states – somewhat hyperbolically – that with *Elizabeth Costello* Coetzee had 'invented a new form of novel' (quoted in Kannemeyer 2012: 549).

11 See the Tanner website for more details: https://tannerlectures.utah.edu/overview/lectures.php (accessed 1 April 2021).
12 Derrida: 'We are all – vegetarians as well – carnivores in the symbolic sense' (cited in Birnbaum and Olsson 2009: n.p.); 'Vegetarians, too, partake of animals, even of men. They practice a different mode of denegation' (1992: 282).

4

Mahasweta Devi's creaturely love

The double task

In the closing pages of Mahasweta Devi's *Pterodactyl, Puran Sahay and Pirtha* (henceforth *Pterodactyl*), a drought-stricken forest-dwelling community immerse themselves in a cleansing oil bath, the first of many rites they will perform in order to leave behind a period of collective mourning. Mahasweta's readers witness this scene through the eyes of the story's journalist protagonist, Puran Sahay. Puran is bathed by a taciturn child, Bikhia, whose apparent sightings and wall engravings of a mysterious winged creature had attracted Puran to Bikhia's remote and pesticide-ravaged village at the story's beginning. Having arrived in Pirtha with his camera and notepad, eager to report on the engravings and, perhaps, discover the pterodactyl for himself, Puran is immediately met with the hostility, hunger and desperation – described in Mahasweta's compound-accumulating *dvandva* style as the 'skeleton men-women-boys-girls' (1995: 136) – of an impoverished community sounding their emergency drums. Puran has assumed that the pterodactyl's arrival will eventually lead to the village's protection by the state. Yet for these adivasis, or first peoples, the pterodactyl is both an impossible marvel of the earth's geological past and a spiritual embodiment of their ancestors' restless souls, stirred into movement by the government's imminent plans to build 'broad arrogant roads' (109) over the community's sacred burial grounds. The people of Pirtha thus see the pterodactyl-spirit as a monstrous omen, an apparition of extinct life whose sudden presence portends their own looming extinction as a people. Its arrival sends them cascading into mourning rituals.

But as *Pterodactyl* reaches its conclusion, there are reasons for hope. The rain has come. The pterodactyl has now perished and been laid to rest. And Puran is set to leave the village and return to the city. Mahasweta's story will even end with something of a call to arms, as her authoritative narrative voice insists on a form of love that is sufficient to sustain political commitment to adivasi life, a 'tremendous, excruciating, explosive love' (196). Reflecting on the book a decade later, Mahasweta writes that she wished to communicate here a 'double task', 'to resist "development" actively and learn to love' (xxii). But before this final call for politics and love, Puran bathes with the people of Pirtha, thinking over his time in the village:

> Puran realizes that the crisis of the menaced existence of the tribals, of the extinction of their ethnic being, pushed and pushed them towards the dark.
> Looking at Bikhia's tawny matted hair, freshly shaven face, he understood that they were being defeated as they were searching in this world for a reason for the ruthless unconcern of government and administration. It was then that the shadow of that bird with its wings spread came back as at once *myth* and analysis.
>
> (193)

With this sudden eruption of anagnorisis, or plotted recognition, Mahasweta dramatizes Puran's newfound appreciation of a deepening crisis for indigenous peoples in postcolonial India. The pterodactyl becomes a 'new myth' (193) and a mode of analysis. Myth: the story of the pterodactyl will be folded into the community's oral tradition. Analysis: it offers an opportunity for thought; it delivers a message to be incorporated into collective memory, something to be taken forward in the struggle for justice to come. The pterodactyl, in the first place a harbinger of certain extinction, turns out to also serve as a guide for future survival.

Why is it, then, that in this story of abandoned human life, Mahasweta decides to not just incorporate but hinge her text on a mysterious creature, a living-yet-extinct and embodied-yet-phantom literary presence? Why is that, throughout her writing in fact, Mahasweta often looks to the figure of the nonhuman as a way of articulating the socio-ecological problems of postcolonial India? What relationship does this suggest between postcolonial governmentality, first peoples and nonhuman life? And how does Mahasweta's writing itself, with its self-imposed double task to resist development and learn to love, thematize and formalize the lives of other creatures?

*

Up until her death in 2016, Mahasweta Devi was committed to an emancipatory project for subaltern autonomy, land sovereignty and ecological survival across the Indian subcontinent.[1] As an investigative journalist, a commissioning editor at the journal *Bortika*, and an organizer with the bonded-labourers movement in Palamau in the 1960s, the *Adim Jati Akiya Parishad* (Tribal Unity Forum) in the 1980s and the Denotified and Nomadic Tribes Rights Action Group (DNT-RAG) in the 1990s, Mahasweta spent decades of her lifetime working in solidarity with India's historically dispossessed and displaced classes, including dalits and low-castes.

Most of Mahasweta's energy was devoted to organizing the movement for adivasi justice. Adivasi, which translates as 'earliest resident' or 'first inhabitant', is a collective noun and functioning political identity first coined by activists in the early twentieth century as a claim to indigeneity.[2] 'Adivasi', as category, is envisioned as a universalizing term, even a strategic essentialism which appropriates the idioms of citizenship in order to build solidarity between those heterogeneous social groups who, according to the 2011 census, make up around 8.6 per cent of the national population: some 100 million people. In 1946, on the eve of independence, adivasi groups appealed to India's Constituent Assembly for the recognition of their indigeneity (Guha 2007a: 318). But this claim went largely unheeded; the Constitution acknowledged adivasis only as 'Scheduled Tribes', and adivasis became newly subjugated by the 'everyday tyranny' (Nilsen 2018: 33) of dispossession, extortion and malnutrition. Adivasis, then, are those communities who 'have gained least and lost most from sixty years of political independence', as historian Ramachandra Guha puts it (2007b: 3309). Virginius Xaxa, an adivasi scholar and member of an Oraon community, writes that adivasis are those groups who have faced waves of colonization: from the Mughal Empire to the East India Company to British rule, and finally to the postcolonial nation, which continued the 'extreme marginalization' of adivasi societies (2016: 49, 51). As adivasi groups negotiated and contested the new political conjunctures of postcolonial nation-building, fighting new battles for *Jal-Jungle-Jameen* (water, forest, land), Mahasweta became an 'extremely active facilitator of tribal unity' (Spivak cited in Burns et al 1990: 82). Mahasweta, like many middle-class intellectual-activists of her generation, wanted to build a social movement informed by a complicated imbrication of indigenous philosophies and Maoist strategies.

Mahasweta's literary project is shaped by and inseparable from these political commitments.[3] In her early work, written in the first two decades after India's independence, she creatively re-writes nationalist historiography and reclaims the previously colonized Indian archive by drawing on the aesthetic repertoire of historical fiction. In *Jhansir Rani* (1956), *Amrita Sanchay* (1964) and *Andhanmalik* (1967), Mahasweta narrates key flashpoints of collective resistance to British colonial occupation in the rebellious century leading up to formal emancipation. Written from the vantage point of recent independence, these historical novels locate the present triumph in the courageous defeats of the past.

Yet from the late 1960s onwards, Mahasweta began to turn her writing back towards the present, and to the unfulfilled promises of the independent nation. Directly tracking the contemporaneous crises of the post-Nehruvian conjuncture, Mahasweta's fiction grappled with the roll-out of the Green Revolution, a commercialization of agriculture which had disastrous socio-ecological impacts on peasant communities and ecologies,[4] the rise and fall of the Naxalite insurgency in 1967, the increasingly authoritarian and corrupt reign of Indira Gandhi, the resultant State of Emergency in 1975, the inadequacy of Gandhi's twenty-point development and redistribution programme, the 1984 Union Carbide gas disaster in Bhopal and later the emergent inequalities of India's globalization. Mahasweta's literary writing, Parama Roy suggests, 'cannot be fully understood except through the idioms of crisis inaugurated by these watershed events' (2010: 121). More than this, to borrow a phrase from Sourit Bhattacharya, Mahasweta's writing became a kind of 'catastrophic realism' (2020: 3). Her texts strained to communicate the complex interrelation of sudden and slow violences in independent India and that consequently pushes at the assumed boundaries of realism itself.

Mahasweta's literary preoccupation with postcolonial crises therefore appears to have necessitated a formal and generic transformation away from the historical novel and towards realist documentation of the present. Indeed, ever since her emergence in the 1990s as an important figure in postcolonial letters, critics have argued that Mahasweta's writing is driven by a 'documentary impulse' (Wenzel 2011: 136) which looks to the affordances of literary realism in order to combine 'diegesis and sociological analysis' (Lazarus 2011: 43). 'The sole purpose of my writing', Mahasweta confirms, 'is to expose the many faces of the exploiting agencies', to 'place this India, a hydra-headed monster, before a people's court' (1998: ix–x). But crucially, Mahasweta achieves this self-styled creative concentration on reportage, exposure and justice not just through a straightforward reflection of the social experience of postcolonial India. Her work is more complex than this, articulating an idiosyncratic combination of documentary realism, in-text authorial-narrative judgement, melodramatic irony and modernism. There is, as Sumanta Banerjee (2009: xxii) points out, a satirical strain of black comedy that runs through many of Mahasweta's stories. Indeed she often uses hyperbole, hammered home through acerbic non-diegetic authorial asides – what Bhattacharya handily describes as an 'interventionist' narrative voice (2020: 127) – in order to attest to and delegitimize the power of the Indian state. This works in tandem with a defamiliarizing modernism, evident especially in Mahasweta's consistent utilization of free indirect discourse and multilingualism, a playfully unfixed literary style which weaves between vernacular Bengali, English bureaucratic officialese, poetic Sanskrit and intertextually incorporated paraphrases from figures as divergent as Marx and Shakespeare.[5]

In more recent years, concomitant with the elaboration of postcolonial ecocriticism, scholars have grappled with the question of how Mahasweta's writing of the nonhuman fits in with her aesthetic blending of serious documentation and playful irony. For some, her mediation of more-than-human phenomena, the natural and the supernatural, produces a peculiarly gothic atmosphere or magical story-world (Roy 2010: 127; Wenzel 2000: 230). For others, her texts develop an *irreal* aesthetics, a form which breaks through realism's boundaries by its description of the sheer unreality – the extraordinary, inexplicable reality – of its own historical situation (WReC 2015: 19, 70; Farrier 2016: 464). Elsewhere, in his lectures on literature and environmental disaster, the novelist Amitav Ghosh classes Mahasweta as being among a number of writers whose work does not reproduce the anthropocentric fiction that humanity is ontologically separate from, and hierarchically towers above, the nonhuman (2016: 80). For Ghosh, in fact, Mahasweta produces a distinctive style that departs from the 'secular code of historical and humanist time' (Chakrabarty 2000: 76) that underpins realist aesthetics.

Yet still, what is missing from these analyses is a sense of how Mahasweta's literary incorporation of nonhuman figures relates to her commitment to adivasi lives. How, then, does her writing of animality intersect with and impact upon her concentration on the lives of those excluded from political humanity? This is the governing question of this chapter, as I wish to home in on how Mahasweta's texts depict the fates of indigenous communities as being conjoined with the fates of other creatures, forests and habitats. By exploring Mahasweta's short stories on the one side, and her longer novella-length story *Pterodactyl* on the other, I will explore how Mahasweta's literary politics is also a literary eco-politics. I want to reveal how, in her texts' depiction of postcolonial India, cultural genocide is inseparable from nonhuman ecocide.

This is not to say that Mahasweta is a straightforwardly pro-animal author, though. Mahasweta's writing does not share Sebald's and Coetzee's sometimes upfront, other times concealed engagement with the post-Enlightenment philosophies of animal ethics and theories of human–animal relations in modernity. In her texts, questions surrounding individualized animal rights and the industrialized slaughter and consumption of animals fade into the background. And yet, much like many adivasi groups' and indigenous rights activists' own political demands (Savyasaachi 2016: 64), Mahasweta's fiction conceives of the fight for subaltern recognition and redistribution as being inextricable from a fight to arrest environmental devastation. The two do not just go together, but are inextricable from one another. This is why Neel Ahuja suggests that Mahasweta pens a form of 'postcolonial critique in a multispecies world' (2009: 556). Against the anthroponormativity of the postcolonial state, Mahasweta's stories powerfully express how real postcoloniality, as a horizon of justice to come, must reconfigure the entrenched divisions between state-recognized political personhood, adivasi subalternity and nonhuman nature. I will be arguing, therefore, that Mahasweta's writing opens up pathways for thinking about a creaturely postcoloniality, a form of justice without anthroponormativity.

Postcolonial justice is precisely what is at stake in Mahasweta's self-designated double task: to resist development and learn to love. With the term 'development' Mahasweta has in mind the material and ideological practices of Indian nation-building, increasingly intertwined with corporate interests, which have become demonstrative of the 'self-definition of the postcolonial state' (Chatterjee 1993: 203). *Materially*, Indian development connotes the uneven alleviation of poverty, the acquisition of resource-rich land for the building of dams and extractive industries, the forced displacement of poor communities, the bulldozing of the commons and thus the destruction of ecosystems. And this is presented *ideologically* as a sometimes regrettable but necessary means to achieve the economic growth required to modernize a supposedly backwards nation. Starting with the Nehruvian, Soviet-inspired Five Year Plans, before its commercialized turn under Indira Gandhi, Indian development is an unequal project, historically enriching some while re-pauperizing adivasis as developmental refugees, severing their relationships with ancestral lands, enforcing unwanted migration and resettlement and proletarianizing many communities into informal work forces. While the work of development has created conservation initiatives such as tiger sanctuaries, these reserves have often come at the cost of displacing poor communities and sanctioning the deforestation of other old-growth areas.

At its core, development is an ambivalent force. It is not an inevitably malicious imposition, but its deployment within capitalism produces uneven and unequal results. In *Capital, Interrupted*, Vinay Gidwani describes development in its prototypical form as 'one of the most powerful anthropological machines of the past two centuries', an improvement machine which in principle but by no means in practice '*reorganizes the conditions – or ecology – of human life for its betterment*' (2008: 70), driving 'human actors into new relations with other human *and* nonhuman actors' (136). And yet, the kinds of development that have played a 'central role in the legitimation strategies of postcolonial regimes' (Gupta 1998: 35) have been motivated by an economic model of growth undergirded by the extraction and appropriation of nature (Chattopadhyay 2014: 70). The policies and programmes of Indian development in particular 'appear to be in direct conflict with safeguarding species, ecosystems and local people' (Kothari and Pathak Broome 2016: 337). Under the dominant 'anthropocentric-economic' (Deb 2009: 510) model, development has been termed 'the scourge of adivasi lives' (Radhakrishna 2016: 372). Adivasis account for under 10 per cent of the national population, but over 40 per cent of all those displaced by developmental projects to make rooms for dams and mines (Debasree 2015: 453). Mahasweta puts it thus: 'India makes progress, produces steel, the tribals give up their land and receive nothing. They are suffering spectators of the India that is travelling toward the twenty-first century.' In short, 'decolonization has not reached the poor' (1995: xi–xx).

When Mahasweta positions her literary project as a kind of writing which resists the nation's developmental agenda, then, she positions her fiction against a system which ruptures socio-ecological relations in its simultaneous pauperization of adivasis, destruction of some habitats *and* conservation of others. Her fiction clearly *stages* the forced reorganization of life in postcolonial India, showing how Indian nation-building renders adivasi and nonhuman lives jointly expendable.

As well as representing the ills of development, Mahasweta's fiction also develops an aesthetics of refusal that refuses India's development. To use the catachrestic phrasing from her short story 'Draupadi', her fiction formally 'kounters' development (Mahasweta 2014: 37). Over the course of this chapter I will argue that Mahasweta's formal repertoire works to arrest the anthropological machine of postcolonial development. Her formal decisions – the use of plotting and endings in her short stories (indeed the sheer shortness of her texts themselves), her metaphorics of animality, her adoption of focalizing lenses and her varied strategies for integrating nonhuman figures within her narratives – destabilize the anthropological machine of literature. There is, as Joseph Slaughter has shown, a sociohistorical alliance between the novel form and modernizing developmentalism, an alliance that is co-constituted alongside the uneven personification of particular humans as rights-bearing subjects (Slaughter 2007: 8, 328). Looked at from this angle way, much of literature becomes a discursive articulation of this developmental apparatus. Yet Mahasweta's stories focus on forms of life whose marginalization is owed to developmentalism. Thus while she works within the bounds of established literary forms, she also repurposes these forms in order to expose the fictions and failures of anthroponormative development.

However, Mahasweta's stories are not simply oppositional. As her stated 'double task' implies, her project is one of both negation *and* proposition. Coincident with her thematic and formal repudiation of developmentalism is also the encouragement of new relations, the building of new forms of solidarity that I will call *creaturely love*. Mahasweta's literary project reanimates and reconfigures development, generating in its place a radical love, a 'minimal communism' (Badiou and Truong 2012: 38) between those humans and nonhumans who are disregarded by the postcolonial state. Mahasweta's writing has been criticized in the past for offering little more than a paternalistic, sentimental and ultimately patronizing vision of indigenous life (Byrd 2011: xxxiii; Weaver 2000: 224). But as we will see below, Mahasweta's texts do not make a liberal-sentimental plea for empathy, nor do they develop an 'antopolitical' and 'unworldly' love, the kind which Hannah Arendt warns can 'destroy the in-between which relates us to and separates from others' (1998: 242). Instead, Mahasweta mobilizes a mode of 'tremendous, excruciating, explosive love' (1995: 196), as she puts it in *Pterodactyl*. The intensity of those three adjectives communicates to us that this love is a barbed feeling, an affect which rips and scratches away, a love whose cultivation verges on the edge of catastrophe, preserving the differences between characters and social experiences while still building solidarity. As much as her work calls for this solidarity, though, it is also set against the backdrop of frictions and tensions within adivasis communities themselves *and* the animals with which they share the forests. Mahasweta's adivasis are not pure victims, nor are her animals. As we will see, her writing suggests that the failures of postcoloniality – developmentalism and the uneven actualization of political humanity – have actually strained the relationships between humans and nonhumans.

Finally, a word on translation and *littérisation*, Pascale Casanova's term for the process by which structurally peripheral texts become perceived as sufficiently 'literary' by agenda-setting authorities in the core (2007: 136). Anyone who writes about Mahasweta must confront the fact that her writing has gained a foothold in the postcolonial canon because of Gayatri Spivak's translations, framings and interpretations. Spivak, for her part, has written reflexively about the methodological problems of translating Mahasweta's writing, as well as the responsibility of being the so-called doorkeeper (1998: 349) of her work. Mahasweta, too, spoke positively of collaborating with Spivak (Collu 1998: 143). Yet critics have justifiably warned that 'reading Mahasweta in English is, to some degree, reading Spivak' (Wenzel 2000: 230). Just as Mahasweta has been criticized for ventriloquizing adivasi voices, so too has Spivak been accused of ventriloquizing Mahasweta, deliberately mistranslating her work so that it reflects Spivak's own critical concerns.[6] When analysing Mahasweta's work in English translation, then, it is crucial to recognize Spivak as a co-author, as a figure who has shaped the work considerably. Such is the conclusion of Minoli Salgado's (2000) even-handed comparison of various translations of Mahasweta's texts, which reveals how important aspects of Mahasweta's poetics are often smoothed over or transformed in their English-language equivalents. This chapter focuses on a number of Mahasweta's texts, some translated by Spivak, some not. Without satisfactory comprehension of Bengali, I acknowledge that my readings will capture only a partial version of 'Mahasweta'.

Inhuman narratives: constituting creatureliness in the short story form

In 1998, in response to the death in police custody of a young adivasi man, Budhan Sabar, Mahasweta co-authored and submitted to the United Nations a damning report on the state of social inequities in India. 'On behalf of 60 million tribals', Mahasweta writes as representative of the Denotified and Nomadic Tribes of India, 'we wish to draw your attention to the violation of [adivasis'] basic human rights and to request with your immediate intervention in the matter in accordance with Clause XXII of the UN Charter of Human Rights' (DNT-RAG 1999: 591). In her report, Mahasweta locates these contraventions of transnational law within the specific sociohistorical context of India, positioning the present situation as part of a historical continuum that includes the 1857 rebellion, the British counter-revolutionary crackdown enshrined by the Criminal Tribes Act of 1871 and the Act's subsequent extensions beyond the northern regions in 1911 and 1924. She traces the effects of colonial reaction and suppression into the postcolonial present, noting how even the full repeal of the Criminal Tribes Act in 1952 failed to adequately actualize the recognition of adivasis as full citizens. Worse still, she argues, the law which replaced it, the Habitual Offenders Act, allowed police forces to continue criminalizing whole communities. For Mahasweta, although India's statuary reforms produced a symbolic politico-administrative change – adivasis, previously branded as 'Criminal Tribes', became 'Denotified Tribes' – they also reproduced the material conditions of colonial rule. 'It is unthinkable', she says, 'that a section of people who are among the earliest occupants of this subcontinent... should be deprived of a dignified life, and persecuted in the most *inhuman* manner even after half a century of independence' (DNT-RAG 1999: 593, my emphasis).

On the face of it, Mahasweta's short stories appear to present a fictional counterpart to this kind of political intervention. In works like 'Fundamental Rights and Bhikari Dusad' (henceforth, 'Fundamental'), for example, Mahasweta registers in satirical prose the shortcomings and contradictions of the constitution. Set on the outskirts of Noagarh, 'Fundamental' explores the poverty, hunger and regular police beatings of a lowly goatherd and outcast, Bhikari. 'Nobody gave a damn about Bhikari Dusad. They were not meant to', Mahasweta writes in the opening lines (2006: 92). A 'timid' and 'harmless soul', with no land and no family, Bhikari's livelihood is tied to a flock of goats and the cycle of goat-rearing: 'taking them here and there, in search of pasture. The goats his only means. Goats' (94); 'the goats to tend, sell, tend, sell' (96). Yet for the landlords and the police of Noagarh, 'nothing enrages them as much as those *dusads* who try... to live like human beings in the land of their birth' (108). The police 'destroy [Bhikari's] very method of survival every time' (96).

At the heart of the story lies a conversation between Bhikari and a teacher, Sukhchand, who tells Bhikari of his seven 'fundamental rights in free India' (101), including the right to equality, to freedom of religion, to culture and education, to property and against exploitation. That Mahasweta has Bhikari be oblivious of these rights is demonstrative enough of the constitution's deficiencies. But when he is maliciously beaten and left disabled by the police – 'an efficient, thoroughly professional beating, approved by the law and administration' (106) – he realizes the extent to which the state actively works against him: 'A lie, every syllable Sukhchandji spoke is a lie!... And the Indian Constitution guarantees that fundamental rights cannot be violated? Lies, all lies!' (106–07). While Sukhchand wonders naively whether Bhikari could attain 'a better standard of living' through education, Mahasweta's narrative voice abruptly and ironically rebuts the schoolteacher, stating that the 'Constitution will never tolerate such a blatant violation... No matter where in India such an injustice occurs, the constitutional machinery will at once deploy the police, reserve police, military police, the military, tanks and combat aircraft, everything' (108). For Mahasweta, the Constitution militates against subaltern life.

As much as short stories like 'Fundamental' dramatize the constitution's failings, Mahasweta's political imaginary also expands beyond the strategic and normative horizon of rights and recognition that underlies her work with the DNT-RAG. Indeed, at the end of 'Fundamental' Bhikari discovers a loophole in the Constitution when he decides to leave Noagarh. While the police may have forced him to give up his right to property, he follows his supposed freedom to pursue any occupation by giving up his goats, fleeing to the jungle and taking up the occupation of begging. In so doing, Mahasweta writes, Bhikari will not only evade the police for good – 'they'll never beat up a beggar dusad' (108) – but he will also become part of a new community of homeless beggars, a 'member of a large, large society' (108) who live adjacent to society itself. Mahasweta's story thus implies that, in practice, the fundamental rights of India perversely encourage dusads to seek freedom in homelessness, outside of the jurisdiction of rights. For if Bhikari is to survive, he must become 'a creature of the forest' (97) and embrace that side of himself that cried 'like an animal' (106) when the police assaulted him and seize his goats. To be free, then, he must forsake his claims to the political category of personhood. Thus while Mahasweta's activism with the DNT-RAG retained a pragmatic confidence in institutional politics, petitioning the state for the formal recognition of subaltern lives, short stories like 'Fundamental' recognize the insufficiency of political humanity itself as category. Set on the peripheries of the state in zones of geographical, political, even ontological exclusion, stories like this break free from the state's grasp and unsettle the anthroponormative apparatus of rights and citizenship.

To capture these different literary animations of political humanity, and to take seriously Mahasweta's description of Bhikari as a 'creature of the forest', I want to introduce the figure of the 'inhuman'. When operating as an adjective, the word 'inhuman' describes the violence meted out to subaltern peoples. As Mahasweta puts it in the DNT-RAG report, the Denotified are 'persecuted in the most inhuman manner' (DNT-RAG 1999: 593). Yet when used as a noun, the concept of the inhuman comes to denote a bare humanity which, cast as the abnegated other of the human, as constitutively excluded from the orbit of human rights, exposes the violence of the anthropological machine. Numerous twentieth-century thinkers have, in the words of Giorgio Agamben, sought to 'bear witness to the inhuman' (1999: 121). One of the most prominent, Judith Butler, insists that humanness is an expendable and mutable categorical norm, a political ontology masquerading as species distinction which has been continually 'allocated and retracted, aggrandized, personified, degraded and disavowed, elevates and affirmed' throughout different regimes of power: 'wherever there is the human, there is the inhuman' (Butler 2009: 76).

Inhumanity is not the same thing as dehumanization. While the latter presupposes a process of loss, one in which one's humanity is stolen, denied, withdrawn, sundered or given up, the inhuman accounts for those who can 'make few or no claims whatsoever to political humanity' (Feldman 2010: 115), or those whose rare claims to political recognition rely on their own perceived degradation. Dipesh Chakrabarty thinks that the category of the inhuman was central to India's advent as a nation-state. For him, the concept is associated with the logics of killability which underlaid the bloodshed of Partition (2002: 142). For others, the inhuman can be productively considered in relation to the hierarchies of caste and the subjugation of entire social identities based on entrenched yet contingent perceptions of who counts as a human.[7] But this dichotomy between human and inhuman, this gap between political humanity and unrecognized and subjugated subjectivity, also invokes the figure of the animal, or animality, as the supposed opposition to the human. Inhumanity is, in this way, a perceived or enforced state of creaturely life, of living below humanity, within the non-political space of the nonhuman. When Bhikari becomes a creature of the forest, he appears to find a way out not through any claim to constitutional rights but through giving them up completely.

Mahasweta's literary repudiations of the constitution and her focus on the logics of inhumanity are intensified by her adoption of the short story form, a genre of compression, fragmentation and ellipsis in which characters typically confront 'a crucial event or crisis' (May 2012: 176). The short story form has often been theorized by literary critics as a genre that is generatively suspended in the contradiction between oral tradition and modernist innovation, between the folktale and novelistic discourse (Rydstrand 2019: 20). György Lukács once described the short story as glimpsing a 'human life expressed through the infinite sensual force of a fateful hour' (2010: 92). Terry Eagleton, echoing Lukacs' focus on synecdoche, intensity and fate, has it that the short story is uniquely capable of depicting a 'single bizarre occurrence or epiphany of terror whose impact would merely be blunted by lengthy realist elaboration' (1995: 150). The short story is thus thought to blend tacitly realist narration with fantastic and irreal eruptions which call into question the story's prior register and temporality in relation to the real. We might say, then, that each short story articulates a form of *complete fragmentation*. Its depicted world is complete, and it stands as a single unit, but its content must necessarily remain unfinished and relatively partial. In other words, the short story offers unity but not development.

In *The Lonely Voice*, an early landmark in short story criticism, Frank O'Connor argues that the form tends towards exploring the social alienation of 'submerged population groups' (1963: 18) – outsiders, the alienated, the persecuted, the unrecognized. I do not presume that O'Connor had in mind subaltern subjectivity when he wrote this; his study focuses primarily on authors such as Katherine Mansfield and Rudyard Kipling. But perhaps his claim has been borne out by the proliferation of the short story in postcolonial territories. In the mid-twentieth century especially, the form flourished in both commercial magazines and small, avant-garde and radical journals across the global south (Awadalla and March-Russell 2013: 4). It is only in recent decades that the novel form has truly overtaken the short story as the genre of choice for postcolonial writers. In India, the short story has often served as the aesthetic wing of class struggle. Writers looked to the short story as a means for articulating and quickly disseminating the social experience of peasant and lower-caste peoples.[8] In an instructive essay on the heterogeneity of the short story form in India, Tania Mehta writes that even when setting their story in a postcolonial present, writers often find themselves engaging with 'three Indias – temporally speaking, ancient, medieval, and colonial, contesting, complementing and dialoguing with each other to generate a vision for the future or immediate present' (2004: 156).

In Mahasweta's hands the short story becomes a form which triangulates between this tradition and modernity, which re-writes the mythic into the 'real', and thereby offers a counter discourse where 'archetypical constructs are interrogated and challenged' (Mehta 2004: 157). Often set on or coinciding with fateful, auspicious or anniversary dates – of independence, of uprisings, as we will see throughout this chapter – Mahasweta's short stories create a concentrated temporality in which present actions are connected with historical patterns. Her characters, with their deprived humanity, even take on 'mythological overtones' (Alter 1998: 25) that challenge the continuation of the state, of personhood and of straightforwardly realist narration. In stories like *Mother of 1084*, for example, the death of a son is interpreted as a geological event, the mother's grief 'like one of those explosions that broke up the solid mass of the earth into continents' (2014: 8). The anonymous corpse, inhumanely tortured and killed, takes on an immense revelatory power, as its inhumanity provokes a recognition of the state's organized extermination of dissenting bodies. Naming is an act of humanization. The corpse, reduced to a number, is deprived of its human dignity. Yet Mahasweta indicates that it is this figuration of inhumanity that ruptures the story-world's reality, and with it the state's myth of steady development. I wish to think, then, about how Mahasweta's short stories – their temporality, their plotting, their form — unsettle the linear progress of development. I will argue that Mahasweta utilizes the episodic intensity of the short story form in order to militate against the steady emplotment of postcolonial development.

Within the compressed story-world of 'Fundamental', for instance, Mahasweta in mines the short story form's partial plotting and character development in order to unsettle the constitution, personhood and development. Indeed the story's narrative voice self-consciously insists that the very story we are reading is predetermined. On numerous occasions Mahasweta writes that 'nobody can alter the plot' (2006: 93, 94, 99); 'This has been, this will be. Such occurrences are as old as the ancient soil of Noagarh'; 'This has been, this will be. The fable of rich landlords poor peasant share croppers bataidars is never any different. Nobody can alter the plot' (94). The law, presented here as circumscribed and entrenched, infects both the story's characters *and* the narrative itself. Mahasweta, by formally incorporating Bhikari's restricted and policed life within her story, re-treads the foreclosed plot-paths to which dusads are currently bound. If the mission of human rights is, broadly, to transcend predestination, to constitute the human person's autonomous pursuit of life, then 'Fundamental' uncovers how human rights in India denote little more than a secularized predestination. The 'plot' of Bhikari's life, condensed within the short story form, appears to remain foreclosed and undeveloped, already written out.

But Mahasweta also undermines this refrain, opening her story to the possibility of breaking the fixed plot of subjugation. At one point, as the spread of political agitation against the landowning classes leads to a rebellion, she writes: 'Nobody can alter the plot. But this time somebody did. As they were beaten up… they yelled out slogans' (94). In indented verse which punctures the story's steady paragraphing, Mahasweta incorporates the chants: 'We have | A fundamental right | To one half | Of the product of our labour!' (94). Organized political protest therefore marks one strategy for altering the plot. But for the unorganized, like Bhikari, Mahasweta suggests that their only recourse to survival is through an abandonment of the political category of humanity. Mahasweta ends the story like this:

> Leaning on his stick, Bhikari walks away. Slowly. Unhurriedly. Free of all fears. No longer scared even of the police…

He does not feel lonely either...
Bhikari Dusad walks away, dragging his feet painfully, slowly disappearing round a bend down the road. He has nothing left to lose.

(108)

Recalling Coetzee's Michael K, Bhikari ends his story poised on the threshold between the pain of the present and the potential freedoms of the future, having to discover – however impossibly – how 'one can live' (Coetzee 2004: 184) outside or away from the state's social order. Yet Mahasweta's consistent present-tense narration – unlike Coetzee's future-oriented prolepsis – ultimately fixes Bhikari in the now, holding him in relation to the very fortress of citizenship from which he is kept out. While Bhikari's unhurried walk is depicted as one of minimal freedom, of the only freedom he can find, his future remains determined by the act of reading itself: What do readers take 'nothing left to lose' to mean? Is this to be read as a mark of bare life and vulnerability, as the end of the road, or is this a negative potentiality that might yet flourish elsewhere?

Animal identifications

I have suggested that the figure of the inhuman implies the figure of the animal. By writing of subaltern characters who live on the outskirts of an assigned political humanity, Mahasweta's short stories associate abandoned human life with the lives of animals and other creatures. Nevertheless this figuration of inhumanity, this narrative association of human and nonhuman life, carries with it a risk: the danger of portraying these characters as being somehow essentially or naturally interlinked with nature, thereby tacitly countersigning their own subjugation as creatures. When, for instance, Mahasweta discusses how deforestation erodes adivasi life – 'now that the forests are gone, the tribals are in dire distress' (1995: x) – there is a kind of rhetorical reduction at work here which generalizes adivasis as being wholly reliant on forests. Does this reproduce an image of adivasis as pre-modern peoples, morally and spiritually rooted to forest lands and unadaptable to contemporary life? Alpa Shah writes that such rhetoric contributes towards a longstanding idea that adivasis are 'eco-savages, natural conservationists, the living remnants of India's cultures that once naturally preserved the environment' (Shah 2010: 107). Archana Prasad calls this 'ecological romanticism' (2011: 3). It is a nostalgic and idealistic image, and it traps adivasis as 'primitives' within a kind of 'eco-incarceration' (Shah

2010: 69, 188) as their claims to indigeneity are only taken seriously if they continue to live off the land.

But Mahasweta's literary work is, I think, cognizant of these tensions surrounding the limits of representation, paternalistic advocacy, and eco-incarceration. In fact, her short stories continually incorporate a metaphorics of animality that identifies and disidentifies the subaltern with 'nature'. Let us take, for example 'Douloti, the Bountiful', one of Mahasweta's most widely known short stories. Set in 1975, a few months into India's nationwide State of Emergency, 'Douloti' focuses on the themes of gendered violence and trafficking. It tells the story of an eponymous teenage protagonist who, forced into a decade of indentured sex work in order to re-pay her father's debts, dies on the twenty-eighth anniversary of India's independence. As her body, exhausted, simply gives up, Douloti slumps inside an outline of Indian subcontinent drawn with chalk in a schoolyard: 'Filling the entire Indian peninsula from the oceans to the Himalayas, here lies *bonded labour* spread-eagled, kaniya-whore Douloti Nagesia's tormented corpse' (1995: 93). Mahasweta thus ends 'Douloti' by re-writing the nationalist myth of Mother India, or *Bharat Mata*, in which the Indian subcontinent is imaginatively cartographed and patriotically visualized as an 'anthropomorphic-sacred' goddess (Ramaswamy 2010: 11). Testifying to the internal colonization of subaltern life in the supposedly decolonized nation, Mahasweta writes that it is Douloti, not Mother India, that is 'all over' the nation (1995: 93). Douloti's body, rendered here as an inhuman 'it', comes to haunt the Indian imaginary.

But it is 'Douloti's' lesser discussed first half that requires further examination, as it stages some of the contradictory valences of animality that operate within postcolonial India, in turn reflexively disputing the uncritical yoking of inhumanity with animality. For here, Mahasweta depicts bonded-labourers as conceiving of themselves as animals while their feudal landlords deem them to be less valuable assets than labouring animals themselves; these characters internalize their inhumanity, identifying as degraded animal life, and yet they also come to reject this identification with the animal. The story is set in the district of Seora village and it dramatizes how the 'feudal land-system' (1997: 26) forces the poor, emblematized here by Ganori Nagesia, to choose between starvation and bondage. Ganori is pushed into life as a bonded-labourer (a *kamiya*) after falling into debt with Seora's landowner, Munabar Singh. Humiliated and trapped in the servitude of endlessly repaying his debt, Ganori becomes Singh's 'chattel slave' (1995: 20), and is forced to take on the labour of an ox. As Ganori struggles under the weight of the axle and carriage, unable to supply the same strength of animal muscle, he is 'broke into a crooked misshape' (20). Like Bhikari, 'he will never be able to stand straight in his life' (37). When discussing the story's origins, Mahasweta writes:

> I saw this man, whose right side, from arm to ankle, was deformed. Why?... [Because] his *malik* made him lift a paddy-laden cart... I asked the *malik*, Why not use the bullocks? He answered, if a bullock dies in this heat, I lose a thousand rupees. He is just a bonded labourer. His life is of no value.
>
> (1998: viii)

Mahasweta thus articulates how the relations of value and private property which structure nonhuman lives come to impact upon the lives of those without full political humanity. Ganori becomes known as Crook Nagesia, recognizing his disability as a confirmation of his inhumanity: 'We are all animals. It's good that the master beat me and made me crooked. What should we do with an animal but beat it?' (34). He thinks of another member of his community, Bono, who has escaped bond slavery and moved to a nearby city: 'if there is a real human being in Seora, it is Bono' (34); '[Bono's] seen the world. How brave he is. Not an animal like us' (35). To Crook Nagesia, then, his situation makes him a kind of animal, deprived of political standing.

While Ganori submits to his own imposed inhumanity, other members of the community cast off this equation with animality. When a government census taker arrives in Seora, the community worry that 'various disasters can happen if human beings are counted like cows or sheep' (31). They recall the censuses of colonialism, 'the time of my father's father. And right away a big Hunger, a real famine' (31). For the travelling government employee, the census is an affirmative biopolitical instrument, a classificatory system that would allow for a more equitable allocation of resources. But for the people of Seora village the census epitomizes a form of negative biopolitics, an anthropological machine of knowledge production, inherited from nineteenth-century colonial anthropology and population management, which collects, categorizes and colonizes life. To be counted 'like' domestic farm animals is, for them, a confirmation of their inhumanity rather than the sign of their entrance into the state's purview of concern. Even if they comply with the census, they say, 'everything will be as before. Delhi's rule will not work in Palamau' (1995: 40). Far from reproducing the image of the subaltern as a kind of nonhuman, then, 'Douloti' dramatizes how conflicting notions of animality are projected onto, internalized within and rejected by subaltern peoples.

What then of eco-savagery, the essentializing notion that adivasis are somehow naturally allied with and continuous with nature? Another story of Mahasweta's, 'Salt', complicates any such idea. Set within a state-created forest reserve, 'Salt' depicts the shifting antagonisms between government forest management, landowning sarkars, poor adivasis and protected elephants in conservation areas. The story's plot is propelled by the sarkar's decision to withhold salt distribution from the local food markets, in effect depriving adivasis of a good they consider to be 'indispensable for life' (1998: 131). Faced with this 'saltless darkness' (135), the story's adivasi characters begin stealing dirty, blackened salt-earth from the nearby licks shared by the forest's animals, deer and elephants. Mahasweta describes these elephants as 'very intelligent animals' (137) who understand the 'slow business' (135) of human tourism, gladly meandering over to feast on bamboo as visitors snap photos. Yet Mahasweta's elephants are also calculating and vengeful. When a young adivasi, Purti Munda, pinches the elephants' salt, he is confronted by an '*irresponsible*' (136) elephant, an 'old tusker' and 'rascal' (137) who has been 'exiled from leadership and from the herd' (138). When the villagers discover that Purti is stealing from the reserve's elephants, the elders prompt him to remember that, years ago, when an adivasi child shot an arrow and accidentally killed an elephant calf, 'the elephants, furious, encircled the dead calf, walking around him as if taking an oath incomprehensible to man'. Thus began a 'war of revenge' (136), a three-year period of unrest in which elephants ransacked villages and killed human inhabitants.

In 'Salt' Mahasweta incorporates the figure of the nonhuman in such a way that guards against an uncritical representation of adivasis as harmoniously interconnected with the natural world. Here, adivasis feud with elephants in the struggle for scarce resources. At the story's end, the rogue elephant embarks on a 'hunt for the guilty' (1998: 140), for those who have been stealing his salt. 'The elephant is the largest animal that walks the earth', Mahasweta writes:

> But when a rogue elephant starts a battle of wits with man, then, if he so desires, he can make less noise than an ant. He carefully side-steps each dried leaf… An elephant is an ant – an elephant is a butterfly – an elephant is the breeze! Such a huge body, but when it wants, it can creep up unnoticed and squash your head with its foot.
>
> (141)

The rogue elephant becomes an occasion for thinking about elephants in general, about their unique *elephanticity*, which is explained metaphorically through their transformation into other animals and elements of nature: ant, butterfly, breeze. While the elephant attacks in silence, Purti and his friends 'shriek and shriek' (143). The adivasis soberly accept that they have wronged the elephant: 'how difficult it is to protect wild animals from the greed of humans' (144). But the Forest Department, learning of the elephant's rampage through the adivasi village, commission a hunter to kill the elephant. The adivasis turn out to pay respects to the dead elephant. An elder, regretting Purti's recklessness, ruminates that 'none of this is quite right. The apparent truth is that the elephant died because it killed Purti and the others. But the underlying truth seems to be something else' (144). With this 'something else', Mahasweta alludes to the injustice of the situation, driven by the profound social disparities between landowners and adivasis. By withholding salt, the landowners initiate a chain reaction which causes the unnecessary deaths of human and nonhuman beings.

'Salt' thus ends up suggesting that adivasi rights stand in tension and confluence with ecological conservation. Squeezed between private farmland and state-owned reserves, the adivasis are in effect pitted against elephants in a struggle for space and nourishment. Looked at one way, the story demonstrates how government-sponsored conservation policies have prioritized endangered animals over adivasi communities. Under the conditions of Indian development, eco-tourism trumps adivasi existence. Yet 'Salt' ultimately discloses how the fates of adivasis and elephants are jointly impacted by India's pre-existing inequalities, exacerbated under the aegis of development. As Mahasweta puts it elsewhere, 'the elephant and the tribal, both are expendable to the system' (ix). Mahasweta thus flags up the conflicts between indigenous peoples and nonhuman animals in order to reveal anew just how conjoined their suffering is.

To close this section I want to analyse one more of Mahasweta's short stories in which the arena of political humanity comes to be bound up with the metaphorics of animality. Set in and around the sal forests of Kuruda, 'The Hunt' stages a collision between community and capital, the latter epitomized by a corrupt lumber contractor, Tehsildar Singh. Narrated in three parts, the story begins by introducing its protagonist, Mary Oraon, 'eighteen years old, tall, flat-featured, light copper skin' (1995: 3), a cowherd who works 'like a dog' (4), 'like an animal' (5). A mixed race and illegitimate daughter of an adivasi woman and the son of a colonial patriarch, Mary is portrayed as the knowing product and bearer of a violent colonial history. The sal forest that surrounds Mary's village is also depicted as a product of colonial landholding, a space that still has profound importance for Oraon social relations in spite of it becoming a timber plantation to fuel the British empire and now, under the agro-industrial model of postcolonial development, a natural factory to be grown for selling 'at the highest price' (6).

Mahasweta plots 'The Hunt' in such a way that Tehsildar Singh's attempt to broker a deal to purchase seventy-five acres of sal forest coincides with the Oraons' annual hunting festival, a celebratory communal hunt in which men from neighbouring groups hunt, drink, eat, sing, dance and, crucially, 'bring offenders to justice' (xviii). Every twelve years, this yearly hunt becomes the *Jani Parab*: here women, not men, perform the ancestral ritual, inverting the gender hierarchies of the tribe.[9] 'For twelve years men run the hunt', Mahasweta writes. 'Then comes the women's turn. It's Jani Parab. Like the men they too go out with bow and arrow. They run in the forest and hill. They kill hedgehogs, rabbits, birds, whatever they can get' (12). But because commercial deforestation has dramatically reduced the animal population, the yearly hunt is no longer viable. As Mahasweta writes, in sentences that invert one another: 'Once there were animals in the forest, life was wild, the hunt game had meaning. Now the forest is empty, life wasted and drained, the hunt game meaningless. Only the day's joy is real' (12). Deforestation, by diminishing the forest's animal habitats, also diminishes the social meaning of the tribal ritual.

How to put right these desacralized rites? Mary first encourages her community to reject Tehsildar's offer to buy the forest. But when this fails, she decides to take retributive action herself. Knowing that Tehsildar desires her, Mary organizes to meet him on the night of the hunt. She exploits the festival's ritualized state of exception, meting out her own kind of justice. Shooing away the nearby hares and hedgehogs, she starts to picture Tehsildar as the animal to be hunted:

> Mary caresses Tehsildar's face, gives him love bites on the lips. There's fire in Tehsildar's eyes, his mouth is open, his lips wet with spittle, his teeth glistening. Mary is watching, watching, the face changes and changes into? Now? Yes, becomes an animal.
> — Now take me?
> Mary laughed and held him, laid him on the ground. Tehsildar is laughing, Mary lifts the machete, lowers it, lifts, lowers.
> A few millions moons pass. Mary stands up.
> (16–17)

This, then, is a scene of animal sacrifice, one occasioned by the intensity and fateful hours of the short story form. But it is one performed against a human in the name of socio-ecological justice. Mouthing the word to herself – 'A-ni-mal' (13) – Mary reinscribes the hunting ritual, metamorphosing the masculine sovereign into the beast, and thereby into the story's eponymous *Shikar*, which translates not just as 'the hunt' but also 'the victim' and 'the prey'. There is something of a Fanonian counter-violence to this, unleashing a liberatory 'cleansing force' (Fanon 1990: 74) that temporarily rids the village of its threatened re-colonization. As Spivak writes, 'Mahasweta shows an individual activating ritual into contemporary resistance' (quoted in Mahasweta 1995: 202). Mary's sacrifice of her would-be rapist, the 'biggest beast' (17), re-enchants the desacralized hunting ritual, utilizing the forest law, or 'Law-bir' (xviii), to achieve a result unimaginable in constitutional law. This is why Mary quips triumphantly, 'Let us hunt this way every year' (17). 'The Hunt' thus compels us to consider the fissures between the rhetorical figuration of animality and violence against nonhuman life. By re-projecting the logic of the ritual hunt onto Tehsildar, Mary discursively appropriates the creaturely semiotics of the beast in order to materially save the forest's animals. Where the state continues to treat peasants with inhuman violence, Mahasweta gives her supposedly inhuman characters a retributive power.

Development against developmentalism

Structured in seven parts and set during the fortieth anniversary-year of Indian independence, *Pterodactyl* follows the third-person focalized narration of a well-meaning but naïve journalist, Puran Sahay, a reporter who has travelled from an unnamed cosmopolitan city to the heart of *Madhya Bharat*, or Middle India. A 'self-reliant' (140) character, Puran arrives with a humanitarian ambition: by investigating the 'unearthly terror' (104) of the mysterious winged creature, Puran hopes to pen a captivating story that will put Pirtha 'on the *map*' (137) of national attention and thus expose the starvation, enteric fever, corruption and police violence that blight this famine-laden and agro-chemically polluted village. But while there, Puran encounters two forms of vulnerability which confound and shock him, breaking his belief in humanitarianism: an impoverished adivasi community who face continual dispossession by national development projects, and a prehistoric pterodactyl, suffering from a broken wing, that appears in his room. By the end of the novel, Puran will realize that there are thousands of communities across India whose lives have been abandoned and destroyed by the onward march of colonial and postcolonial modernity: 'we have slowly destroyed a continent in the name of civilization' (195), Mahasweta writes in free indirect speech. More than this, *Pterodactyl* stages Puran's recognition of how extinction can be both an anthropogenic event and a socio-biological affliction, something caused by some human communities that dramatically destroys others, whether human or nonhuman: 'both your existences are greatly endangered', Puran says (156).

Pterodactyl is a much longer work than the short stories I have read above. In fact, at around one-hundred pages long the text is generically indeterminate, and has been described by critics as a long short story, a novella and short novel (*uponyash* in Bengali). However we wish to categorize this story, the fact that Mahasweta adopts a longer prose form is crucial: its length allows her to draw from and unsettle the generic expectations of the ostensibly humanist, third-person narrated coming-of-age novel of development. Indeed, looked at one way, *Pterodactyl* can be read as adhering to the narrative motifs of the *Bildungsroman* as a quintessential modern form of storytelling. Broadly conforming to the genre's dual-focus on psychological depth and social panorama, *Pterodactyl* reads like a story of development. At the beginning of the novel, Mahasweta characterizes Puran as a 'floating' (97), self-interested soul who 'gives money to all political parties' and sees caste politics as a mere business opportunity: 'The newspaper is a business to him. If reporting caste war keeps his paper going, so be it. Nothing will touch him' (97). Yet after witnessing the impacts of India's agro-industrial development initiatives, Puran is 'touched' by his experiences in Pirtha, and thereby commences his own kind of development into a more committed citizen, no longer a disinterested reporter of current affairs but an active participant in history-making. The novel thus plots out Puran's character transformation, an attitudinal coming-of-age story in which self-enclosed autonomy becomes generatively balanced with community-bound citizenship. Put differently, *Pterodactyl* follows a protagonist's subjectivation as they become a responsible subject of the polis.[10]

Yet still, what 'touches' Puran is the suffering of those who have not been granted full personhood, full humanity. More than this, even, Puran is touched by the *dactyl*, or finger, of an entire nonhuman history which remains necessarily unassimilable, incommensurable, bewildering. If the *Bildungsroman* typically functions as a genre of humanization, in which the protagonist undergoes individual development in order to identify with a community of humanity, then *Pterodactyl* unsettles this by opening out onto an ethics that exceeds this community: Puran falls into creaturely responsibility, a kind of ethics concerned with both those adivasis who have been denied political humanity and the nonhuman ecologies that are being bulldozed by development initiatives. On his first night in Pirtha village, Puran is confronted by the pterodactyl. As its quivering body moves across his room, 'half claw scratching, half floating', Puran is invaded by the 'touch of our times' (140–1). But this 'touch', while belonging to Puran's present, is also entirely out of time. It is contemporaneous to the present 'now', but also a touch *across* time:

> From the other side of millions of years the soul of the ancestors of Shankar's people looks at Puran, and the glance is so prehistoric that Puran's brain cells, spreading a hundred antennae, understand nothing of that glance. ...
>
> The creature is breathing, its body is trembling. Puran backs off with measured steps.
>
> (141)

Puran is shaken by the pterodactyl's prehistoric gaze and its silent, trembling body. He finds himself completely 'invaded' (182) by the realities of Pirtha village. But this invasion is never incorporated into the stable bounds of Puran's political humanity. Although he begins the novel as 'a half-man, a rootless weed' (160), Puran's time in Pirtha village does not provide him with the missing half of his humanity. Instead, Mahasweta's narrative unsettles Puran's entire consideration of himself as a 'modern man' (158). If the prototypical *Bildungsroman* is an anthropological machine, a form that constructs the modern human, then *Pterodactyl* rewrites the form into something more creaturely. Puran's putative character development is forged not through an apparent mastery of his surroundings and relations but through giving himself up to the 'inhuman' and nonhuman other.

The pterodactyl remains inaccessible to Puran. He consults dinosaur encyclopaedias, reading about the 'pterosauria class from the Mesozoic era' (154). But Puran begins questioning whether the creature is a pterodactyl at all: 'Their earlier editions, e.g. the Rhamphorhynchus, still had the long tail of a reptile and innumerable teeth. [This creature has no teeth. It does not have a long tail, Puran is certain, for he has taken a good look in the half-light]' (154–5). Rendered here within square brackets which emphasize the 'half-light' of his knowledge, Puran's reflections trouble his and the reader's wish to categorize this nonhuman figure. He soon gives up his desire to report it to the national press. As 'tears stream from his eyes' (142), Puran proleptically imagines the consequences of reporting this 'explosive discovery': 'Newspapers and scientists from the world over are pouring into Pirtha, extinguishing the tribals altogether' (142–3). Against this anticipated 'invasion' of adivasi forest lands, which would turn Pirtha into a paleontological digging site, Puran decides to omit the pterodactyl from his final report, to conceal it from national attention and therefore abandon the compulsion to catalogue life. Because India's forest lands have already been 'invaded and devastated' (161), Puran realizes that it is he who must shoulder the 'intolerable burden' of the discovery (143). Put differently, Puran must be invaded so as to avert further adivasi dispossession: 'You are now invaded', Mahasweta's omniscient narrator tells him (182).

Puran thus learns how to be touched by the nonhuman without himself mastering it: 'I do not wish to touch you, you are outside my wisdom, reason, and feelings, who can place his hand on the axial moment of the end of the third phase of the Mesozoic and the beginnings of the Cenozoic geological ages? That is a story of seventy-five million years' (157). Cautious of the pterodactyl's broken wing, Puran and Bikhia bring it moss, rice, kodo millet, dead gnats, mud, a small fish and a bowl of water. But the pterodactyl does not eat. It soon dies. As Puran and Bikhia bury its body in the nearby caves, Mahasweta's narrative voice enters into the text: 'One has to leave finally without knowing many things' (180). And so this is where the story draws to its conclusion: the pterodactyl is now gone, and Puran will go too:

> Now Puran's amazed heart discovers what love there is in his heart, perhaps he cannot remain a distant spectator anywhere in life.
> Pterodactyl's eyes.
> Bikhia's eyes....
> A *truck* comes by.
> Puran raises his hand, steps up.
>
> (196)

Character development, or *Bildung*, is typically considered to be most visible in crescendos of plotted anagnorisis, in which a protagonist is hailed into humanity as they negotiate self-enclosed autonomy and community-bound citizenship. Yet Puran's 'stepping up' denotes less his entrance into full humanity and more of a way of being in the world that is irrevocably marked by the adivasi and the nonhuman. In contrast to the European novel of development, Joseph Slaughter has theorized the postcolonial *Bildungsroman* as plotting out forms of 'disillusionment, in which the promises of developmentalism and self-determination are revealed to be empty' (2007: 215). *Pterodactyl*, undergirded by Mahasweta's double task, stages this negation while also pushing towards the propositional: towards new commitments, towards love. Indeed, this is intensified by the story's generic combination of the short story's compression and fatefulness with the novel form's longer temporality of plot development. What emerges out of this juxtaposition of forms is futurity, as Mahasweta ends by looking towards a political horizon for both adivasis and the planet. Puran 'steps up' with his gaze turned towards 'the primordial forest, water, living beings' (196).

Literary de-extinction

As *Pterodactyl* has become a paradigmatic text of postcolonial literary studies, critics have puzzled over the peripheral textual presence of its nonhuman being. For some readers, the pterodactyl's radical alterity – a sort of alterity-beyond-alterity, beyond the otherness of the animal – makes an impossible demand of hospitality which Puran must answer to.[11] The pterodactyl is a test of commitment that undergirds the plot. For others, though, the pterodactyl is a distraction, exemplary of not just Puran's but even postcolonial criticism's obsession with a supposedly inaccessible radical alterity. For Neil Lazarus, 'it is presumably easier for the "modern" consciousness to rest with the absurd suggestion that the creature is an extant pterodactyl than with the idea – diegetically framed as true – that it is the embodied form of the soul of the ancestors of the inhabitants of Pirtha' (2011: 250 fn. 67). Read this way, 'Pterodactyl' ironizes its protagonist; Mahasweta suggests that it is easier for Puran to cathect to this late-Jurassic alterity-beyond-alterity, this lost object, rather than the 'mere' alterity of adivasi communities. In much the same way, Lazarus is suggesting that Mahasweta's Anglophone readers fixate on the pterodactyl and thus forget the adivasis.

As a figure, as figuration, the pterodactyl has consequently been read as a call to an ethics of alterity *and* as an ironic indictment of this ethics. But both of these accounts share a tacit humanism, as they ultimately argue that the pterodactyl is merely a triangulator of human concerns. For them, the pterodactyl functions as something akin to what Fredric Jameson has termed a 'vanishing mediator', a catalytic agent which 'disappears from the historical scene' after facilitating an 'exchange of energies between two otherwise mutually exclusive terms' (78). For Spivak, for example, the pterodactyl is 'no more than an occasion for "responsibility" between members of two groups that would otherwise be joined by the abstract collectivity of Indian citizenship' (2003: 80), between the caste Hindu and the adivasi, the protagonist and the minor character.

This has led critics to neglect Mahasweta's figuration and formal incorporation of the pterodactyl. Questions therefore remain: If the pterodactyl is unassimilable to Puran, if it stupefies his 'brain cells' (142), then what are we – as readers – to make of it? What relationship does Mahasweta's text suggest between the pre-historic extinction of the pterodactyl on the one side and the modern deforestation of forest lands and destruction of 'endangered' (156) adivasi communities on the other? How does Mahasweta integrate the pterodactyl into the text, and what effects does its symbolization have on the plot as well as on us, the readers? Through the figure of the pterodactyl, I want to suggest, Mahasweta operationalizes a discursive terrain of extinction, a metaphorical field of endangerment, which communicates the dramatic, world-historical and planetary stakes of adivasi genocide and nonhuman ecocide. To do this, though, she first has to write the pterodactyl into the text. And I want to call this process *literary de-extinction*, a mode of writing which reanimates extinct life forms within the text's diegetic present.

With the word 'de-extinction' I do not mean to call forth the shadow of that divisive bio-technical process of archive fever in which previously extinct species, harnessed as biological resources, are genetically regenerated into the present. That form of de-extinction is a kind of resurrection biology which aims to de- and re-code the preserved DNA of lost species, recovered from the preserved archives of museum storehouses, frozen zoos and the melting archives of permafrost: think of charismatic megafauna such as woolly mammoths and thylacines. Over the past decade, de-extinction has received extravagant investments and has, in its own way, begun to capture the popular imagination. But it has also come under justifiable scrutiny as a nostalgic practice, a techno-fix to mass extinction, an extension of anthropocentric mastery and as a new frontier for capital accumulation. Ursula Heise asks: 'What ecological consequences would ensue, given that, even in the case of the relatively recent extinction of the passenger pigeon, a century has gone by without it and its ecological niche has been occupied by other species? Would this in fact turn the de-extincted species into an introduced, possibly even invasive one?' (2016: 210). Ashley Dawson argues that de-extinction promises to 'wind evolutionary time backwards' (2016: 75), a 'seductive but dangerously deluding techno-fix for an environmental crisis generated by the systemic contradictions of capitalism' (79) that 'takes the extinction crisis as an opportunity to ratchet up the commodification of life itself' (82).

De-extinction is also pervaded by a melancholic attachment to the lost object, an elegiac impulse fixated on the sublimity of charismatic megafauna. This produces an archive fever: a returning to the past so as to salvage the present. This fascination with the spectacular bigness and pastness of extinct creatures structures a particular kind of modern obsession with dinosaurs, crystallized today by the *Jurassic Park* franchise. Over half a century ago, Theodor W. Adorno diagnosed this melancholic attachment to the extinct as a further 'rationalization of culture' which, by 'opening its doors to nature, thereby completely absorbs it, and eliminates... the possibility of reconciliation' (2005: 115–16). More recently, W. J. T. Mitchell argues that the dinosaur-sign is so integral to the Americanized global imaginary that it has become a 'totem animal of modernity' (1998: 5). A 'rare, exotic, and extinct animal that has to be "brought back to life" in representations' (79), Mitchell writes, the dinosaur 'epitomizes a modern time sense – both the geological "deep time" of paleontology and the temporal cycles of innovation and obsolescence endemic to modern capitalism' (77). The project of de-extinction is therefore driven by a melancholic attachment to the lost object and a bio-capitalist desire to techno-fix anthropogenic extinctions, two powerful desires which will not so much rescind but continue the war against animals as a form of ecological, material and cultural devastation.

Mahasweta's literary de-extinction diverges from this melancholic cathexis and bio-capitalist archive fever. Mahasweta's text 'brings back to life' the pterodactyl in such a way that disobeys the sublime dinosaur-sign. In the novel's opening pages the pterodactyl is portended as a 'monstrous shadow' with a 'gaping mouth' (102–3). When visiting Bikhia's stone engraving, Puran observes how the outline depicts the pterodactyl as having wings that are 'webbed like a bat's, the body like a gigantic iguana, four clawed feet, no teeth in the yawning terrible mouth' (128). However, these prefigurations hyperbolically betray rather than portray the dominant symbolization of the pterodactyl. When the pterodactyl finally arrives, it does so as little more than a 'quivering' body with 'faded eyes' (143). Rather than effortlessly gliding through the sky, a figure of sublimity, Mahasweta's pterodactyl is fatigued and grounded, a homeless 'unknown tired bird' that soon passes away (193). The pterodactyl also remains peripherally formalized: it is rarely anthropomorphized and depicted exclusively from Puran's outsider focalization. Mahasweta thus evades straightforwardly representing the pterodactyl. And in those moments in which the pterodactyl is indeed figured in the text, it simply crumples and deteriorates. Even the pterodactyl's death is described ambiguously, with Mahasweta enlisting the metaphor 'darkness opened its mouth' (181) to denote what we assume is its cave burial. Against the sublime Americanized aesthetic of the dinosaur that Adorno and Mitchell rally against, Mahasweta writes the pterodactyl as passive and ambiguous.

At the very same time, Mahasweta utilizes the figure of the pterodactyl in order to admonish the development-sanctioned patenting, privatization, and commodification of life. In rapid, paratactic clauses, Mahasweta lists off 'deadly

DDT greens,/charnel-house vegetables,/uprooted astonished onions, radioactive potatoes' (157). Apostrophizing the pterodactyl as a representative of extinct species, she writes:

> What does [the pterodactyl] want to tell? We are extinct by the inevitable natural geological evolution. You too are endangered. You too will become extinct in nuclear explosions, or in war, or in the aggressive advance of the strong as it obliterates the weak, which finally turns you naked, barbaric, primitive, think if you are going forward or back. Forests are extinct, and animal life is obliterated outside of zoos and protected forest sanctuaries. What will finally grow in the soil, having murdered nature in the application of man-imposed substitutes?... The collective being of the ancient nations is crushed. Like nature, like the sustaining earth.
>
> (157)

For Mahasweta, at stake in the proliferation of nuclear weapons and the failures of the Green Revolution is the endangerment of life, the extinction of humanity and the obliteration of the wild. The pterodactyl's 'wordsoundless message' conveys to Puran that he 'is a newcomer in the history of the earth's revolution' (155): 'The human being is only a few million years old' (154). The pterodactyl thus conjures up a kind of memory of the planet which, by predating humanity, unsettles it, revealing to Puran that he is not exempt from extinction.

Pterodactyl's metaphorics of extinction therefore creates space for Puran to see how his life is knotted together with adivasi life. The pterodactyl disabuses the ideology of the human as the pinnacle of evolution by opening up a plurality of other nonhuman worlds and times. As Puran confesses, 'if we acknowledge the pterodactyl, where will homo-sapiens-mapiens be?' (159). Importantly, the pterodactyl's apostrophic formulations directly address Puran, calling on him to 'think', to witness and recognize his participation in the 'aggressive advance' of human history. The anaphoric repetition of 'you too' insists that human history is contingent; it is as finite as the pterodactyl. Mahasweta thus bestows the pterodactyl with a kind of textual force which begins from its vulnerability.

Later, Mahasweta returns to these questions of vulnerability, extinction and deep time by adopting a zoomed-out, planetary perspective:

> Having seen history from beyond pre-history, continental drift, seasonal changes after much geological turbulence, the advent of the human race, primordial history, the history of the ancient lands, the Middle Ages, the present age, two World Wars, Hiroshima-Nagasaki, holding under its wing this entire history

and the current planetary arms race and the terror of nuclear holocaust, it came to give some sharply urgent news.

(180)

Mahasweta turns the history of anthroponormative 'progress' into a catastrophic teleology of technological militarization which brings about its own extinction. The pterodactyl's deep perspective places an urgent demand on Puran and the reader. In a word, they must recalibrate their relationship with the planet. Puran thus asks of the pterodactyl, without a response: 'Have you come up from the past to warn us, are you telling us that this man-made poverty and famine is a crime, this widespread thirst is a crime, it is a crime to take away the forest and make the forest-dwelling peoples naked and endangered?' (157). Mahasweta further rebukes this 'crime' against life when she writes that the 'collective being of the ancient nations is crushed. Like nature, like the sustaining earth, their sustaining ancient cultures received no honor, they remained unknown, they were only destroyed, they are being destroyed' (157).

With this, Mahasweta echoes Sebald's vision of modernity as a continual piling up of ruins. But despite this catastrophic tone, which risks a resigned melancholia for a disappearing world, *Pterodactyl* does not slip into the despondency. Instead the text foregrounds the present as the site of resistance for multispecies justice. Mahasweta knows that the clock cannot be wound backwards. 'Listen, man, I can't turn the clock back by five hundred years', Pirtha's Block Development Officer, Harisharan, says to Puran (120). And just as the story suggests that the only way for Puran to take responsibility would be to give up his intention to document and publicize the pterodactyl, so too does Mahasweta's writing perform this very injunction. Her literary de-extinction is soon eclipsed by a re-extinction:

> The body seemed slowly to sink down, a body crumbling on its four feet, the head on the floor, in front of their eyes the body suddenly begins to tremble steadily. It trembles and trembles, and suddenly the wings open, and they go back in repose, this pain is intolerable to the eye.
> About an hour later Puran says, 'Gone.'

(180)

The fragile pterosaur is not thought of as a lost object that must be preserved. Instead, Mahasweta lets it be, which is to say, lets it die, so that 'the human being' can 'enter life' again (158). Like Coetzee's *Disgrace*, then, Mahasweta gives up her text's nonhuman figure. But where for Coetzee this act of giving up denotes the end of the novel itself, *Pterodactyl* continues to follow the story beyond the scene of giving up. Puran learns to give up the pterodactyl so that he can reshape his politics in the service of human and nonhuman life, against developmental modernity. And Mahasweta's text itself, by rendering the pterodactyl as small and minor, and by ultimately giving it up completely, similarly reconciles itself to letting go of the sublime aesthetics of the dinosaur-sign. By rendering the nonhuman in such a way, Mahasweta ensures that the pterodactyl remains unincorporated into the orbit of understanding. Both Puran and the reader must relinquish the pterodactyl. By doing this, Mahasweta's literary de-extinction activates a kind of history which is no longer anchored to the human subject, and a kind of postcolonial writing which also interrupts the logics of the novel as an anthropological machine.

Planetary alongsideness

To conclude this chapter I wish to home in on one final formal-thematic node of *Pterodactyl* which opens out onto a world beyond anthroponormativity: the asymptote. In geometric terms, asymptotes are those lines which are closed in on by – but never ultimately intersect with – a curve as it tends towards infinity. The asymptote approaches zero but is infinitely deferred from ever reaching it. Metaphorically, then, the asymptotic connotes a sense of intimacy without intersection, a closeness that brushes up against irreducible difference. In *Pterodactyls*' first half, Mahasweta invokes the asymptote in order to thematize a seemingly uncrossable gulf which separates Puran from both the adivasis at Pirtha village and the elusive pterodactyl. When Puran speaks at cross-purposes with the regional officer responsible for Pirtha's relief package, Mahasweta interjects: 'Are the two placed on two islands and is one not understanding the urgent message of the other, speaking with vivid gestures on the seashore? This asymptote is a contemporary contagion' (102). By drawing on the figure of the asymptote, Mahasweta stresses that there is an insurmountable obstacle of untranslatability that lies between Puran and the district. Society, she is saying, is infected with a disease that splits it into distant islands of experience, into distinct sections that cannot communicate with one another: 'Puran's Hindi and theirs come from two different worlds… There is no meeting-point. Language too is class divided' (162–3). Mahasweta invokes the asymptote as a symptom of the ossification of unequal social relations. It is a 'communication gap', a 'tremendous (mental and linguistic) suspension of contact' (102) that thematizes a political, linguistic and ontological abyss which separates the cosmopolitan protagonist subject from the subaltern minor characters, and hence keeps the reader at arm's length.

Yet across the story Mahasweta shifts the metaphorics of the asymptote: from affliction to remedy, from a disease of postcolonial inequality to a symbol of future decolonization. When Puran and Bikhia witness the pterodactyl's death, for instance, they do so from supposedly incommensurable perspectives. But Mahasweta emphasizes the important fact that, despite their difference, they are nevertheless brought together in this encounter. Mahasweta constructs two consecutive paragraphs which convey and formally mark out this moment as conjoined but distinct: 'Bikhia is witnessing that their ancestors' soul embodied itself and flew in one day… Puran is witnessing his own futility' (180). Mahasweta's anaphoric formulations pull Puran and Bikhia into asymptotic proximity with one another. Their disparity is no longer insinuated as pure negativity, as malady, but is instead installed as a generative difference that founds solidarity. Indeed, in one of the story's final passages Mahasweta writes:

> Now Bikhia's eyes explain that this strange situation had made them one but they were never really one. As if in a strange situation of war two people from separate worlds and lives, who do not understand one another's language, were obliged to cross some icy ravine, or to pass an unknown and violent desert, and then complete mutual help became necessary. A time of danger has brought them together.
>
> (182)

Turning, here, to the rhetoric of wartime, Mahasweta analogizes Puran and Bikhia as two travellers from different lands who must lean on one another. The asymptote, now conceptually reclaimed and reconstructed, becomes a symbol for a provisional 'clasp' of hands in this 'heavy phase' of history (182), not as a becoming-one but a becoming-two.

It is the pterodactyl that prompts this becoming-two. The story suggests that it is through the nonhuman, through the relation to nature and to the planet, through the fundamental vulnerability of the human as a species among other species, that Puran and Bikhia – as representatives of the cosmopolitan and the rural, the Hindu and the adivasi – can stand in relation to one another. Recalling Adorno's writing on the 'possibility of reconciliation' (2005: 116) which I introduced in Chapter 1, I want to argue that the pterodactyl hastens an *asymptotic reconciliation* between Puran and Bikhia, a paradoxical meeting-point between what is constructed here as normative humanity and its constitutively excluded inhuman other. Indeed, as Adorno put it elsewhere, 'the image of what is oldest in nature reverses dialectically into the cipher of the not-yet-existing, the possible' (2013: 73). If, at the beginning of the story, the pterodactyl is introduced as an omen of adivasi extinction, then by the end it becomes a harbinger of a future reconciliation between normative humanity and all of its others, human and nonhuman. The pterodactyl, an extinct pre-historic being, becomes the symbol of future possibility.

In her many reflections on *Pterodactyl*, Spivak reads the story's commitment to futurity via the concept of 'planetarity'. Spivak conceptualized this term, planetarity, in the late 1990s, in response to what she saw as the flattening globalization of international finance and information technology. Writing at a time in which 'the gridwork of electronic capital' (2003: 72) was even throwing into question the entire Westphalian model of nation states, as governmental power was increasingly conceded to finance, Spivak proposes the term 'planetarity' as a 'catachresis for inscribing collective responsibility as right. Its alterity, determining experience, is mysterious and discontinuous – an experience of the impossible' (72). Planetarity, for Spivak, names a reappropriation of the global for ethics, a kind of globalization-from-below which embraces transnational solidarity as a bulwark against globalized capital: 'If we imagine ourselves as planetary subjects rather than global agents, planetary creatures rather than global entities, alterity remains underived from us' (73). Put differently, planetarity is a creaturely ethics, one which directs us towards other creatures with whom we share a differential inhabitation of the planet.

As we have seen, Mahasweta's metaphorics of extinction requires a planetary perspective. As a being that holds 'under its wing this entire history and the current planetary arms race and the terror of nuclear holocaust', the pterodactyl brings with it a reevaluation and humbling of human modernity through its embodied invocation of extinction across deep time and contemporary existential threats, from 'geological turbulence' to 'Hiroshima-Nagasaki' (1995: 180). What we have then is a story motivated by a desire to warn against both the planetary risk of nuclear catastrophe *and* the ongoing destruction of adivasi peoples as an unrecognized 'continent' within the Indian nation. Mahasweta uses the spectres of mutually assured destruction and species extinctions as occasions for staging a planetary ethics. In animal studies and postcolonial theory alike, hybridity has been celebrated as an intermingling of subjectivities which reveals not just the porousness of individual identity but also the constitutive relation between the subject and its others. Yet

Mahasweta's *Pterodactyl*, with its emphasis on asymptotic reconciliation, suggests a different path. It suggests, to borrow a formulation from Joanna Latimer, a form of *alongsideness*, of being-alongside (2013: 93). Planetarity is not a hybrid ethics but an asymptotic one: it sustains relationality precisely through difference.

Let us conclude, then, with these three keywords: 'asymptotic planetary alongsideness'. In *Pterodactyl*, I want to finally argue, Mahasweta reveals how despite not inhabiting the same world, her characters nevertheless share the same planet. They remain separate from one another, yet bound together as creatures on the same journey, like two lines that run towards infinity, into the future beyond the text. *Pterodactyl* stresses this paradoxical inseparability and asymptotic disjunction. This is, as I have argued, both a thematic and ethical commitment. But it is also encoded in literary form: Mahasweta gives form to the pterodactyl without assimilating or domesticating its otherness. Ultimately, what we are faced with in this text is two people from separate worlds joining together to care for a suffering pre-historic being. This form of creaturely care-taking inspires a vision of postcoloniality as planetarity, as multispecies love which preserves difference while also transcending the entrenched ontological divisions between human, inhuman and nonhuman. Mahasweta's writing tackles the anthropological machine of development through an attention to indigeneity and adivasi survival, bonded labour and trafficking, the murdering of nature by deforestation and chemical technologies and the extinction of lifeforms. All of these compel us to conceive of a planetary justice which would leave behind the humanist political ontologies of anthroponormativity. Against the socio-ecological catastrophes of modernity, Mahasweta's writing insists on creaturely love.

Notes

1 The term 'subaltern' has a specific and complex history, from Gramscian theory to the Subaltern Studies Group's intervention into postcolonial historiography. Here, I use the term to invoke the marginalized and disenfranchised classes, mostly peasants, with whom Mahasweta worked.
2 Mahasweta, for her part, tended to use the word 'tribal' rather than adivasi. But throughout this chapter I follow the work of David Hardiman (1995: 15–16), Ajay Skaria (1999: 277–81), Meena Radhakrishna (2016) and Alpa Shah (2010: 31) by adopting 'Tribe' as a purely politico-administrative category, or when quoting Mahasweta herself. I also follow these scholars by not italicizing adivasi.

3 Madhurima Chakraborty puts it that Mahasweta is 'understood in leftist communities in India, as well as in global literary circles, as one of the few writers whose literary and political endeavours are coterminous' (2014: 282).
4 Vandana Shiva writes that Green Revolution was an internationally sanctioned 'techno-political' experiment in agricultural production which promised the alleviation of poverty and hunger. By courting US agriculturalists, Indira Gandhi's government responded to the country's agrarian crisis by importing subsided grain, fertilizers and seeds. But these reforms ended up being 'conflict-producing instead of conflict-reducing' (Shiva 1991: 14–15), leading to human dispossession and impoverishment on the one side, and nonhuman monocultures and extinctions on the other. For further research on the origins and impacts of the Green Revolution, see Patel (2013).
5 For more on Mahasweta's multilingual narration, see Salgado (2000).
6 On this, see Lazarus (2011: 155, 250 fn. 66) and Gopal (2005: 3).
7 Following Vinay Gidwani's synthesis of prominent theories of caste – from Louis Dumont to G. S. Ghurye to Nicholas Dirks – I take caste to be a mutable and 'overdetermined entity, enabled by historically and geographically contingent articulations of class, gender, political, and religious elements' (2008: 38). Following Partha Chatterjee, I also think of caste as an increasingly secular category of social identity (2014: 182).
8 See Alter (1995: 26).
9 For more on the *Jani Parab* as a space of female assertion, see the conclusions of Toppo (2018).
10 My characterizations of the *Bildungsroman* synthesize the work of Buckley (1974: 17), Redfield (2006: 193), and Esty (2012).
11 For various iterations of this argument, see Spivak (2012: 210), Roy (2010: 148), Menozzi (2014: 62) and Farrier (2016: 464).

Conclusion: from anthropological machines to creaturely forms

Reconstructing creatureliness

As I write today, the war against animals shows no signs of ending. There are new extinctions every day. The meat, dairy and fish industries are expanding further and deeper into nature. Immense wildfires are tearing through the planet's old-growth forests, incinerating billions of endangered animals: koalas, spiders, cockatoos and dunnarts in Australia; spider monkeys, jaguars, giant river otters and poison dart frogs in Brazil; pygmy rabbits and sage grouse in the United States. Other effects of climate change – flooding, drought, extreme weather events – are already devastating many of the world's poorest people in the global south and destroying nonhuman habitats in the process. And now, due to the continuing human encroachment into a commodified nature, a vicious infectious disease has jumped from species to species, unlocking host cells, causing acute respiratory distress and failure, and reaching pandemic proportions. Zoonotic diseases like Covid-19 are not unforeseen accidents. They are long-anticipated symptoms of the war against animals, emerging from human contact with critters whose habitats have been fragmented, depleted or razed.

It is already late. Even before climate change and zoonotic disease became part of our everyday vocabulary, Jacques Derrida understood that we were entering a 'critical phase' (2008: 29) of the war against the animal, a significant conjuncture in which the instrumentalization of the natural world reaches new breaking points. Modernity's supposed mastery of nature, totalizing but not complete, is today rebounding onto humanity, implicating and injuring us, calling on us to respond. Environmentalists, ecosocialists and journalists alike have heeded this call by making the case for a radical transformation of economy, wealth and power. Naomi Klein, one of the sharpest public intellectuals of our time, has put it that what is needed in this moment of crisis is nothing short of a 'fundamental shift in power relations between humanity and the natural world on which we depend' (2015: 460), a shift towards alternative kinds of social relations and economic production 'embedded in interdependence rather than hyperindividualism, reciprocity rather than dominance, and cooperation rather than hierarchy' (462). But what Klein misses in her otherwise powerful account is that any such redistribution of power and reorganization of production – whether a green new deal or de-growth – must also transform human–animal relations. Whether we are making a strategic eco-political case for the future flourishing of human life on planet Earth, or an ethical claim about our responsibility to other beings, the abolition of animal industries must surely be a foundational demand of any green future.

But we also need a cultural revolution in the way we think about animals in relation to our own peculiar subject position as a species that is related yet different, distinct yet not superior, to other forms of life. In the words of Adorno and Horkheimer, the mastery of nature will end when the human subject develops a clearer sense of itself as a being which 'as nature, is more than mere nature' (2002: 165). In other words, the human is an animal among other animals *and also* an animal with its own specific capacity to act, and thus its own obligation to the planet. At stake in realizing this is not just the potential overthrow of anthroponormativity and its attendant exclusions of other genres of life but also the construction of new kinds of responsibility and community. Working through human supremacy, then, is a reconciliatory project of humility and reconstruction that requires thought as well as action, stories as well as organizing.

This is what I have wanted to show. In these pages I have argued that literature plays an active cultural and discursive role, and hence important ideological function, in recording and producing our sense of what it means to be human. Although literature tends to function as an anthropological machine, with literary devices working as 'device[s] for producing the recognition of the human' (Agamben 2004: 26), the practice of writing also carries with it the possibility of undermining the manifold constructions of human superiority. Literary forms can thus form and deform anthroponormativity. Forms afford writers the opportunity to strategically *mis*recognize human subjectivity's apparent opposition to and supremacy over animal life. My readings of works by W. G. Sebald, J. M. Coetzee and Mahasweta Devi have sought to demonstrate this. Over the past two decades, these three writers have been subject to near-constant literary-critical scrutiny. Such scrutiny, however, has mostly come from scholars invested in explicitly humanist modes of reading. For my part, then, by bringing these authors into dialogue with one another under the banner of the creaturely, I have sought to reveal how their distinctive literary projects are formally and thematically attentive towards a shared animality that undermines humanism itself.

I have argued, in other words, that their texts are creaturely forms: their writing sometimes bears witness to, and other times seeks to arrest or suspend, the decisionist logic of the anthropological machine as it fictionalizes modes of human life that rely on the mass production and mass extinction of other creatures. In this, these authors might be said to write *as* animals. That is, they write in the knowledge that they are human animals, using their literary texts to dramatize the lives of human characters who, subject to forms of vulnerability and interdependence, assume different modes of relationality towards other forms of life. These creaturely forms of writing therefore articulate a response and challenge to the existing war against animals while also generating new imaginaries for thinking and acting differently alongside nature. Sebald, Coetzee and Mahasweta each write in such a way that makes imaginative sense of the scale of the war against animals, the colonial impulse to obliterate forms of life deemed insufficiently human and the urgent need for a surrendering of human supremacy. Creaturely forms trouble ingrained species hierarchies and encourage solidarities that extend beyond anthroponormativity.

I have made this argument by invoking and reconstructing the concept of the creaturely. Under my reading, the 'creaturely' has become a critical term which, working through the logics of inhumanity, dehumanization and animalization, deconstructs the category of the human. Despite the concept's shifting meanings across the last century of intellectual thought, the creaturely has remained relatively stable in two important aspects: it disrupts the logic by which animality is cast as the other to anthroponormativity, and it calls for new modes of relationality. The texts I have analysed in *Creaturely Forms in Contemporary Literature* all differently engage with this sense of the creaturely, whether we think, at a sentence-by-sentence level, of the authors' particular uses of the word itself or, at a thematic level, of their preoccupations with human–animal relations. Sebald, Coetzee and Mahasweta all tell stories about human characters who, when encountering other creatures, undergo their own forms of dehumanization. Chapter 2 attended to how Sebald depicts his narrator-protagonists as 'prone bodies' (2002b: 79), so sensitive to modernity's destructive progress that they melancholically identify with nonhumans, whether those animals survive in Europe's zoos, suffer from over-fishing or are displayed as taxidermy specimens in British country houses. In Chapter 3, I explored how Coetzee's texts routinely abject, diminish and deform their protagonists in the face of animal life. In *Disgrace*, both David Lurie and his daughter Lucy become undone, unmoored. But while David holds on to a tacitly humanist 'idea of the world' (2000: 146), Lucy chooses to 'give up' (205) the trappings of a liberal personhood made possible by colonial conquest. With his concurrent invention of Elizabeth Costello, Coetzee also develops a character-persona who is so overwhelmed by the dizzying scale of industrial animal agriculture that she begins to recognize herself not as a human but as a creature, a 'branded, marked, wounded animal' (2004a: 70–1). My fourth chapter considered how Mahasweta stages the dissolution of anthroponormative subjectivity, of 'modern man' (1995: 158), through a call to ethics from those whom (post) colonial modernity has seemingly left behind. In texts like 'Fundamental Rights and Bhikari Dusad' and *Pterodactyl*, the creaturely stands as a process by which plotted dehumanizations of character make possible new ethical engagements that exceed the exclusions of human rights.

Under my reading, Sebald, Coetzee and Mahasweta set their creaturely ethics against capitalist modernity's war against animals. For these writers, modernity is founded on the destruction of creaturely life; it variously and contradictorily obliterates, instrumentalizes, commodifies, reifies, deadens and conserves other beings. Sebald's melancholy narrators are peculiarly alert to how the progress of modernity, as a 'relentless conquest of darkness' (2002b: 59), is concomitant with the elimination and exhaustion of both human and nonhuman lives. Trees are incessantly reduced to charcoal, herring are pushed to the brink of extinction, labourers in eighteenth-century Norfolk are tortured by the industrial working day, and the architecture of Belgium's cities is built on the foundation of colonial genocide. Sebald's wide natural-historical perspective recasts modernity's progress as an interminably long period of decline. A similar counter-narrative is at play in Mahasweta's work, in which India's post-Independence development initiatives are shown to simultaneously 'crush' adivasis and 'destroy' habitats (1995: 157). Sebald's and Coetzee's texts interrogate modernity as a time of increasing animal production and extinction, from over-fishing to factory farming to animal experimentation. Elizabeth Costello calls this an 'enterprise without end, self-regenerating, bringing rabbits, rats, poultry, livestock ceaselessly into the world for the purpose of killing them' (Coetzee 2004a: 65). While I have argued that Sebald and Coetzee foreground vegetarianism and the ethics of consuming animals, it is also the case that all three writers are concerned with the systems of production that *precede* consumption. While Sebald and Coetzee focus in on animal industries, Mahasweta's fiction turns to the privatization of the commons and what she describes as the Green Revolution's 'murdering' (1995: 157) of nature through the spraying of chemicals, the proliferation of monocultures, deforestation and extinction – what we saw Rachel Carson call a war against nature in this book's introduction. For these authors, then, the continual development of modernity is founded on the mastery, homogenization, production and annihilation of other forms of life.

Yet what *Creaturely Forms in Contemporary Literature* has also wanted to emphasize is *how* these authors narrate modernity's war against animals. In Chapter 2, for example, I put it that Sebald's signature stylistic motifs – his texts' slow narrative temporality, generic indeterminacy, non-indexical images, and lists and hypotaxis – can all be said to militate against what he dismisses as the mechanical grinding of the plot-reliant novel. By articulating a kind of novelistic form that is digressive, unhurried and peripatetic, Sebald creates a literary breathing space which allows him to concentrate on beings and ideas that might otherwise go unnoticed. In so doing, Sebald's forms give attention to forms of life that might for other authors simply be left out, or articulated as mere description subsumed into background environment. In Chapter 3, I suggested that Coetzee, critically invested in novelistic theory, often uses and ab-uses (Spivak 2021: 395) the central tenets of novel forms in order to undermine literature as an anthropological machine. I argued that texts like *Disgrace* and *Elizabeth Costello* can be understood as literary experiments in which realism and metafiction are tested out to see whether and to what extent they can accommodate animals and a human affinity with fellow creatures. Coetzee's animal turn, his period of intense literary engagement with the war against animals, thus stages a tension between literary form and pro-animal ethics. The final scene of *Disgrace* is a case in point. As Coetzee rearranges his novel's synchronic tense, indefinitely suspending any final ending to the novel, it is as if he recognizes that his writing is hurtling towards a scene of animal death, a decision between the human and the animal: for David Lurie to live on, the novel seems to suggest, the animal must die as a material and symbolic victim of plotted resolution. *Disgrace*'s final indeterminacy therefore uncovers, within literary form itself, how much the novel is compelled towards sacrifice. In Chapter 4, I juxtaposed *Disgrace* with Mahasweta's *Pterodactyl*. While both texts relinquish their literary creatures and, in doing so, call attention to the limits of incorporating nonhumans into fiction, Mahasweta's letting-go does not bring the novel to a close, but instead opens up new plotted pathways that lead towards a horizon of more-than-human love and justice. This creaturely horizon, I suggested, unsettles the confluences between characterization and anthroponormativity. Indeed, Mahasweta's short fictions can all be said to thematically trouble, as well as structurally prevent, the steady build-up of character development which is deemed to be contiguous with the development of postcolonial subjectivity.

By underlining the importance of form, I have sought to shed light on how the writing of human–animal relations calls into question the borders and conventions of literature itself. Formal constraints are, from this perspective, *generatively limiting* in that they offer bounded possibilities for incorporating animals into fiction, staging species relations and reflecting on the war against animals. Writers like Sebald, Coetzee and Mahasweta creatively negotiate the boundaries of literary form each and every time they write animals. Ultimately, their literary encounters with animality lead to a rewriting of novelistic forms as their texts attest to and fracture literature's production of species difference.

One upshot of this argument's attention to the politics of form is that it forges new paths for literary animal studies, which has until now focused overwhelmingly on how writers represent animals. By closely reading formal patterns, structures, motifs and styles in conjunction with representational and thematic content, we come to see how the incorporation of creatures into literature is shaped not just by particular social ideas about animals but also by the inherited structures and capacities of forms that are available to writers at any given time.

Yet the implications of this argument also extend beyond animal studies. For if literature has played an important cultural role in capitalist modernity, a sprocket within the anthropological machine, then that means that literature too is part of the war against animals. Just as modernity organizes and reorganizes human–animal relations for the betterment of some humans, so too does literature's realization of its imagined social worlds rest on particular organizations of human–animal life. At stake in every work of literature is, in a sense, a decision about whether to discursively reproduce the war against animals.

This is not to say that literature is irreversibly or inevitably speciesist. Rather, it is to acknowledge that the literary construction of human character tends to take for granted a dominant contemporary vision of social life premised on the direct and indirect mastery of nature. It is also, importantly, to call attention to the difficulty of writing differently. As I have argued throughout this book, even though Sebald, Coetzee and Mahasweta might be said to narrate the war against animals, their texts do not escape anthroponormativity. They do not ever fully subdue, leave behind or transcend the category of the 'human'. Instead, their creaturely forms dramatize a dialectical tension between a drive or willingness to undermine anthroponormativity on the one hand and an awareness of its hegemonic stranglehold on the other. Creaturely forms are thus countervailing texts that, as texts, push up against the very limitations of this deconstructive gesture. In fact, because the creaturely is concerned with revealing the domination of life under modernity, with positing a joined-up way of thinking about mastery, creaturely forms also carry the possibility of collapsing or forgetting crucial differences between the kinds of life that are historically dominated. Sebald and Coetzee have both received criticism for associating the Nazi genocide of Jewish life in relation to the industrialized slaughter of animals. Sebald's closely paired images of the Holocaust and the herring appear to offer the reader no road map for critically understanding their connection. Looked at one way, then, the images' visual resemblance conflates genocide and fishing. Coetzee has likewise been faulted for using Elizabeth Costello as a stand-in or puppet, an invented persona to conveniently hide behind when voicing strong opinions. Mahasweta, too, has been accused of paternalism towards adivasis, and of recapitulating rather than contesting romanticized notions of adivasis as pre-modern subjects. Thus while Sebald, Coetzee and Mahasweta each come up with innovative literary techniques for linking nonhuman animals and marginalized humans, such linking also risks a suspension of specificity that might jeopardize this entire project.

Criticisms like these remind readers to guard against the logic of equivalence, to be cautious about metaphorical and rhetorical imprecision and to remain critically receptive to the ways in which the subjugation of particular human communities relates to the subjugation of other creatures. But if my analysis has been persuasive, then I may have convinced you that the stakes are too high for us to shy away from articulating the connections between human and nonhuman oppression. Through my study of Sebald's, Coetzee's and Mahasweta's writing, I have come to think of their texts as taking literary risks in order to unearth deep grammars of anthroponormativity that sanction the destruction of creaturely life. Sebald's non-identical images, Coetzee's metafictional strategies and Mahasweta's literary de-extinction of the pterodactyl are attempts to discover novel ways of writing about the historical yoking of inhumanity and animality. I hope to have shown that, even when these texts reach formal limitations or thematic contradictions, they nonetheless bear witness to the intractability of the war against animals. They make sensible, or perceptible, the exclusions of anthroponormativity, thereby offering powerful stories of modernity's mastery of nature. Just as fiction is an apparatus for producing a recognition of the human, it also turns out to be a vehicle for recognizing that this production of the human rests on the mass production and mass extinction of nonhuman life.

Creaturely forms in more contemporary literature

In writing this book, I have wanted to offer a comprehensive analysis of how three literary projects differently narrate the war against animals. I have wanted, in other words, to write about how writers write about animals, to craft a mode of reading that attends to the possibilities of formalizing the war against animals, paying special attention to how particular authors' stylistic concerns develop in conversation with their ideas about the fate of animal life. Yet Sebald, Coetzee and Mahasweta are just three writers among many who utilize literary forms in order to reflect and reconsider contemporary human–animal relations. Absent from my account are a number of other noteworthy texts which, articulating their own kinds of creatureliness, intriguingly draw out the limits and possibilities of their specific literary forms.

Texts like Amitav Ghosh's *The Hungry Tide* and Indra Sinha's *Animal's People*, for example, both echo this book's concerns with how the war against animals is inseparable from the allocation of humanity, the discourse of rights and the legacies of colonial thought. *The Hungry Tide* has become a paradigmatic text within postcolonial ecocriticism for its novelistic dramatization of the tensions between international nature conservation efforts and the unrecognized human rights of the very poorest. The novel is set in the flood-prone mangrove forests of the Sundarbans, a fragile ecosystem located between India and Bangladesh in which pressure to safeguard a tiger sanctuary led to the eviction and massacre of refugees on Marichjhapi island in 1979. Ghosh juxtaposes and, ultimately, seeks to reconcile the worldviews and experiences of Piyali Roy, an American marine biologist, with the local groups of social activists, displaced peoples and indigenous fishermen whom her scientific and liberal-universalist commitments are said to disregard. Ghosh adopts a reflective and critical realism, constructing a cast of characters who, by voicing what Pablo Mukherjee calls 'subaltern resentment' (2010: 118), challenge Piya's managerial conservationism by bringing the reality of human misery to her attention; Kusum, a refugee, expresses disbelief at animal enthusiasts like Piya for forgetting that 'this is how humans have always lived – by fishing, by clearing land and by planting soil' (2005: 262). *The Hungry Tide*'s plotted associations between political and ecological crises culminate with a reconciliation of social justice and animal protection, as Piya – in the novel's final scene – decides to call the Sundarbans home and pursue a locally sensitive kind of environmental study: 'I don't want to do the kind of work that places the burden of conservation on those who can least afford it' (397). Yet the novel's apparent resolution of the tensions between human dignity and nonhuman conservation is only achieved by eliding the tensions *internal to* conservation, as Ghosh shifts the novel's focus away from endangered tigers and towards Piya's original research focus, the Irrawaddy dolphins.[1] Thus although Piya develops a kind of multispecies postcolonial environmentalism ('Once we decide we can kill off other species, it'll be people next' (301)), Ghosh secures this provisionally stable ending by leaving unresolved the decades-long grievances between forest management, endangered tigers and displaced peoples.

Where Ghosh seeks to assert the dignity of the human, the refugee, in the face of state violence and international environmentalism, Sinha's *Animal's People* embraces the figure of the inhuman as a way to register social and ecological injustice without appealing to human rights.[2] Through the monologue of Animal, a caustic teenage narrator-figure left disabled by Union Carbide's poisoning of Bhopal in 1984, Sinha's novel invents a protagonist who brashly asserts his creatureliness: walking on all forms and scavenging for food, Animal announces that he 'used to be human once' (2007: 1). Speaking to an Australian journalist, Animal derides the bureaucratic and legalistic 'talk of *rights, law, justice*' (3), saying that these words 'are choking us' like the poison of the gas explosion. Across the novel, Animal comes to see himself as a lonely creature, at once human and nonhuman and, at the same time, neither human nor nonhuman. Yet come the end, he discovers in this liminality a connection to a wider 'people', to the many fellow orphans, the human and nonhuman victims, of the Bhopal tragedy and beyond. Animal refuses the surgery that would make him 'upright, true' (366), declining the anthroponormative ideology of rectitude that, as we saw in Chapter 3, figures the human through its ability and autonomy. He ends the novel by articulating a creaturely welcoming that is also a warning: 'Tomorrow there will be more of us' (366).

More recently, Jean-Baptiste Del Amo's *Animalia* is a brutally realist novel which conveys how the force-feeding, neutering, slaughter and butchery of pigs transforms across the twentieth century as *raising* becomes *processing*. By adopting a multi-generational narrative mode, Del Amo leverages a form of literary naturalism in which peasant farmers and their pigs are trapped in a cycle of suffering, with both species becoming 'haggard, spent creature[s]' (2019: 15). There is in this book a deeply miserable sense of determinism which functions as a kind of multispecies heredity: 'In the same time, the same space, men and beasts are born, struggle, and pass away' (71); 'they come into the world like livestock, scrabble in the dust in search of meagre sustenance, and die in miserable solitude' (121). Indeed the novel builds a vision of today's intensive animal agricultural practices as being 'at the heart of some much greater disturbance', 'like some machine that is unpredictable, out of kilter, by its nature uncontrollable' (292). Del Amo thus reimagines naturalism in light of the anthropological machine, picturing how human and nonhuman beings are bound together by inexorable laws of violence. The crucial question thus becomes: does Del Amo's naturalism work to counteract these violent relations, or does it ultimately lock them in place as inevitable and unchangeable aspects of life?[3]

In contrast to *Animalia*'s rurally isolated setting and bleak outlook, both Sarah Hall's *The Wolf Border* and Aminatta Forna's *Happiness* envision hope for human–animal futures. More than many of the works I have explored in this book, *The Wolf Border* and *Happiness* tend to utilize their literary creatures – re-introduced wolves in Cumbria and urban foxes in London – in order to dramatize human concerns. Indeed, Hall and Forna might be said to instrumentalize these creatures, incorporating them into their plots so as to ultimately stage the budding romances between their protagonists.[4] And yet, both novels also look towards wolves and foxes as border-crossing beings that, in their survival and flourishing within and beyond the built environment, bring to light the limits of the British nation state, the inequalities of private land-use and the violence of immigration enforcement. Hall pays special attention to England as a private island, with her novel's zoologist protagonist Rachel yearning for 'a place, again, where the streetlights end and wilderness beings. The wolf border. And if this is where it has to begin in England, she thinks, this rich, disqualifying plot, with its private sponsorship and antiquated hierarchy, so be it' (Hall 2015: 234). Forna's depiction of London, however, points out that the wilderness already exists underneath the capital city's lights, as parakeets, owls, foxes, rats and ants dwell in the cracks between city and nature. By foregrounding the lives of animals who interact with, adapt to and disobey human-made boundaries, both The Wolf Border and Happiness usher in forms of interspecies kinship that promise to push past the limits of citizenship and rights. Despite their surface-level conventionality as works of humanizing literary fiction, both novels affirm a kind of borderless internationalism that is also a more-than-human cosmopolitanism. In both works, rewilding is not just a conservationist strategy – it also proposes a wider ethics of co-existence.

This brief survey alone shows how contemporary writers continue to navigate some of the same challenges that I identified in the works of Sebald, Coetzee and Mahasweta. But to more fully articulate this, I will briefly turn to three other texts. These three close readings are intended to extend and challenge the analysis of *Creaturely Forms in Contemporary Literature*, pointing towards different literary-formal engagements with animality and the question of anthroponormativity.

Of vultures and ice cream: Arundhati Roy's *The Ministry of Utmost Happiness*

Arundhati Roy's much-anticipated second novel is concerned with the consolidation of Hindu authoritarianism, the ongoing military occupation of Kashmir, and India's embrace of capitalist-industrial modernity. Addressed at the outset to 'The Unconsoled', *The Ministry of Utmost Happiness* is a geographically sprawling and linguistically acerbic text at pains to point out the 'price for Progress' (2017: 99) in Narendra Modi's India. Here, the kinds of uneven postcolonial development that we saw in Mahasweta Devi's work become newly accelerated in a period of twenty-first-century neoliberal globalization. Roy depicts India, and Delhi in particular, as undergoing a rapid American-style urbanization, one in which landscapes and ecosystems are dramatically reshaped:

> Skyscrapers and steel factories sprang up where forests used to be, rivers were bottled and sold in supermarkets, fish were tinned, mountains mined and turned into shining missiles. Massive dams lit up the cities like Christmas trees. Everyone was happy.
>
> Away from the lights and advertisements, villages were being emptied. Cities too. Millions of people were being moved, but nobody knew where to.
>
> (98)

When Roy addresses her novel to the 'Unconsoled', then, she is referring to the losers of globalization: to the capital city's poorest, whose homes are flattened by bulldozers imported from Australia, and to the environment itself, now leaden with the 'smog and mechanical hum of the city' (101). When Tilo, one of the novel's two major protagonists, tours the city, she is struck – just like Sebald's narrators – by a spectacle of horrors at the capital's busy zoo. Visitors throw litter into enclosures. A Bornean gibbon clings on to a tree 'as though his life depended on it' (234). A hippo swims in a 'scummy pond' full of plastic bottles, empty cigarette packets and razor blades flicked by a 'knot of noisy young men' (235). The zoo claims to care for a host of exotic snakes, sambar deer and a Siberian tiger, but these animals are nowhere to be seen. 'Most of the birds in the aviary were ones you could see on the trees anyway. Bird scam' (235), Tilo thinks, the word 'scam' linking the widespread corruption of India's political classes to its wildlife industries.

Later, Tilo considers how the world's farmed animals are becoming increasingly genetically modified and turned into living factories. Pigs given growth hormones can no longer bear their own weight. Gigantic trout require more feed than ever before. Even cows, the very beings that Hindutva purports to protect, are pumped with painkillers in order to ease their daily labours as 'dairy machines' (1). Tilo scoffs: 'But perhaps this is the path to genuine modernity?' (299). Roy maintains this ironic tone as Tilo turns to the poultry industry, which pays scientists to figure out how 'to excise the mothering instinct in hens [...] Their goal, apparently, is to stop chickens wasting time on unnecessary things and thereby to increase the efficiency of egg production' (299). Tilo wonders whether this business model will be applied to the grief-stricken Maaji, 'The Mothers of the Disappeared in Kashmir' (300), who live as 'inefficient, unproductive units, living on a mandatory diet of hopeless hope'. Here, Roy joins together the battery-farming of India's hens to the anguish of Kashmiri mothers. The novel therefore appears to assert a form of more-than-human love that sits in contradiction to the machinations of commodification and military occupation.

Roy's reviewers were, by and large, left baffled and unconvinced by *The Ministry*'s length, polyphony, non-synchronism, episodic emplotment and diverse cast of minor characters.[5] Yet as critics like Lorna Burns (2019: 134) and Romy Rajan (2021: 93) have pointed out, the novel's scale is a conscious choice, an attempt by Roy to gather together a variety of stories, characters and literary techniques that reflect a nationwide fragmentation 'as the saffron tide of Hindu Nationalism rises in our country like the swastika once did in another' (165). Hindutva's fascistic promise of an undivided India is premised on a deliberate exacerbation of extant inequalities and grievances. Its ideology of unity rests on extreme repression: restricting the citizenship of Muslims, extending police powers, deepening economic deprivation, worsening political disenfranchisement and inciting communal violence.[6]

How, then, might a novel narrate Hindutva's shattering of an already shattered society? Roy poses this question in the novel's final act as Tilo notes down: 'How to tell a shattered story? By slowly becoming everybody. No. By slowly becoming everything' (436). Tilo's answer is not to be read as a literary expression of new materialist philosophy. Roy does not assume the viewpoint or identity of the nonhuman, nor does she endorse the allegedly agentic power of objects. Rather, 'becoming everything' necessitates the adoption of a panoramic and vertiginous standpoint, a world-systemic angle that maps space, surveys time and follows the money. Telling a shattered story thus involves literary form in political resistance. But Roy's novel also doubts its own ability to become everything, even emphasizing its failure, as literature, to face the crisis of Hindutva. As Filippo Menozzi has argued, Roy frequently foregrounds 'literature's inability to represent a reality of suffering in full, and to right the wrongs being done in the real world' (2019: 31). *The Ministry*'s polyphonic social panorama is thus articulated but questioned, enacted but destabilized.

Even so, Roy's search for an 'everything' perspective remains powerful as a mode of description, particularly so in the novel's fragmentary opening paragraph, a short, scene-setting preface, typeset in italics, which tracks an ecological-industrial chain-reaction that begins with the artificially stimulated production of milk and ends with the chemical poisoning of white-backed vultures:

> The vultures died of diclofenac poisoning. Diclofenac, cow-aspirin, given to cattle as a muscle relaxant, to ease pain and increase the production of milk, works – worked – like nerve gas on white-backed vultures. Each chemically relaxed, milk-producing cow or buffalo that died became poisoned vulture-bait. As cattle turned into better dairy machines, as the city ate more ice cream, butterscotch-crunch, nutty-buddy and chocolate chip, as it drank more mango milkshake, vultures' necks began to droop as though they were tired and simply couldn't stay awake. Silver beards of saliva dripped from their beaks, and one by one they tumbled off their branches, dead.
>
> (1)

Writing in prose that recalls Sebald's natural-historical style and Mahasweta's planetary perspective, but which nonetheless develops her long-standing linguistic attention to Indian snack culture and the everyday, Roy begins *The Ministry* by mapping the ways in which globalization deepens the war against animals. Through the paratactic repetition of the conjunction 'as', Roy suggests that the forces of mass production and mass consumption (the city consumes en masse as an 'it') are temporally and causally paralleled with anthropogenic extinction. Cows and white-backed vultures are dying so that the city's wealthy consumers can munch their way through dairy products. The novel's narrative form, of 'becoming everything', thus glimpses the totality of the war against animals.

Vultures occupy a crucial ecological position in Southeast Asia. Because they scavenge on carcasses, they act as an important buffer for the possible spread of pathogens. Because they prevent zoonotic spillover, their sudden decline due to diclofenac poisoning – one of the fastest collapses of bird populations ever recorded – is a concern for public health as much as it is biodiversity loss.[7] But Roy also draws attention to the symbolic role of vultures. As 'custodians of the dead' (1), vultures not simply feast on carcasses but, in doing so, safeguard the memory of fallen animals. In the web of life, vultures transform lifeless bodies into new liveliness. Who else will be able to turn death into life, Roy implies, when these creatures are gone? And who will shoulder the memory of the white-backed vultures now that they are caught in the extinction vortex? Roy begins *The Ministry* by noting that 'not many noticed the passing of the friendly old birds' (1). Yet the vultures' ending is also the novel's beginning. Roy elects to be the one who notices. Thus although her novel cannot prevent the war against animals, and although it cannot do justice to the region's 'Unconsoled', Roy nonetheless chooses to bear witness to the abiding socio-ecological conflicts of neoliberalizing India.

Of postcolonial pests: Henrietta Rose-Innes's *Nineveh*

Where *The Ministry* opens with avian extinction, Henrietta Rose-Innes's *Nineveh* begins *in medias res* with a scene of insect conservation: 'Caterpillars? Easy, thinks Katya' (2011: 4). Katya Grubbs is the daughter of a once-respected Cape Town pest exterminator. We readers join her on a job as she attends to a thick infestation of caterpillars on a garden tree. After surveying the swarm and locating the chief invertebrate among the multitude, Katya and her assistant Toby construct an elaborate bridge of tin-cans leading away from the tree bark and into a cigar-box. Prodding the swarm lightly with a stick, Katya cajoles the 'modest caravan of furry beasts' (6) so that they crawl away from the tree. As the last of the caterpillars drops into her container, a gardener asks how Katya intends to exterminate them. 'We release them into the wild', she replies. 'It's a strictly no-kill policy' (8). While many people pay to have such creatures poisoned, Katya thinks of pests and vermin as wanderers who unknowingly cross boundaries only perceptible to human society, as 'small sojourners in a strange land' (19). Katya's clients may laugh confusedly, but she affirms her 'philosophy [...] to respect any creature that gets by in the city' (14).

In *Nineveh*, then, Rose-Innes gently reimagines human-pest relations through the labour and care of painless pest relocation. Because Katya recognizes invasive species as critters with their own desires and claims to safety, 'day by day negotiating new truces with the humans among whom they live' (14), she too seeks to reach provisional truces with these critters by relocating wasps' nests, rerouting caterpillar swarms, wrangling cats and catching rats. In this work Katya thinks of herself as 'policing borders' (14) between the wild and the tame, and thus between nonhuman nature and human society. But if Katya is something of a border guard who patrols the boundary between society and nature, she does not do so in order to enforce human superiority over animal others. Rather, her Painless Pest Relocation service aims for an alternative to the armed response of extermination. By creating and preserving physical boundaries between society and nature, Katya in fact cultivates an alternative ethics towards other creatures. Paradoxically, then, the novel begins by articulating how the preservation of some human–animal boundaries can break down the borders of human superiority. *Nineveh* trains our attention on the injustices of invertebrate extermination. Caring for caterpillars becomes another creaturely relation.

And yet any reading of *Nineveh* must account for its particular setting: a post-apartheid South Africa riven by inequalities, in which luxury real estate and neoliberal urban planning sustains the social borders between the rich and the poor, white and black. Rose-Innes's metaphorics of pestilence, connoting ideas of invasion, overabundance, parasitism and alienness, invokes simultaneously the colonial invasions of southern Africa, the colonial project's figuration of race as a natural, inhuman ontology, *and* the post-apartheid era's conflictual politics of belonging, planning, eviction and housing. The novel's plot centres on a half-built luxury residence, Nineveh, a business venture drawn up by a conveniently named capitalist, Mr Brand. A fenced and guarded territory, replete with servants' quarters, Nineveh aspires to be a mini-city and gated community that stands in marked contrast to the townships and swamps that lie beyond it. Yet Mr Brand has a problem. The site is constructed on shaky foundations. Worse, an infestation of elusive metallic longhorn small beetles – *goggas*, as the novel calls them – has colonized the model apartments. Haemorrhaging money and investors, Brand hires Katya to dispose of the complex's unwanted autochthonous guests, folding her into the logics of accumulation and dispossession that underpin both the expulsion of wildlife *and* the displacement of poor, racialized humans from the city.

Through the work of vermin relocation, *Nineveh* might be read as manifesting a posthumanist feminist care ethics positioned against the novel's two patriarchal figures. Rose-Innes plots the novel in such a way that challenges Katya's abusive pest exterminator father's and her landlord employer's 'belief in the fixed nature of things, in walls and floors' (188), as pests expose the fissures and overlaps in-between the abstractions of humanity and nature. But because the novel emphasizes this so strongly, it also finds itself dramatizing the limits of Katya's idealistic vision of 'humane conquest' (93). As the novel's men recognize the inequality and permeability of a supposedly protected humanity, so too does Katya eventually realize that her work of mastery is impossible because beetles, ants and rats are inextricable from the built environment. In the novel's final pages, Rose-Innes focalizes Katya's disillusionment:

> Everything's in motion, changed and changing. There is no way to keep the shape of things. […] Even human skin, Katya has read, is porous and infested, every second letting microscopic creatures in and out. Our own bodies are menageries. Short of total sterility, there is no controlling it.
> (207)

Katya, then, while still committed to a 'humane' pest service, ultimately comes to see her job as 'the fruitless work of trying to keep things in their proper place' (207). Focusing on the human as a holobiont, a creature who is home to other creatures, who contains multitudes, Rose-Innes compels her readers to discover a form of emancipation in this disenchantment with a 'proper' humanity and its unequal propertied relations.

Nineveh's critics have thus far disagreed about whether Rose-Innes's pest semantics can be read as a form of joined-up postcolonial-ecocritical critique. One side argues that, because pest invasion is not a metaphor but a real aspect of the plot, the novel literalizes postcolonial justice beyond the human (Menozzi 2014: 199). Yet the other side says that it remains ultimately 'unclear whether the novel's metaphoric resourcefulness and wider tragicomic tenor can wholly reclaim the discourse of vermin' (Williams 2018: 425). In other words, does the novel really evince an ecological postcolonial ethics, or does it finally side with ecological concerns over and above social inequalities, ably revealing how 'human skin' (Rose-Innes 2011: 207) is always already more-than-human yet failing to account for how such skin has been historically racialized and animalized? This is an open question that requires further thought. For now, though, I wish to close this section by reaffirming that what *Nineveh* does so well is imagine an alternative sense of home: no longer the unequally allocated, heavily policed, sanitized space of colonial domination, but a multispecies zone in which many beings, living in mutual but provisional relation with one another, stake a claim for shelter and their flourishing.

Of stories and trees: Richard Powers's *The Overstory*

This has been a book about literature and animals. Yet my critique of anthroponormativity and my analyses of creaturely forms have necessarily involved the question of nature, a nature that includes the figure of the animal but extends beyond it towards other nonhuman forms of life. Sebald and Mahasweta are, as we have seen, both preoccupied with trees and forests. In texts like *The Rings of Saturn* and 'The Hunt' they propose that the supposed progress of capitalist modernity largely depends on the extensive and exploitative felling of trees. For them, mass deforestation is constitutive of the war against animals, a predatory appropriation of nature that simultaneously induces human displacements and widespread biodiversity loss.

In *The Overstory*, the American novelist Richard Powers also thinks of mass deforestation as a form of conflict. In interviews, Powers remarks that the book arose out of his insight that 'we had been at war for a long time, trees and people, and I wondered if it might be possible for things ever to go any other way' (Brady 2018: n.p.). Powers's point is not that all human interactions with trees are necessarily violent, nor still that trees have been conspiring and fighting against the human species. The war against trees, like the war against animals, is acutely one-sided, and *The Overstory* situates this war geographically and historically within a North American landscape shaped by centuries of capitalist and colonialist expansion. Yet at the same time Powers's novel depicts trees not as passive victims but as fellow creatures, as subjects who move and communicate with intentionality, who build the environment we humans inhabit. Thinking, then, in a geological time frame that has been largely absent within the novel form, Powers attempts to 'turn the story on its head. This is not our world with trees in it. It's a world of trees, where humans have just arrived' (2019: 530).

Powers welcomes the reader into this world in the novel's opening section, 'Roots'. A miniature scene of apparent ecological stability, 'Roots' carefully balances its verbs between human and nonhuman figures as they rest on one another: 'A woman *sits* on the ground, *leaning* against a pine. Its bark *presses* hard against her back, as hard as life. Its needles *scent* the air and a force *hums* in the heart of the wood. Her ears *tune down* to the lowest frequencies. The tree is *saying* things, in words before words' (3; my emphasis). A chorus of trees begins speaking, whispering the alders' memories of 'long-ago disasters' and the oaks' anticipation of 'future weather' (3). The chorus then addresses the reader: 'All the ways you imagine us… are always amputations. Your kind never sees us whole. You miss the half of it, and more. There's always as much below ground as above' (4). Humanity is thus said to have a 'root problem' (4).

The Overstory therefore marks a literary attempt to recognize tree life, to more fully imagine trees from the roots up in a time in which they are being 'sacrificed to silicon' (114). One of Powers's nine protagonists is a biologist, Patricia Westerford, who is convinced that trees are 'social creatures' (152) long before she embarks on years of dendrological research that will culminate in her book *The Secret Forest*. At first derided by the scientific community, Westerford's work is later embraced as offering a path-breaking theory of arboreal intelligence and intentionality: 'The biochemical behaviour of individual trees may make sense only when we see them as members of a community' (158). Westerford's key ideas are that 'everything in the forest, is the forest' (179); that 'there are no individuals in a forest, no separable events' (272); that 'eco-systems tend toward diversity, and markets do the opposite' (354); and that trees actually 'want something from us, just as we've always wanted things from them. This isn't mystical. The "environment" is alive – a fluid changing web of purposeful lives dependent on each other' (567).

Powers thus builds an idea of the forest as a collective being, a 'threatened creature' (355) that creates the stable environmental conditions for earthly life's flourishing. *The Secret Forest* has a profound effect on the novel's eight other protagonists, and Westerford is invited to testify as an expert educating witness on commercial logging on federal land. There is something of Coetzee's Elizabeth Costello, here, when Westerford's deliberate calm gives way, 'her words come out of hiding', as her love for trees 'pours out of her' (354). Both Cosatello and Westerford leave their dramatized public appearances in a state of personal turmoil, as if the act of committing oneself to nonhuman life is a form of betrayal of their social ties to human community. But Westerford, sometimes characterized by Powers in quite heroic terms, has much more success than Costello in persuading her interlocutors. *The Overstory* is more optimistic than *The Lives of Animals*, its cast of characters each finding their own way towards an ethical obligation to trees.

It is precisely through this recognition of trees that Powers's novel arrives at its own particular re-writing of the novel form. It is as if Powers asks: how does the novel itself change once it is viewed from the standpoint of trees? Or, as one critic puts it, 'what does the novel need to learn or unlearn in order to "do" trees?' (Schoene 2021: 1). This is a multi-plot and multi-character work, a polyphonic work narrated within two historical temporalities: on the one side, the novel takes place during the social time of the 'timber wars' of the 1990s, a protracted conflict between Californian logging companies and environmental activists, and ends with the emergence of Occupy Wall Street in the wake of the global financial crash of 2007/8; on the other, Powers adopts a deeper temporality of past generations of humans and trees, a natural-historical perspective which traces biological and even geological shifts at a planetary scale. Because of this, critics have described the novel's narrative as building a concentric structure in which individual characters and plots encircle one another (Saint-Amour 2020; Schoene 2021). But Powers's novel ultimately frustrates this desire for a looping, converging narrative of resolution. Better, I think, to imagine *The Overstory*'s character arcs and timelines as a series of roots, interlocking with one another at some points and branching off into new directions at others. Powers's characters drift in and out of each other's worlds. Some never meet at all. Some characters are given multiple, divergent endings. With others, we come to wonder whether they are entirely imagined by characters within the novel.[8]

The narrative process of *storying* thus becomes essential, and Powers incorporates this arboreal metaphor into the novel's shape: the forest's understory and overstory come to signify the novel's social and ecological temporalities, as well as society's inseparability from nature; the novel's structure of roots, trunk, crown and seeds offers a regenerative rather than teleological conclusion. With this, Powers's novel might be said to fantasize that storytelling is the hidden root that, if followed, would lead towards a greener ethics: 'The best arguments in the world won't change a person's mind', one character states. 'The only thing that can do that is a good story' (336). Powers is, to be sure, wary of the novel's formal limitations. In one scene, Adam Appich throws an unnamed novel against a wall after trying, and failing, to care for 'privileged people having trouble getting along with each other in exotic locations' (444). In another, Ray Brinkman thinks that 'the world is failing precisely because no novel can make the contest for the world seem as compelling as the struggles between a few lost people' (477–8). And yet despite this continuous hesitation about its own formal inheritance, *The Overstory* ends up crafting an idea of storytelling as an ecological act: good stories 'kill you a little. They turn you into something you weren't' (515). In this, the novel is more optimistic than Roy's *The Ministry of Utmost Happiness*, encouraging its readers – perhaps too implicitly, too belatedly – to listen out for these stories from others, to treat humans and nonhumans as potential storytellers. When Nick Hoel is struck by 'how much [trees] say, when you let them', a man textually coded as Native American quips back that 'we've been trying to tell you that since 1492' (613).

Although Powers idealistically emphasizes storytelling as a process of individualized ethical transformation, *The Overstory* is equally invested in collective environmental action. Its plots revolve around characters who are radicalized – rooted and uprooted – by trees, and who commit themselves to serious political struggles to stave off logging: 'A people! United! Can never be defeated! A forest! Once blighted! Can never be re-seeded!' (372). Occupying corporate property, facing down bulldozers, the protestors are met with police violence, repression, espionage, jail sentences, even death. The novel dramatizes their defeat, but it does so without finally coming down on the side of a foreclosing fatalism. Rather, Powers ends his novel with the sentence 'This will never end' (625), an idea of perpetual if fragile opportunity, a hope against hope.

A creaturely reconciliation?

Writing in 1972 during the first wave of radical ecology movements, Herbert Marcuse questioned the idea of a future reconciliation between humans and other species. How would it be possible, Marcuse asked, for any human society to flourish without the cruel appropriation of the natural world? Can we even envision a planet in which the 'physical reproduction of the human race' (1972: 68) does not also rely on some forms of violence towards other beings? Like many of the thinkers we have encountered across this book, including his Frankfurt School neighbours Adorno and Horkheimer, Marcuse describes capitalist modernity's systemic cruelty towards animals as a conflict, a war that objectifies nature as mere means, mere substance. He argues, too, that any radical transformation of society must also entail a radical transformation of society's relationship to nature. Yet he cautions his readers that the struggle against the natural world may well continue into any utopian project. Even a free society might not necessarily call an end to the war against animals. Perhaps this battle is 'unconquerable' (68), Marcuse continues. Perhaps it is, in fact, just a myth of the end of history:

> The end of this war, the perfect peace in the animal world – this idea belongs to the Orphic myth, not to any conceivable historical reality. In the face of the suffering inflicted by man on man, it seems terribly premature to campaign for universal vegetarianism or synthetic foodstuffs; as the world is, priority must be on human solidarity among human beings. And yet, no free society is imaginable which does not… make the concerted effort to reduce consistently the suffering which man imposes on the animal world.
>
> (68)

Marcuse's dialectical thought pivots on this negation, 'And yet … '. Reaffirming his foundational proposition in a new light, Marcuse commits again to the idea that any truly free society is also one which works to liberate nature, both the nature of the human and the nature that is out there in the planet. There may always be a structural difference between humanity and nature, he says, but the current relations of hostility and struggle must be brought to an end in favour of 'peace, tranquility, fulfillment. In this case, not appropriation but rather its negation would be the nonexploitative relation: surrender, "letting-be", acceptance' (69).

And it is art, the aesthetic, *form*, that Marcuse turns to as something that already offers a promise of peaceful reconciliation through its power of 'recollection' (70). Recollection is not a nostalgic remembrance of things past, a falsified memory of a previously pristine nature that we might one day return to. Recollection instead names an aesthetic process of imaginative reassembly, of re-collection, one in which modernity's many distortions of humanity and nature are reconstructed in new ways. The aesthetic, as a mode of formalized re-collection, prefiguratively imagines future horizons of transformation, freedom and tranquillity for human society and human–animal relations. Put differently, aesthetic forms offer a formal instantiation of reconciliation, an assembly of creatures, human and nonhuman, that conjure nonexploitative relations. Literary writing may not be able to concretely reduce the suffering of animals. Yet this does not mean that literature should continue to sustain the abiding fictions of human supremacy. By narrating the war against animals, literary forms can call for peaceable futures between humans and other animals, redressing the commodification of animal life and conjuring alternate genres of planetary relations. We will need these other genres of living if we are to call time on the war against animals and begin again.

Notes

1   Graham Huggan and Helen Tiffin articulate a similar argument in *Postcolonial Ecocriticism*, writing that *The Hungry Tide*'s tiger 'is not sacrificed to anthropocentric narrative expectation but rather to its pre-designated ideological positioning between the rights of local peoples and western conservationist objectives' (2015: 202).

2   *Animal's People* has, like *The Hungry Tide*, attracted a wealth of postcolonial-ecocritical scholarship. Pablo Mukherjee's (2010) writing on the novel is especially

sharp in its fusion of close reading, historical contextualization and literary-sociological analysis of the text's publication and circulation. Anthony Carrigan's (2012) work is also noteworthy for its attention to how Sinha's use of genre and form informs its figuration of disaster.

3 I explore this question in much more detail in an article for the comparative literature journal *TRANS*, forthcoming at the time of writing.
4 On *The Wolf Border* specifically, I recommend Anna Cottrell's essay on how Hall's use of genre depends on her texts' differing representations of interpersonal relationships. I agree with Cottrell that Hall's depiction of romance, love and parenthood 'is not a crude parable about learning to love, or not being "the lone wolf"' (2019: 689). But Cottrell leaves unexamined the novel's animal metaphorics, its figuration of animals and how these are, in effect, subordinated to protagonicity.
5 Allan Massie's review for *The Scotsman* (2017) is exemplary of this reaction.
6 On the characteristics of Hindu nationalism, see Vanaik (2017).
7 Research indicates that approximately 97 per cent of India's three main vulture species are now gone. See Swan et al. (2006).
8 For more on *The Overstory*'s metaleptic ambiguities, see Saint Amour (2020: 141).

Bibliography

Abbott, Matthew (2008), 'The Creature Before the Law: Notes on Walter Benjamin's *Critique of Violence*', *COLLOQUY*, 16: 80–96.
Adams, Carol J. (2010), *The Sexual Politics of Meat: A Feminist-Vegetarian Critical Theory*, Twentieth anniversary edn., New York: Continuum.
Adorno, Theodor W. (1973), *Negative Dialectics*, trans. E. B Ashton, London: Routledge.
Adorno, Theodor W. (2005), *Minima Moralia*, trans. Edmund Jephcott, London: Verso.
Adorno, Theodor W. (2006), 'The Idea of Natural-History', in Robert Hullot-Kentor (ed.), *Things Beyond Resemblance: Essays on Theodor W. Adorno*, 252–69, New York: Columbia University Press.
Adorno, Theodor W. (2013), *Aesthetic Theory*, trans. Robert Hullot-Kentor, London: Bloomsbury.
Adorno, Theodor W., and Max Horkheimer (2002), *The Dialectic of Enlightenment*, trans. John Cumming, London: Verso.
Agamben, Giorgio (1998), *Homo Sacer: Sovereign Power and Bare Life*, trans. Daniel Heeler-Roazen, Stanford: Stanford University Press.
Agamben, Giorgio (1999), *Remnants of Auschwitz: The Witness and the Archive*, trans. Daniel Heller-Roazen, New York: Zone Books.
Agamben, Giorgio (2004), *The Open: Man and Animal*, trans. Kevin Attell, Stanford: Stanford University Press.
Ahmed, Sara (2010), 'Feminist Killjoys (And Other Willful Subjects)', *S&F Online*, 8. Available online: http://sfonline.barnard.edu/polyphonic/ahmed_01.htm (accessed 29 March 2021).
Ahmed, Sara (2014), *Willful Subjects*, Durham: Duke University Press.
Ahmed, Sara (2017), *Living a Feminist Life*, Durham: Duke University Press.
Ahuja, Neel (2009), 'Postcolonial Critique in a Multispecies World', *PMLA*, 124 (2): 556–63.
Alter, Stephen (1995), 'The Short Story in India', *Wasafiri*, 10 (21): 26–8.
Alter, Stephen (1998), 'A Few Thoughts on Indian Fiction, 1947–1997', *Alif*, 18: 14–28.
Anderton, Joseph (2016), *Beckett's Creatures: Art of Failure after the Holocaust*, London: Bloomsbury.
Arendt, Hannah (1998), *The Human Condition*, trans. Margaret Canovan, Chicago: University of Chicago Press.
Armstrong, Nancy (2005), *How Novels Think: The Limits of Individualism from 1719–1900*, New York: Columbia University Press.
Armstrong, Philip (2008), *What Animals Mean in the Fiction of Modernity*, London: Routledge.

Attridge, Derek (2004), *J. M. Coetzee and the Ethics of Reading: Literature in the Event*, Chicago: University of Chicago Press.
Attwell, David (1993), *J. M. Coetzee: South Africa and the Politics of Writing*, Berkeley: University of California Press.
Attwell, David (2002), 'Race in Disgrace', *Interventions*, 4 (3): 331–41.
Attwell, David (2006), 'The Life and Times of Elizabeth Costello: J. M. Coetzee and the Public Sphere', in Jane Poyner (ed.), *J. M. Coetzee and the Idea of the Public Intellectual*, 25–41, Athens: Ohio University Press.
Attwell, David (2015), *J. M. Coetzee and the Life of Writing: Face to Face with Time*, Oxford: Oxford University Press.
Auerbach, Erich (1991), *Mimesis: The Representation of Reality in Western Literature*, Princeton: Princeton University Press.
Awadalla, Maggie, and Paul March-Russell (2013), 'Introduction', in Maggie Awadalla and Paul March-Russell (eds), *The Postcolonial Short Story: Contemporary Essays*, 1–14, Basingstoke: Palgrave.
Badiou, Alain, and Nicolas Truong (2012), *In Praise of Love*, New York: The New Press.
Baker, Timothy C. (2019), *Writing Animals: Language, Suffering, and Animality in Twenty-First-Century Fiction*, Basingstoke: Palgrave.
Bakhtin, Mikhail (1981), *The Dialogic Imagination: Four Essays*, trans. Caryl Emerson and Michael Holquist, Austin: University of Texas Press.
Barnosky, Anthony D., et al. (2011), 'Has the Earth's Sixth Mass Extinction Already Arrived?', *Nature*, 471 (7336): 51–7.
Barthes, Roland (1989), *The Rustle of Language*, trans. Richard Howard, Berkeley: University of California Press.
Bauman, Zygmunt (1989), *Modernity and the Holocaust*, Cambridge: Polity.
Baxter, Jeannette, Valerie Henetiuk, and Ben Hutchinson (2013), 'Introduction: "A Quoi Bon la Littérature?"', in Jeannette Baxter, Valerie Henetiuk, and Ben Hutchinson (eds), *A Literature of Restitution: Critical Essays on W. G. Sebald*, Manchester: Manchester University Press.
Bellamy Foster, John, and Brett Clark (2018), 'Marx and Alienated Speciesism', *Monthly Review*, 70 (7). Available online: https://monthlyreview.org/2018/12/01/marx-and-alienated-speciesism/ (accessed 25 March 2021).
Benjamin, Andrew (2005), *Walter Benjamin and History*, London: Bloomsbury.
Benjamin, Andrew (2010), *Of Jews and Animals*, Edinburgh: Edinburgh University Press.
Benjamin, Walter (1928), *Einbahnstraße*, Berlin: Ernst Rowohlt.
Benjamin, Walter (1997), *One-Way Street*, trans. Edmund Jephcott and Kingsley Shorter, London: Verso.
Benjamin, Walter (2003), *Walter Benjamin: Selected Writings, Vol. 2, Part 1, 1927–1930*, ed. Michael W. Jennings, Howard Eiland and Gary Smith, Cambridge: Harvard University Press.
Benjamin, Walter (2005), *Walter Benjamin: Selected Writings, Vol. 2, Part 2, 1931–1934*, ed. Michael W. Jennings, Howard Eiland and Gary Smith, Cambridge: Harvard University Press.

Benjamin, Walter (2006), *Walter Benjamin: Selected Writings, Vol. 4, 1938–1940*, ed. Michael W. Jennings, Howard Eiland and Gary Smith, Cambridge: Harvard University Press.

Benjamin, Walter (2009), *Origin of German Tragic Drama*, trans. John Osborne, London: Verso.

Benton, Ted (1993), *Natural Relations: Ecology, Animal Rights and Social Justice*, London: Verso.

Benton, Ted (2019), 'Marx, Animals, and Humans: A Reply to My Critics', *Monthly Review*, 71 (1). Available online: https://monthlyreview.org/2019/05/01/marx-animals-and-humans/ (accessed 25 March 2021).

Berger, John (2009), *About Looking*, London: Bloomsbury.

Bernstein, J. M. (2009), 'Mad Raccoon, Demented Quail, and the Herring Holocaust: Notes for a Reading of W. G. Sebald', *Qui Parle*, 17 (2): 31–57.

Bewes, Timothy (2014), 'Against Exemplarity: W. G. Sebald and the Problem of Connection', *Contemporary Literature*, 55 (1): 1–31.

Bhattacharya, Sourit (2020), *Postcolonial Modernity and the Indian Novel on Catastrophic Realism*, Basingstoke: Palgrave.

Bigsby, Christopher (2001), *Writers in Conversation with Christopher Bigsby. Volume Two*, Norwich: Arthur Miller Centre for American Studies.

Birnbaum, Daniel, and Anders Olsson (2009), 'An Interview Jacques Derrida on the Limits of Digestion', *e-flux*, 2. Available online: https://www.e-flux.com/journal/02/68495/an-interview-with-jacques-derrida-on-the-limits-of-digestion/ (accessed 30 March 2021).

Blanchard, Pascal, et al. (2008), *Human Zoos: Science and Spectacle in the Age of Colonial Empires*, Liverpool: Liverpool University Press.

Boehmer, Elleke (2002), 'Not Saying Sorry, Not Speaking Pain: Gender Implications in Disgrace', *Interventions*, 4 (3): 342–51.

Boggs, Colleen Glenney (2013), *Animalia Americana: Animal Representations and Biopolitical Subjectivity*, New York: Columbia University Press.

Boisseron, Bénédicte (2018), *Afro-Dog: Blackness and the Animal Question*, New York: Columbia University Press.

Boxall, Peter (2011), 'The Threshold of Vision: The Animal Gaze in Beckett, Coetzee and Sebald', *Journal of Beckett Studies*, 20 (2): 123–48.

Brady, Amy (2018), 'Richard Powers: Writing "The Overstory" Quite Literally Changed My Life', *Chicago Review of Books*, 18 April. Available online: https://chireviewofbooks.com/2018/04/18/overstory-richard-powers-interview (accessed 1 April 2021).

Brouillette, Sarah (2007), *Postcolonial Writers in the Global Literary Marketplace*, Basingstoke: Palgrave.

Buber, Martin (1996), *The Letters of Martin Buber: A Life of Dialogue*, ed. Nahum N. Glatzer and Paul Mendes-Flohr, New York: Syracuse University Press.

Buber, Martin, Viktor von Weizsäcker, and Joseph Wittif (1926), 'Vorwort', *Die Kreatur*, 1: 1–2.

Buckley, Jerome Hamilton (1974), *Season of Youth: The Bildungsroman from Dickens to Golding*, Cambridge: Harvard University Press.
Buck-Morss, Susan (1977), *The Origin of Negative Dialectics*, London: Macmillan.
Burns, Judy, et al. (1990), 'An Interview with Gayatri Spivak', *Women & Performance*, 5 (1): 80–92.
Burns, Lorna (2019), *Postcolonialism after World Literature: Relation, Equality, Dissent*, London: Bloomsbury.
Butler, Judith (2009), *Frames of War: When Is Life Grievable?*, London: Verso.
Byrd, Jodi A. (2011), *The Transit of Empire: Indigenous Critiques of Colonialism*, Minneapolis: University of Minnesota Press.
Calarco, Matthew (2015), *Thinking through Animals: Identity, Difference, Indistinction*, Stanford: Stanford University Press.
Carrigan, Anthony (2012), '"Justice Is on Our Side"? *Animal's People*, Generic Hybridity, and Eco-Crime', *Journal of Commonwealth Literature*, 47 (2): 159–74.
Carson, Rachel (2000), *Silent Spring*, London: Penguin.
Casanova, Pascale (2007), *The World Republic of Letters*, trans. M. B. DeBevoise, Cambridge: Harvard University Press.
Cavarero, Adriana (2016), *Inclinations: A Critique of Rectitude*, trans. Amanda Minervini and Adam Sitze, Stanford: Stanford University Press.
Ceballos, Gerardo, Paul R. Ehrlich, and Rodolfo Dirzo (2017), 'Biological Annihilation via the Ongoing Sixth Mass Extinction Signaled by Vertebrate Population Losses and Declines', *PNAS*, 114 (30): E6089–E6096.
Celan, Paul (2011), *The Meridian: Final Version–Drafts–Materials*, ed. Bernhard Böschenstein and Heino Schmull, trans. Pierre Joris, Stanford: Stanford University Press.
Chakrabarty, Dipesh (2000), *Provincializing Europe: Postcolonial Thought and Historical Difference*, Princeton: Princeton University Press.
Chakrabarty, Dipesh (2002), *Habitations of Modernity: Essays in the Wake of Subaltern Studies*, Chicago: University of Chicago Press.
Chakraborty, Madhurima (2014), '"The Only Thing I Know How to Do": An Interview with Mahasweta Devi', *Journal of Postcolonial Writing*, 50 (3): 282–90.
Chatterjee, Partha (1993), *The Nation and Its Fragments: Colonial and Postcolonial Histories*, Princeton: Princeton University Press.
Chatterjee, Partha (2014), 'There Is an Indian Ideology, but It's Not This', *Constellations*, 21 (2): 175–85.
Chattopadhyay, Sutapa (2014), 'Postcolonial Development State, Appropriation of Nature, and Social Transformation of the Ousted Adivasis in the Narmada Valley, India', *Capitalism Nature Socialism*, 25 (4): 1–20.
Cheney, Dorothy L., and Robert M. Seyfarth (1997), *Why Animals Don't Have Language*. Available online: http://tannerlectures.utah.edu/_documents/a-to-z/c/Cheney98.pdf (accessed 30 March 2021).
Ciobanu, Calina (2012), 'Coetzee's Posthumanist Ethics', *MFS*, 58 (4): 668–98.

Clarkson, Carrol (2009), *J. M. Coetzee: Countervoices*, Basingstoke: Palgrave.
Clingman, Stephen (2009), *The Grammar of Identity: Transnational Fiction and the Nature of the Boundary*, Oxford: Oxford University Press.
Coetzee, J. M. (1991), *Age of Iron*, London: Vintage.
Coetzee, J. M. (1992), *Doubling the Point: Essays and Interviews*, ed. David Attwell, Cambridge: Harvard University Press.
Coetzee, J. M. (1998), 'The Novel Today', *Upstream*, 6 (1998): 2–5.
Coetzee, J. M. (1999), *The Lives of Animals*, Princeton: Princeton University Press.
Coetzee, J. M. (2000), *Disgrace*, London: Vintage.
Coetzee, J. M. (2004a), *Elizabeth Costello*, London: Vintage.
Coetzee, J. M. (2004b), *Life and Times of Michael K*, London: Vintage.
Coetzee, J. M. (2004c), *Waiting for the Barbarians*, London: Vintage.
Coetzee, J. M. (2005), *Slow Man*, London: Vintage.
Coetzee, J. M. (2007a), 'Exposing the Beast', *Sydney Morning Herald*, 22 February 2007, 17.
Coetzee, J. M. (2007b), *Inner Workings: Literary Essays 2000–2005*, London: Penguin.
Coetzee, J. M. (2010), *Summertime: Scenes from Provincial Life*, London: Vintage.
Coetzee, J. M., and Arabella Kurtz (2015), *The Good Story: Exchanges on Truth, Fiction and Psychotherapy*, London: Harvill Secker.
Collard, Rosemary-Claire (2020), *Animal Traffic: Lively Capital in the Global Exotic Pet Trade*, Durham: Duke University Press.
Collu, Gabrielle (1998), 'Speaking with Mahasweta Devi: Mahasweta Devi Interviewed by Gabrielle Collu', *Journal of Commonwealth Literature*, 33 (2): 143–8.
Cornwell, Gareth (2008), 'An Image of Animals: Speciesism in Coetzee's Disgrace', *English Academy Review*, 25 (1): 133–8.
Cosgrove, Mary (2011), 'W. G. Sebald's *Austerlitz*', in Stuart Taberner (ed.), *The Novel in German Since 1900*, 226–40, Cambridge: Cambridge University Press.
Cottrell, Anna (2019), 'The Power of Love: From Feminist Utopia to the Politics of Imperceptibility in Sarah Hall's Fiction', *Textual Practice*, 33 (4): 679–93.
Couper, Alastair, Hance D. Smith, and Bruno Ciceri (2015), *Fishers and Plunderers: Theft, Slavery and Violence at Sea*, London: Pluto.
Couttenier, Maarten (2014), '"We Can't Help Laughing": Physical Anthropology in Belgium and Congo (1882–1914)', in Nicholas Bancel et al. (eds), *The Invention of Race: Scientific and Popular Representations*, 101–16, London: Routledge.
Creature, n. (2020), OED. Available online: https://www.oed.com/view/Entry/44082?redirectedFrom=creature#eid (accessed 25 March 2021).
Crownshaw, Richard (2010), *The Aftermath of Holocaust Memory in Contemporary Literature and Culture*, London: Palgrave.
Culler, Jonathan (2008), 'The Most Interesting Thing in the World', *Diacritics*, 38 (2): 7–16.
Danta, Chris (2007), '"Like a Dog… Like a Lamb": Becoming Sacrificial Animal in Kafka and Coetzee', *New Literary History*, 38 (4): 721–37.
Davis, Mike (2005), *The Monster at Our Door: The Global Threat of Avian Flu*, New York: The New Press.

Davis, Thomas S. (2015), *The Extinct Scene: Late Modernism and Everyday Life*, New York: Columbia University Press.

Dawson, Ashley (2016), *Extinction: A Radical History*, New York: OR Books.

Deane-Drummond, Celia, and David Clough (2009), *Creaturely Theology: On Gods, Humans and Other Animals*, London: SCM Press.

Deb, Debal (2009), *Beyond Developmentality: Constructing Inclusive Freedom and Sustainability*, London: Earthscan.

Debasree, De (2015), 'Development-induced Displacement: Impact on Adivasi Women of Odisha', *Community Development Journal*, 50 (3): 448–62.

Deckard, Sharae, and Stephen Shapiro (2017), *World Literature, Neoliberalism and the Culture of Discontent*, Basingstoke: Palgrave.

Del Amo, Jean-Baptiste (2019), *Animalia*, trans. Frank Wynne, London: Fitzcarraldo.

Derrida, Jacques (1992), '"Eating Well" or the Calculation of the Subject', in Jacques Derrida, *Points…: Interviews, 1974–1994*, ed. Elisabeth Weber, trans. Peggy Kamuf and others, 255–87, Stanford: Stanford University Press.

Derrida, Jacques (2008), *The Animal That Therefore I Am*, ed. Marie-Louise Mallet, trans. David Wills, New York: Fordham University Press.

Derrida, Jacques (2009), *The Beast and the Sovereign: Volume 1*, trans. Geoffrey Bennington, Chicago: Chicago University Press.

Derrida, Jacques, and Elisabeth Roudinesco (2004), *For What Tomorrow…: A Dialogue*, trans. Jeff Fox, Stanford: Stanford University Press.

Diamond, Cora (2009), 'The Difficulty of Reality and the Difficulty of Philosophy', in Stanley Cavell, Cora Diamond, John McDowell, Ian Hacking, and Cary Wolfe, *Philosophy and Animal Life*, 43–90, New York: Columbia University Press.

Doerry, Martin, and Volker Hage (2001), 'Ich fürchte das Melodramatische', *Der Spiegel*, 12 March: 228–34.

Dorahy, James F. (2014), 'Mimesis, Critique, Redemption: Creaturely Life in and Beyond *Dialectic of Enlightenment*', *COLLOQUY*, 27: 89–103.

Durrant, Sam (2004), *Postcolonial Narrative and the Work of Mourning: J. M. Coetzee, Wilson Harris, and Toni Morrison*, Albany: SUNY Press.

Eagleton, Terry (1995), *Heathcliff and the Great Hunger: Studies in Irish Culture*, London: Verso.

Easton, Kai (2007), 'Coetzee's *Disgrace*: Byron in Italy and the Eastern Cape c. 1820', *Journal of Commonwealth Literature*, 42 (3): 113–30.

Eshel, Amir (2003), 'Against the Power of Time: The Poetics of Suspension in W. G. Sebald's *Austerlitz*', *New German Critique*, 88: 71–96.

Eshel, Amir (2013), *Futurity: Contemporary Literature and the Quest for the Past*, Chicago: University of Chicago Press.

Esposito, Roberto (2012), *Third Person: Politics of Life and Philosophy of the Impersonal*, trans. Zakiya Hanafi, Cambridge: Polity.

Esty, Jed (2012), *Unseasonable Youth: Modernism, Colonialism, and the Fiction of Development*, Oxford: Oxford University Press.

Fanon, Frantz (1960), *The Wretched of the Earth*, trans. Constance Farrington, London: Penguin.
FAO (2018), *The State of World Fisheries and Aquaculture 2020: Meeting the Sustainable Development Goals*, Rome. Available online: http://www.fao.org/3/i9540en/i9540en.pdf (accessed 20 March 2021).
Farrier, David (2016), 'Disaster's Gift: Anthropocene and Capitalocene Temporalities in Mahasweta Devi's *Pterodactyl, Puran Sahay, and Pirtha*', *Interventions*, 18 (3): 450–66.
Federici, Sylvia (2004), *Caliban and the Witch: Women, the Body and Primitive Accumulation*, New York: Autonomedia.
Felbab-Brown, Vanda (2017), *The Extinction Market: Wildlife Trafficking and How to Counter It*, Oxford: Oxford University Press.
Feldman, Allen (2010), 'Inhumanitas: Political Speciation, Animality, Natality, Defacement', in Ilana Feldman and Miriam Ticktin (eds), *In the Name of Humanity: The Government of Threat and Care*, 115–50, Durham: Duke University Press.
Fiber-Ostrow, Pamela, and Jarret S. Lovell (2016), 'Behind a Veil of Secrecy: Animal Abuse, Factory Farms, and Ag-Gag Legislation', *Contemporary Justice Review*, 19 (2): 230–49.
Fish, Kenneth (2012), *Living Factories: Biotechnology and the Unique Nature of Capitalism*, Montreal: McGill-Queen's University Press.
Foer, Jonathan Safran (2009), *Eating Animals*, New York: Little, Brown.
Foote, Bonnie (2007), 'The Narrative Interactions of *Silent Spring*: Bridging Literary Criticism and Ecocriticism', *New Literary History*, 38 (4): 739–53.
Forna, Aminatta (2018), *Happiness*, London: Bloomsbury.
Foucault, Michel (2002), *The Order of Things*, London: Routledge.
Frow, John (2014), *Character and Person*, Oxford: Oxford University Press.
Fuchs, Anne (2006), 'W. G. Sebald's Painters: The Function of Fine Art in His Prose Works', *Modern Language Review*, 101: 167–83.
Fuchs, Anne (2007), '"Ein Hauptkapitel der Geschichte der Unterwerfung": Representations of Nature in W. G. Sebald's *Die Ringe des Saturn*', in Anne Fuchs and Jonathan Long (eds), *W. G. Sebald and the Writing of History*, 121–38, Wurzburg: Königshausen and Neumann.
Gal, Noam (2006), 'A Note on the Use of Animals for Remapping Victimhood in J. M. Coetzee's *Disgrace*, *African Identities*, 6 (3): 241–52.
Garrard, Greg (2004), *Ecocriticism*, London: Routledge.
Gell, Lachlan, Harry Glass, and Ezekiel Morgan (2016), 'Creaturely Life', *POLLEN*, 2 September.
Ghosh, Amitav (2005), *The Hungry Tide*, London: Vintage.
Ghosh, Amitav (2016), *The Great Derangement: Climate Change and the Unthinkable*, Chicago: University of Chicago Press.
Gidwani, Vinay (2008), *Capital, Interrupted: Agrarian Development and the Politics of Work in India*, Minneapolis: University of Minnesota Press.

Glick, Megan H. (2018), *Infrahumanisms: Science, Culture, and the Making of Modern Non/Personhood*, Durham: Duke University Press.

Gopal, Priyamvada (2005), *Literary Radicalism in India: Gender, Nation, and the Transition to Independence*, London: Routledge.

Graham, Lucy (2002), '"Yes, I Am Giving Him Up": Sacrificial Responsibility and Likeness with Dogs in J. M. Coetzee's Recent Fiction', *Scrutiny2*, 7 (1): 4–15.

Gray, Richard T. (2009), 'Sebald's Segues: Performing Narrative Contingency in *The Rings of Saturn*', *The Germanic Review*, 84 (1): 26–58.

Gray, Richard T. (2010), 'Writing at the Roche Limit: Order and Entropy in W. G. Sebald's *Die Ringe des Saturn*', *German Quarterly*, 83 (1): 38–57.

Greene, Roland, et al. (2012), *The Princeton Encyclopedia of Poetry and Poetics*, 4th edn., Princeton: Princeton University Press.

Grooten, Monique, and Rosamunde E. A. Almond (2018), *Living Planet Report – 2018: Aiming Higher*, Gland: WWF.

Groves, Jason (2017), 'Writing after Nature: A Sebaldian Ecopoetics', in Caroline Schaumann and Heather I. Sullivan (eds), *German Ecocriticism in the Anthropocene*, 267–92, Basingstoke: Palgrave.

Guha, Ramachandra (2007a), *India after Gandhi: The History of the World's Largest Democracy*, London: Picador.

Guha, Ramachandra (2007b), 'Adivasis, Naxalites and Indian Democracy', *Economic and Political Weekly*, 42 (32): 3305–12.

Gunderson, Ryan (2011), 'Marx's Comments on Animal Welfare', *Rethinking Marxism*, 23 (4): 534–48.

Gupta, Akhil (1998), *Postcolonial Development: Agriculture in the Making of Modern India*, Durham: Duke University Press.

Hall, Sarah (2015), *The Wolf Border*, London: Faber and Faber.

Hall, Stuart (2019), *Essential Essays Volume 1: Foundations of Cultural Studies*, Durham: Duke University Press.

Hanssen, Beatrice (1998), *Walter Benjamin's Other History: Of Stones, Animals, Human Beings, and Angels*, Berkeley: University of California Press.

Haraway, Donna (1989), *Primate Visions: Gender, Race, and Nature in the World of Modern Science*, London: Routledge.

Haraway, Donna (2008), *When Species Meet*, Minneapolis: University of Minnesota Press.

Haraway, Donna (2016), *Staying with the Trouble: Making Kin in the Chthulucene*, Durham: Duke University Press.

Hardiman, David (1995), *The Coming of the Devi: Adivasi Assertion in Western India*, Delhi: Oxford University Press.

Hardy, Thomas (2002), *Jude the Obscure*, Oxford: Oxford University Press.

Hayes, Patrick (2010), *J. M. Coetzee and the Novel: Writing and Politics after Beckett*, Oxford: Oxford University Press.

Herman, David, ed. (2016), *Creatural Fictions: Human–Animal Relationships in Twentieth and Twenty-First Century Literature*, Basingstoke: Palgrave.

Herrick, Margaret (2016), 'The "Burnt Offering": Confession and Sacrifice in J. M. Coetzee's *Disgrace*', *Literature and Theology*, 30 (1): 82–98.
Herron, Tom (2005), 'The Dog Man: Becoming Animal in Coetzee's *Disgrace*', *Twentieth Century Literature*, 51 (4): 467–90.
Hirsch, Marianne (2008), 'The Generation of Post-Memory', *Poetics Today*, 29 (1): 103–28.
Huber, Irmtraud (2016), *Present Tense Narration in Contemporary Fiction*, Basingstoke: Palgrave.
Huehls, Mitchum, and Rachel Greenwald Smith (2017), *Neoliberalism and Contemporary Literary Culture*, Baltimore: Johns Hopkins University Press.
Huggan, Graham, and Helen Tiffin (2015), *Postcolonial Ecocriticism: Literature, Animals, Environment*, 2nd edn., London: Routledge.
Hullot-Kentor, Robert (2006), *Things beyond Resemblance: Essays on Theodor W. Adorno*, New York: Columbia University Press.
Hungerford, Amy (2008), 'On the Period Formerly Known as the Contemporary', *American Literary History*, 20 (1–2): 410–9.
Hutchinson, Ben (2009a), '"Ein Penelopewerk des Vergessens"? W. G. Sebald's Nietzschean Poetics of Forgetting', *Forum for Modern Language Studies*, 45 (3): 325–36.
Hutchinson, Ben (2009b), *W. G. Sebald: Die dialektische Imagination*, Berlin: De Gruyter.
Hutchinson, Ben (2011), 'The Shadow of Resistance: W. G. Sebald and the Frankfurt School', *Journal of European Studies*, 41 (3–4): 267–84.
IPBES (2019), *Global Assessment Report on Biodiversity and Ecosystem Services*, Bonn: IPBES.
James, David (2016), *Discrepant Solace: Contemporary Literature and the Work of Consolation*, Oxford: Oxford University Press.
Jameson, Fredric (1996), 'On Literary and Cultural Import-Substitution in the Third World: The Case of the Testimonio' in G. M. Gugelberger (ed.), *The Real Thing: Testimonial Discourse and Latin America*, 172–91, Durham: Duke University Press.
Jameson, Fredric (2007), *Late Marxism: Adorno, or The Persistence of the Dialectic*, London: Verso.
Janes, Regina (1997), '"Writing Without Authority": J. M. Coetzee and His Fictions', *Salmagundi*, 114 (5): 103–21.
Johnson, Lindgren (2017), *Race Matters, Animal Matters: Fugitive Humanism in African America, 1840–1930*, London: Routledge.
Kaakinen, Kasia (2017), *Comparative Literature and the Historical Imaginary*, Basingstoke: Palgrave.
Kannemeyer, J. C. (2012), *J. M. Coetzee: A Life in Writing*, trans. Michael Heyns, Melbourne: Scribe.
Keiffer, Katy (2017), *What's the Matter with Meat?*, London: Reaktion.
Kennedy, Rosanne (2012), 'Humanity's Footprint: Reading *Rings Of Saturn* and *Palestinian Walks* in an Anthropocene Era', *Biography*, 35 (1): 170–89.

Kilbourn, Russell J. A. (2018), *W. G. Sebald's Postsecular Redemption: Catastrophe with Spectator*, Evanston: Northwestern University Press.

Kim, Claire Jean (2015), *Dangerous Crossings: Race, Species, and Nature in a Multicultural Age*, Cambridge: Cambridge University Press.

Kingsford, Richard T., et al. (2009), 'Major Conservation Policy Issues for Biodiversity in Oceania', *Conservation Biology*, 23 (4): 834–40.

Klein, Naomi (2014), *This Changes Everything: Capitalism vs. The Climate*, London: Penguin.

Kolbert, Elizabeth (2014), *The Sixth Extinction*, London: Bloomsbury.

Korsgaard, Christine M. (2016), *Fellow Creatures: Our Obligations to the Other Animals*, Oxford: Oxford University Press.

Kothari, Ashish, and Neema Pathak Broome (2016), 'Conservation and Rights in India: Are We Moving towards Any Kind of Harmony?', in Meena Radhakrishna (ed.), *First Citizens: Studies on Adivasis, Tribals and Indigenous Peoples in India*, 337–69, New Delhi: Oxford University Press.

Kreilkamp, Ivan (2018), *Minor Creatures: Persons, Animals, and the Victorian Novel*, Chicago: University of Chicago Press.

Lanser, Susan (1981), *The Narrative Act: Point of View in Prose Fiction*, Princeton: Princeton University Press.

Latimer, Joanna (2013), 'Being Alongside: Rethinking Relations amongst Different Kinds', *Theory, Culture & Society*, 30 (7–8): 77–104.

Lazarus, Neil (2011), *The Postcolonial Unconscious*, Cambridge: Cambridge University Press.

Lee, Tom McInnes (2012), 'The Lists of W. G. Sebald', *M/C Journal*, 15 (5). Available online: https://doi.org/10.5204/mcj.552 (accessed 26 March 2021).

Lodge, David (2003), 'Disturbing the Peace', *New York Review of Books*, 20 November. Available online: http://www.nybooks.com/articles/2003/11/20/disturbing-the-peace (accessed 9 January 2021).

Long, J. J. (2007), *W. G. Sebald: Image, Archive, Modernity*, Edinburgh: Edinburgh University Press.

Longo, Stefano B., Rebecca Clausen, and Brett Clark (2015), *The Tragedy of the Commodity: Oceans, Fisheries, and Aquaculture*, New Brunswick: Rutgers University Press.

Lubow, Arthur (2007), 'Crossing Boundaries', in Lynne Sharon Schwartz (ed.), *The Emergence of Memory*, 159–73, New York: Seven Stories.

Lukács, György (1971), *The Theory of the Novel*, Cambridge: MIT Press.

Lukács, György (2010), *Soul and Form*, trans. Anna Bostock, New York: Columbia University Press.

Lupton, Julia (2000), 'Creature Caliban', *Shakespeare Quarterly*, 51 (1): 1–23.

Macherey, Pierre, and Etienne Balibar (1978), 'Literature as an Ideological Form: Some Marxist Propositions', *Oxford Literary Review*, 3: 4–12.

Mahasweta, Devi (1995), *Imaginary Maps*, trans. Gayatri Chakravorty Spivak, London: Routledge.

Mahasweta, Devi (1997), *Dust on the Road: The Activist Writings of Mahasweta Devi*, ed. and trans. Maitreya Ghatak, Calcutta: Seagull.
Mahasweta, Devi (1998), *Bitter Soil*, trans. Ipsita Chanda, Calcutta: Seagull.
Mahasweta, Devi (2006), 'Fundamental Rights and Bhikari Dusad', *Index on Censorship*, 4 (4): 92–108.
Mahasweta, Devi (2014), *Breast Stories*, trans. Gayatri Chakravorty Spivak, Calcutta: Seagull.
Malabou, Catherine (2012), *Ontology of the Accident: An Essay on Destructive Plasticity*, trans. Carolyn Shread, Cambridge: Polity.
Malm, Andreas (2018), *The Progress of This Storm: On the Dialectics of Society and Nature in a Warming World*, London: Verso.
Marais, Mike (2006), 'J. M. Coetzee's *Disgrace* and the Task of the Imagination', *Journal of Modern Literature*, 29 (2): 75–93.
Marchesini, Roberto (2016), 'Zoomimesis: Animal Inspiration', *Angelaki*, 21 (1): 175–97.
Marcuse, Herbert (1972), *Counterrevolution and Revolt*, Boston: Beacon Press.
Martin, James R. (2013), 'On Misunderstanding W. G. Sebald', *Cambridge Literary Review*, 4 (7): 123–38.
Martin, Theodore (2017), *Contemporary Drift: Genre, Historicism, and the Problem of the Present*, New York: Columbia University Press.
Marx, Karl (1975), *Collected Works*, vol. 3, London: Lawrence & Wishart.
Marx, Karl (1993), *Grundrisse: Foundations of the Critique of Political Economy*, London: Penguin.
Marx, Karl, and Freidrich Engels (1998), *German Ideology*, New York: Prometheus Books.
Massie, Allan (2017), 'Review: *The Ministry of Utmost Happiness*', *The Scotsman*, 14 June. Available online: http://www.scotsman.com/lifestyle/culture/books/book-review-the-ministry-of-utmost-happiness-by-arundhati-roy-1-4469121 (accessed 11 July 2017).
Masson-Delmotte, Valérie, et al. (2018), *Global Warming of 1.5 ºC: An IPCC Special Report*, Geneva: IPCC.
Massumi, Brian (2014), *What Animals Teach Us About Politics*, Durham: Duke University Press.
May, Charles E. (2012), 'The Short Story's Way of Meaning: Alice Munro's "Passion"', *Narrative*, 20 (2): 172–82.
Mbembe, Achille (2005), *On the Postcolony*, Berkeley: University of California Press.
McCormack, Fiona (2017), *Private Oceans: The Enclosure and Marketisation of the Seas*, London: Pluto.
McCulloh, Mark R. (2003), *Understanding W. G. Sebald*, Columbia: University of South Carolina Press.
McHugh, Susan (2009), 'Literary Animal Agents', *PMLA*, 124 (2): 487–95.
McHugh, Susan (2011), *Animal Stories: Narrating across Species Lines*, Minneapolis: University of Minnesota Press.

McKay, Robert (2010), 'Metafiction, Vegetarianism, and the Literary Performance of Animal Ethics in J. M. Coetzee's *The Lives of Animals*', *Safundi*, 11 (1–2): 67–85.

McKay, Robert (2014), 'What Kind of Literary Animal Studies Do We Want, or Need?', *MFS*, 60: 636–44.

Mehta, Tania (2004), 'The Changing Configurations of the Indian Short Story: Sites, Space and Semantics', *Indian Literature*, 48 (2): 151–60.

Menely, Tobias (2015), *The Animal Claim: Sensibility and the Creaturely Voice*, Chicago: Chicago University Press.

Menozzi, Filippo (2013), 'Invasive Species and the Territorial Machine: Shifting Interfaces between Ecology and the Postcolonial', *ariel*, 44 (4): 181–204.

Menozzi, Filippo (2014), *Postcolonial Custodianship: Cultural and Literary Inheritance*, London: Routledge.

Menozzi, Filippo (2019), '"Too Much Blood for Good Literature": Arundhati Roy's *The Ministry of Utmost Happiness* and the Question of Realism', *Journal of Postcolonial Writing*, 55 (1): 20–33.

Mitchell, W. J. T. (1998), *The Last Dinosaur Book: The Life and Times of a Cultural Icon*, Chicago: University of Chicago Press.

Moore, Stephen, ed. (2014), *Divinanimality: Animal Theory, Creaturely Theology*, New York: Fordham University Press.

Morgan, Peter (2005), 'The Sign of Saturn: Melancholy, Homelessness and Apocalypse in W.G. Sebald's Prose Narratives', *German Life and Letters*, 58 (1): 75–92.

Mukherjee, Pablo Upamanyu (2010), *Postcolonial Environments: Nature, Culture and the Contemporary Indian Novel in English*, Basingstoke: Palgrave.

Mullan, John (2006), *How Novels Work*, Oxford: Oxford University Press.

Murphet, Julian (2011), 'Coetzee and Late Style: Exile Within the Form', *Twentieth-Century Literature*, 57 (1): 86–104.

Mwangi, Evan Maina (2019), *The Postcolonial Animal: African Literature and Posthuman Ethics*, Ann Arbor: University of Michigan Press.

Nägele, Rainer (2004), 'Dialectical Materialism between Brecht and the Frankfurt School' in David S. Ferris (ed.), *The Cambridge Companion to Walter Benjamin*, 152–76, Cambridge: Cambridge University Press.

Neyrat, Frédéric, and Elizabeth Johnson (2014), 'The Political Unconscious of the Anthropocene', *Society & Space*. Available online: https://www.societyandspace.org/articles/on-the-political-unconscious-of-the-anthropocene (accessed 26 March 2021).

Nietzsche, Friedrich (1997), *Untimely Meditations*, trans. R. J. Hollingdale, Cambridge: Cambridge University Press.

Nilsen, Alf Gunvald (2018), *Adivasis and the State: Subalternity and Citizenship in India's Bhil Heartland*, Cambridge: Cambridge University Press.

Norris, Margot (1985), *Beasts of the Modern Imagination: Darwin, Nietzsche, Kafka, Ernst, and Lawrence*, Baltimore: Johns Hopkins University Press.

O'Connor, Frank (1963), *The Lonely Voice: A Study of the Short Story*, Cleveland: World.

Ogden, Benjamin H. (2010) 'The Coming into Being of Literature: How J. M. Coetzee's *Diary of a Bad Year* Thinks through the Novel', *Novel*, 43 (3): 466-82.
O'Key, Dominic (2019), 'Animal Borderlands: An Introduction', *parallax*, 25 (4): 351-7.
Ortiz Robles, Mario (2016), *Literature and Animal Studies*, London: Routledge.
Painter, Corinne (2016), 'Non-human Animals Within Contemporary Capitalism: A Marxist Account of Non-human Animal Liberation', *Capital & Class*, 40 (2): 327-45.
Parry, Benita (1996), 'Speech and Silence in the Fictions of J. M. Coetzee', in Graham Huggan and Stephen Watson (eds), *Critical Perspectives on J. M. Coetzee*, 37-65, Basingstoke: Palgrave.
Parry, Catherine (2017), *Other Animals in Twenty-First Century Fiction*, Basingstoke: Palgrave.
Patel, Raj (2013), 'The Long Green Revolution', *The Journal of Peasant Studies*, 40 (1): 1-63.
Pauly, Daniel (2009), 'Beyond Duplicity and Ignorance in Global Fisheries', *Scientia Marina*, 73 (2): 215-24.
Petuchowsk, Elizabeth (1995), '*Die Kreatur*, an Interdenominational Journal, and Martin Buber's Strange Use of the Term "Reality" ("Wirklichkeit")', *Deutsche Vierteljahrsschrift für Literaturwissenschaft und Geistesgeschichte*, 69: 766-87.
Pick, Anat (2011), *Creaturely Poetics: Animality and Vulnerability in Literature and Film*, New York: Columbia University Press.
Powers, Richard (2019), *The Overstory*, London: Vintage.
Prasad, Archana (2011), *Against Ecological Romanticism: Verrier Elwin and the Making of an Anti-Modern Tribal Identity*, New Delhi: Three Essays Collective.
Pratt, Mary Louise (2008), *Imperial Eyes: Travel Writing and Transculturalism*, London: Routledge.
Quammen, David (2012), *Spillover: Animal Infections and the Next Human Pandemic*, New York: Norton.
Qureshi, Sadiah (2011), *Peoples on Parade: Exhibitions, Empire, and Anthropology in Nineteenth-Century Britain*, Chicago: Chicago University Press.
Radhakrishna, Meena (2016), 'Epilogue: Violence of "Development" and Adivasi Resistance – An Overview', in Meena Radhakrishna (ed.), *First Citizens: Studies on Adivasis, Tribals and Indigenous Peoples in India*, 370-408, New Delhi: Oxford University Press.
Rajan, Romy (2021), 'Where Old Birds Go to Die: Spaces of Precarity in Arundhati Roy's *The Ministry of Utmost Happiness*', *ariel*, 52 (1): 91-120.
Ramaswamy, Sumathi (2010), *The Goddess and the Nation: Mapping Mother India*, Durham: Duke University Press.
Rancière, Jacques (2011), *The Politics of Literature*, trans. Julie Rose, Cambridge: Polity.
Redfield, Marc (2006), 'The Bildungsroman' in David Scott Kastan (ed.), *Oxford Encyclopedia of British Literature*, 191-4, Oxford: Oxford University Press.
Robbins, Bruce (2012) 'Many Years Later: Prolepsis in Deep Time', *The Henry James Review*, 33 (3): 191-204.

Rose, Gillian (2014), *The Melancholy Science: An Introduction to the Thought of Theodor W. Adorno*, London: Verso.
Rose-Innes, Henrietta (2011), *Nineveh*, Cape Town: Umuzi.
Rose, Jacqueline (2013), *The Last Resistance*, London: Verso.
Roy, Arundhati (2017), *The Ministry of Utmost Happiness*, London: Penguin.
Roy, Parama (2010), *Alimentary Tracts: Appetites, Aversions, and the Postcolonial*, Durham: Duke University Press.
Ruti, Mari (2015), 'The Posthumanist Quest for the Universal: Butler, Badiou, Žižek', *Angelaki*, 20 (4): 193–210.
Rydstrand, Helen (2019), *Rhythmic Modernism: Mimesis and the Short Story*, London: Bloomsbury.
Said, Edward (1994), *Culture and Imperialism*, New York: Vintage.
Saint Amour, Paul K. (2020), 'There is Grief of a Tree', *American Imago*, 77 (1): 137–55.
Saito, Kohei (2016), 'Why Ecosocialism Needs Marx', *Monthly Review*, 68 (6). Available online: https://monthlyreview.org/2016/11/01/why-ecosocialism-needs-marx/ (accessed 24 March 2021).
Salgado, Minoli (2000), 'Tribal Stories, Scribal Worlds: Mahasweta Devi and the Unreliable Translator', *Journal of Commonwealth Literature*, 35 (1): 131–45.
Sanders, Mark (2002), 'Disgrace', *Interventions*, 4 (3): 363–73.
Santner, Eric (2006), *On Creaturely Life: Rilke, Benjamin, Sebald*, Chicago: University of Chicago Press.
Santner, Eric (2011), *The Royal Remains: The People's Two Bodies and the Endgames of Sovereignty*, Chicago: University of Chicago Press.
Savyasaachi (2016), 'Primitive Accumulation, Labour, and the Making of "Scheduled Tribe", "Indigenous" and Adivasi Sensibility', in Meena Radhakrishna (ed.), *First Citizens: Studies on Adivasis, Tribals and Indigenous Peoples in India*, 53–76, New Delhi: Oxford University Press.
Schmidt-Hannisa, Hans-Walter (2007), 'Aberration of a Species: On the Relationship between Man and Beast in W. G. Sebald's Work', in Anne Fuchs and Jonathan Long (eds), *W. G. Sebald and the Writing of History*, 31–43, Wurzburg: Königshausen and Neumann.
Schmidt, Alfred (2014), *The Concept of Nature in Marx*, trans. Ben Fowkes, London: Verso.
Schoene, Berthold (2021), 'Arborealism, or do Novels do Trees?', *Textual Practice*, 1–24. Available online: https://doi.org/10.1080/0950236X.2021.1900379 (accessed 3 June 2021).
Scholtmeijer, Marian (1993), *Animal Victims in Modern Fiction: From Sanctity to Sacrifice*, Toronto: University of Toronto Press.
Schreiner, Olive (1988), *The Story of an African Farm*, Oxford: Oxford University Press.
Schütte, Uwe (2011), *W. G. Sebald: Einführung in Leben und Werk*, Göttingen: Vandenhoeck and Ruprecht.
Schütte, Uwe (2020), *W. G. Sebald: Leben und literarisches Werk*, Berlin: De Gruyter.

Sebald, W. G. (1973), Review of Franz Hubmann, *Dream of Empire: The World of Germany in Original Photographs 1840–1914*, *Journal of European Studies*, 3: 286.
Sebald, W. G. (1994), *Die Beschreibung des Unglücks. Zur österreichischen Literatur von Stifter bis Handke*, Berlin: Fischer.
Sebald, W. G. (1995a), *Nach der Natur: Ein Elementargedicht*, Frankfurt am Main: Eichborn.
Sebald, W. G. (1995b), *Die Ringe des Saturn: Eine englische Wallfahrt*, Frankfurt am Main: Eichborn.
Sebald, W. G. (2001a), *Austerlitz. Roman*, Munich: Carl Hanser.
Sebald, W. G. (2001b), 'Zerstreute Reminiszenzen: Gedanken zue Eröffnung eines Stuttgarter Hauses', *Stuttgarter Zeitung*, 18 November.
Sebald, W. G. (2001c), 'Mit einem klenin Strandspaten: Abschied von Deutschland nehmen', *Süddeutsche Zeitung*, 22 December.
Sebald, W. G. (2002a), *Austerlitz*, trans. Anthea Bell, London: Penguin.
Sebald, W. G. (2002b), *The Rings of Saturn*, trans. Michael Hulse, London: Vintage.
Sebald, W. G. (2002c), *Vertigo*, trans. Michael Hulse, London: Vintage.
Sebald, W. G. (2003), *After Nature*, trans. Michael Hamburger, London: Penguin.
Sebald, W. G. (2004), *On the Natural History of Destruction*, trans. Anthea Bell, New York: Modern Library.
Sebald, W. G. (2006), *Campo Santo*, trans. Anthea Bell, London: Penguin.
Sebald, W. G. (2014), *A Place in the Country*, trans. Jo Catling, London: Penguin.
Sebald, W. G., and Gordon Turner (2006), 'Introduction and Translation of an Interview Given by Max Sebald', in Scott Denham and Mark McCulloh (eds), *W. G. Sebald: History – Memory – Trauma*, 21–9, Berlin: de Gruyter.
Shah, Alpa (2010), *In the Shadows of the State: Indigenous Politics, Environmentalism, and Insurgency in Jharkhand, India*, Durham: Duke University Press.
Sheppard, Richard (2005), 'Dexter – Sinister: Some Observations on Decrypting the Mors Code in the Work of W. G. Sebald', *Journal of European Studies*, 35 (4): 419–63.
Shiva, Vandana (1991), *The Violence of the Green Revolution: Agriculture, Ecology, and Politics in the South*, London: Zed Books.
Shukin, Nicole (2009), *Animal Capital: Rendering Life in Biopolitical Times*, Minneapolis: University of Minnesota Press.
Silverblatt, Michael (2007), 'A Poem of an Invisible Subject', in Lynne Sharon Schwartz (ed.), *The Emergence of Memory: Conversations with W. G. Sebald*, 77–86, New York: Seven Stories Press.
Simons, John (2002), *Animal Rights and the Politics of Literary Representation*, Basingstoke: Palgrave.
Singer, Peter (1975), *Animal Liberation*, New York: HarperCollins.
Singh, Julietta (2018), *Unthinking Mastery: Dehumanism and Decolonial Entanglements*, Durham: Duke University Press.
Sinha, Indra (2007), *Animal's People*, New York: Simon and Schuster.
Skaria, Ajay (1999), *Hybrid Histories: Forests, Frontiers and Wildness in Western India*, New Delhi: Oxford University Press.

Slaughter, Joseph (2007), *Human Rights, Inc: The World Novel, Narrative Form, and International Law*, New York: Fordham University Press.
Smil, Vaclav (2013), *Harvesting the Biosphere: What We Have Taken from Nature*, Cambridge: MIT Press.
Sontag, Susan (2003), *Regarding the Pain of Others*, London: Penguin.
Soper, Kate (1995), *What is Nature?: Culture, Politics and the Non-Human*, Oxford: Blackwell.
Soper, Kate (2012), 'The Humanism in Posthumanism', *Comparative Critical Studies*, 9 (3): 365–78.
Spiegel, Marjorie (1988), *The Dreaded Comparison: Human and Animal Slavery*, London: Heretic.
Spivak, Gayatri Chakravorty (1998), *In Other Worlds: Essays in Cultural Politics*, London: Routledge.
Spivak, Gayatri Chakravorty (2002), 'Ethics and Politics in Tagore, Coetzee, and Certain Scenes of Teaching', *Diacritics*, 32 (3–4): 17–31.
Spivak, Gayatri Chakravorty (2003), *Death of a Discipline*, New York: Columbia University Press.
Spivak, Gayatri Chakravorty (2012), *An Aesthetic Education in the Era of Globalization*, Cambridge: Harvard University Press.
Stache, Christian (2018), 'On the Origins of Animalist Marxism: Rereading Ted Benton and the Economic and Philosophic Manuscripts of 1844', *Monthly Review*, 70 (7). Available online: https://monthlyreview.org/2018/12/01/on-the-origins-of-animalist-marxism/ (accessed 25 March 2021).
Steiner, Gary (2005), *Anthropocentrism and Its Discontents: The Moral Status of Animals in the History of Western Philosophy*, Pittsburgh: University of Pittsburgh Press.
Stone, Alison (2006), 'Adorno and the Disenchantment of Nature', *Philosophy and Social Criticism*, 32 (2): 231–53.
Swan, Gerry E., et al. (2006), 'Toxicity of Diclofenac to Gyps vultures', *Biology Letters*, 2 (2): 279–82.
Taylor, D. J. (2003), 'Prize Fights', *The Guardian*, 14 October. Available online: https://www.theguardian.com/books/2003/oct/14/bookerprize2003.thebookerprize (accessed 30 March 2021).
Taylor, Jane (1999), 'The Impossibility of Ethical Action', *Mail & Guardian*, 23 July: 25.
Taylor, Sunaura (2017), *Beasts of Burden: Animal and Disability Liberation*, New York: The New Press.
Telesca, Jennifer (2020), *Red Gold: The Managed Extinction of the Giant Bluefin Tuna*, Minneapolis: University of Minnesota Press.
The Denotified and Nomadic Tribes of India (DNT-RAG) (1999), 'Appeal for Justice and Struggle for Rights', *Interventions*, 1 (4): 590–604.
Theisen, Bianca (2006), 'A Natural History of Destruction: W. G. Sebald's *The Rings of Saturn*', *MLN*, 121 (3): 563–81.
Thompson, Hilary (2018), *Novel Creatures: Animal Life and the New Millennium*, London: Routledge.

Toppo, Anju Oseema Maria (2018), 'Jani Shikar and Its Contemporary Relevance', *Journal of Adivasi and Indigenous Studies*, 8 (1): 16–28.
Tremaine, Louis (2003), 'The Embodied Soul: Animal Being in the Work of J. M. Coetzee', *Contemporary Literature*, 44 (4): 587–612.
Twidle, Hedley (2014), 'Rachel Carson and the Perils of Simplicity: Reading Silent Spring from the Global South', *ariel*, 44 (4): 49–88.
Vanaik, Achin (2017), *The Rise of Hindu Authoritarianism: Secular Claims, Communal Realities*, London: Verso.
Vermeulen, Pieter (2015), *Contemporary Literature and the End of the Novel: Creature, Affect, Form*, Basingstoke: Palgrave.
Vermeulen, Pieter, and Virginia Richter (2015), 'Introduction: Creaturely Constellations', *European Journal of English Studies*, 19 (1): 1–9.
Wadiwel, Dinesh (2015), *The War against Animals*, Leiden: Brill.
Walkowitz, Rebecca (2015), *Born Translated: The Contemporary Novel in an Age of World Literature*, New York: Columbia University Press.
Warwick Research Collective (WReC) (2015), *Combined and Uneven Development: Towards a New Theory of World-Literature*, Liverpool: Liverpool University Press.
Watt, Ian (1968), *The Rise of the Novel: Studies in Defoe, Richardson and Fielding*, London: Penguin.
Weaver, Jace (2000), 'Indigenousness and Indigeneity', in Henry Schwarz and Sangeeta Ray (eds), *A Companion to Postcolonial Studies*, 221–35, Malden: Blackwell.
Weheliye, Alexander (2014), *Habeas Viscus: Racializing Assemblages, Biopolitics, and Black Feminist Theories of the Human*, Durham: Duke University Press.
Weigandt, Kai (2019), *J. M. Coetzee's Revisions of the Human: Posthumanism and Narrative Form*, Basingstoke: Palgrave.
Weigel, Sigrid (2013), *Walter Benjamin: Images, the Creaturely, and the Holy*, Stanford: Stanford University Press.
Weil, Kari (2012), *Thinking Animals: Why Animal Studies Now?*, New York: Columbia University Press.
Weis, Tony (2013), *The Ecological Hoofprint: The Global Burden of Industrial Livestock*, London: Zed Books.
Weis, Tony (2016), 'Towards 120 Billion: Dietary Change and Animal Lives', *Radical Philosophy*, 199: 8–13.
Wenzel, Jenifer (2000), 'Grim Fairy Tales: Taking a Risk, Reading Imaginary Maps', in Amal Amireh and Lisa Suhair Majaj (eds), *Going Global: The Transnational Reception of Third World Women Writers*, 229–51, London: Routledge.
Wenzel, Jennifer (2011), 'Forest Fictions and Ecological Crises: Reading the Politics of Survival in Mahasweta Devi's "Dhowli"', in Elizabeth DeLoughrey and George B. Hadley (eds), *Postcolonial Ecologies: Literature of the Environment*, 136–55, Oxford: Oxford University Press.
Wicomb, Zoë (2002), 'Translations in the Yard of Africa', *Journal of Literary Studies*, 18 (3–4): 209–23.

Wilde, Lawrence (2000), '"The Creatures, too, Must Become Free": Marx and the Animal/Human Distinction', *Capital & Class*, 24 (3): 37–53.
Williams, Daniel (2018), 'Life among the Vermin: *Nineveh* and Ecological Relocation', *Studies in the Novel*, 50 (3): 419–40.
Wilm, Jan (2016), *The Slow Philosophy of J. M. Coetzee*, London: Bloomsbury.
Wolfe, Cary (2003), *Animal Rites: American Culture, the Discourse of Species and Posthumanist Theory*, Chicago: University of Chicago Press.
Wolfe, Cary (2010), *What Is Posthumanism?*, Minneapolis: University of Minnesota Press.
Wolff, Lynn L. (2014), *W. G. Sebald's Hybrid Poetics: Literature as Historiography*, Berlin: De Gruyter.
Woloch, Alex (2003), *The One vs. the Many: Minor Characters and the Space of the Protagonist in the Novel*, Princeton: Princeton University Press.
Wood, James (2017), 'W. G. Sebald: Humorist', *New Yorker*, 5 & 12 June.
Wright, Laura (2006), 'A Feminist-Vegetarian Defense of Elizabeth Costello: A Rant from an Ethical Academic on J. M. Coetzee's *The Lives of Animals*', in Jane Poynor (ed.), *J. M. Coetzee and the Idea of the Public Intellectual*, 193–216, Athens: Ohio University Press.
Wynter, Sylvia (2003), 'Unsettling the Coloniality of Being/Power/Truth/Freedom: Towards the Human, after Man, Its Overrepresentation – An Argument', *CR*, 3 (3): 257–337.
Xaxa, Virginius (2016), 'Formation of Adivasi/Indigenous People's Identity in India', in Meena Radhakrishna (ed.), *First Citizens: Studies on Adivasis, Tribals and Indigenous Peoples in India*, 33–52, New Delhi: Oxford University Press.
Zimbler, Jarad (2014), *J. M. Coetzee and the Politics of Style*, Cambridge: Cambridge University Press.

Index

activism and advocacy 1–2, 16, 86, 87, 125, 133, 175
Adams, Carol J. 19, 116
Adorno, Theodor W. 35, 36, 39 n.17, 44, 45, 56–7, 60, 62, 67, 68, 71, 72, 106, 149, 153, 154, 158, 176
Agamben, Giorgio 4, 27, 28, 38 n.11, 133
Ahmed, Sara 115
Ahuja, Neel 128
Anatomy Lesson of Dr Nicolaes Tulp, The (Rembrandt) 53
animal agriculture
  factory farming 17, 116, 118, 160
  industrial 6, 13–16, 47, 55, 56, 58, 59, 61, 66, 72, 114, 116, 117, 128, 141, 144, 160, 163, 167, 169
Animalia (Del Amo) 165–6
animality 3, 6, 7, 10, 17, 19, 21, 27, 29, 51–3, 55, 67, 86, 87, 90, 92–4, 96–8, 107, 111, 112, 129, 134, 138, 139, 141, 143, 158, 159, 162, 163, 166
Animal Rites (Wolfe) 19
animals 3, 11, 27, 30, 112
  annihilation of 55
  Coetzee's 161
  death 105, 112, 161
  and disability 15
  ethics 6, 9, 20, 66, 86–9, 114, 120, 120 n.4, 127, 154, 160
  farmed 16, 17, 37, 167
  figurations of 6, 17, 18, 25, 42, 91–2, 110, 143, 178 n.4
  flesh 116
  forest 140, 142, 143
  higher 61
  human and 2–3, 5, 7–9, 11, 12, 19, 20, 23, 27–9, 32, 37 n.1, 42, 52, 64, 66, 70, 71, 74, 80, 85, 86, 97, 106, 127, 158, 162, 164, 177
  identifications 137–43
  Kafka's 33
  liberation 3, 5, 15, 21, 30, 70, 86

life 2, 5, 8, 9, 13, 16, 26, 27, 37 n.1, 42, 55, 69, 71, 85, 87, 93, 94, 96, 110, 138, 160, 162, 164, 166, 177
  literature and 173
  Marx 37 n.1
  meat 14, 15, 19, 116, 157
  metaphorics of 141
  noisy 24, 27, 101
  nonhuman 14, 21, 23, 33, 54, 67, 75, 90, 93, 111, 141, 163
  pictures of 62
  population 142
  production 16, 160
  reading for 22–9
  rights 3, 9, 20, 21, 35, 86, 128, 171
  sacrifice 142–3
  vulnerability 34
  war against 3, 5–10, 12–23, 27, 28, 33, 35, 37, 42, 44, 54, 62, 71, 80, 87–9, 105, 106, 113, 115, 118, 119, 149, 157, 159–64, 169, 170, 173, 176, 177
  wild 16, 17, 141
  zoo 67–74, 80, 167
Animal's People (Sinha) 164, 165
Animal Stories (McHugh) 23
animal studies 3, 18–22, 65, 72, 93, 154, 162
  literary 2, 4, 5, 22, 23, 86, 162, 171
anthropocentrism 19–20, 23, 38 n.8, 38 n.10
anthropological machine 4, 5, 26–9, 42, 47, 80, 85, 97, 98, 103, 108, 120, 128, 129, 133, 139, 145, 152, 155, 158, 159, 161, 162, 166
anthroponormativity 20, 21, 28, 29, 33, 43, 53, 55, 67, 81, 87, 89, 91, 96, 105, 113, 114, 119, 120, 128, 152, 155, 158, 159, 162, 163, 166, 173
Armstrong, Nancy 25
asymptotic reconciliation 153–5
attentiveness 5, 8, 10, 29, 32, 33, 37, 100, 159

Attridge, Derek 88, 90, 99, 119
Attwell, David 84, 86
Auerbach, Erich 38–9 n.15, 76–7
Austerlitz (Sebald) 41–3, 48, 67–80

Baker, Timothy C. 23
Bakhtin, Mikhail 24
Balibar, Etienne 24
Banerjee, Sumanta 126
Bauman, Zygmunt 44
Beasts of Burden (Taylor) 19
Benjamin, Andrew 31
Benjamin, Walter 31–5, 37, 38 n.15, 46, 47, 67
Berger, John 14, 72–3
Bewes, Timothy 41, 81 n.1
Bildungsroman 25, 98, 144–6
biodiversity 13, 16, 17, 42, 79, 169, 173
biologico-literary experiment 89
Boehmer, Elleke 93
Boggs, Colleen Glenney 22
bovine spongiform encephalopathy (BSE) 16
Brouillette, Sarah 107
Buber, Martin 30–1
Buck-Morss, Susan 57
Burns, Lorna 168
Butler, Judith 18, 113, 133–4

Calarco, Matthew 20
Capital, Interrupted (Gidwani) 128–9
capitalism 9, 13, 21, 25, 37 n.1, 44, 128, 148, 149
capitalist modernity 8, 14, 30, 31, 160, 162, 173, 176
Carrigan, Anthony 178 n.2
Carson, Rachel 1–3, 10 n.1, 11
Chakrabarty, Dipesh 134
Chakraborty, Madhurima 156 n.3
Clarkson, Carrol 89
climate change 26, 157
Coetzee, J. M. 6–9, 46
  aesthetic shift 106–7
  Age of Iron 85, 91, 99
  animal-centred works 90
  animal turn 9, 87, 89, 90, 107, 161
  characters 84–5, 88
  closer to the ground 91–2, 99
  critics 85–6, 92–3

Disgrace 6, 34, 86–90, 92–107, 111, 116, 120, 151, 160, 161
Doubling the Point 87–8
Driepoot death 99–106, 119
Elizabeth Costello 87–90, 105–16, 118, 120, 160, 161, 163, 174
GOD-DOG 106
inclination 85, 87, 92, 94
Life and Times of Michael K 101–2
Lives of Animals, The 6, 33, 86, 87–90, 107, 113–19, 174
Novel in Africa, The 112
novels 83–90, 93, 96, 100, 107, 120 n.4
situational metafiction 84
Slow Man 89
Summertime 84
Tanner Lectures 113, 114, 117
vegetarian killjoy 113–20
Waiting for the Barbarians 85
colonial domination 83, 84, 100, 172
consumption 169
contemporary
  capitalism 21
  contagion 152
  the contemporary 8
  life 74–5, 137
  literature 2, 4, 5, 8–10, 12, 22, 26, 37, 86, 164–76
  meat production 116
  novel 80, 127
Cornwell, Gareth 120 n.9
Cottrell, Anna 178 n.4
Covid-19 16, 157
creatura 30
creaturely 7–8, 29–37, 159
  affinity 89
  awareness 42
  care-taking 155
  ethics 34, 67, 154, 160
  existence 91
  forms 5, 23–4, 29, 62, 79, 159, 162–76
  horizon 161–2
  life 5, 7, 9, 10, 33, 34, 36, 42, 44, 91–2, 98, 134, 160, 163
  love 130, 155
  melancholia 43, 47, 80–1
  politics 32
  reconciliation 176–7
  responsibility 97, 144
  semiotics 143

sympathy 75
transformation 93
trouble 114–15
vulnerability 51–2
Creaturely Poetics (Pick) 33–4
Criminal Tribes Act 131
critters (Haraway, Donna) 7
Crownshaw, Richard 65–6
cultural revolution 24, 158

Davis, Mike 16
Dawson, Ashley 13, 148
de-extinction 148–9
  literary 147–9, 151–2, 163
deforestation 13, 16, 17, 42, 48, 56, 128, 137, 142, 148, 155, 161, 173
dehumanization 6, 7, 37, 91, 134, 159, 160
Del Amo, Jean-Baptiste 165–6
Denotified and Nomadic Tribes of India, The (DNT-RAG) 125, 132, 133
depopulation 16
Derrida, Jacques 10 n.2, 11–12, 17–18, 68, 118, 157
Dialectic of Enlightenment (Adorno and Horkheimer) 35, 67
Die Kreatur 30–1
domestication 26
Durrant, Sam 85, 88

Eagleton, Terry 134
ecological romanticism 137
Esposito, Roberto 96–7
Esty, Jed 25
Extinction: A Radical History (Dawson) 13

factory farming 17, 116, 118, 160
Federici, Silvia 53
fishing 15–16, 42, 56–61, 63, 64, 160, 163, 164
Fish, Kenneth 16
Foer, Jonathan Safran 16
Food and Agriculture Organization (FAO) 15
form
  creaturely 5, 23–4, 29, 62, 79, 159, 162–76
  fiction 2, 9, 26, 27, 29, 43, 80, 84, 86–9, 125–9, 161–3

literary 1–2, 4, 6, 7, 10, 22, 25, 28, 29, 37, 41, 42, 62, 80, 88, 89, 108, 111, 130, 155, 158, 161, 162, 164, 168, 177
metafiction 7, 84, 89, 106, 108–11
narrative 27, 49, 51, 169
novel 2, 4, 23–6, 47, 80, 84, 85, 94, 99–101, 103, 105, 120, 129, 135, 146, 161, 173, 174
short story 7, 108, 129, 134–6, 138, 142
Forna, Aminatta 166
Foucault, Michel 18, 60
Frankfurt School 35, 37, 38 n.13, 44, 176
Fuchs, Anne 47, 66–7

Gandhi, Indira 126, 128, 156 n.4
Ghosh, Amitav 26, 127, 164–5
Gidwani, Vinay 128–9, 156 n.7
Glick, Megan H. 19
Great Derangement, The (Ghosh) 26
Green Revolution 126, 150, 156 n.4, 161
Groves, Jason 81 n.5
Guha, Ramachandra 125

Habitual Offenders Act 131
Hall, Sarah 166, 178 n.4
Hall, Stuart 27–8
Hanssen, Beatrice 32
Happiness (Forna) 166
Haraway, Donna 7, 19
Hardy, Thomas 98
Heise, Ursula 148
Hindutva 168
Horkheimer, Max 35, 36, 44, 67, 158, 176
How Novels Think (Armstrong) 25
human
  community 1, 20, 34, 114, 117, 144, 163, 174
  differentiation 19
  exceptionalism 11, 27, 34, 95
  history 12, 17, 46, 49, 56, 62, 66, 144, 150
  life 34, 35, 45, 55, 68, 69, 124, 134, 137, 152, 158, 159
  and nonhuman 1, 7, 19, 21, 29, 30, 35, 37, 67, 69, 71, 74, 85, 88, 93, 99, 129, 137, 141, 145, 152, 154, 155, 158, 160, 163, 165, 166, 173, 177
privilege 96
superiority 4, 12, 20, 158, 171

human–animal relations 2, 3, 5, 7–9, 11, 12, 19, 20, 23, 27–9, 32, 37 n.1, 42, 52, 64, 66, 70, 71, 74, 80, 85, 86, 97, 106, 127, 158, 162, 164, 177
humanity 3, 17, 85
  and animality 6, 158, 163
  and inhumanity 18, 134–9, 159, 163
  mastery 12, 21, 32, 35, 36, 76, 79, 145, 148, 157, 158, 162, 163, 172
  and nature 13, 27, 37 n.1, 45, 46, 172, 177
  political 18, 127, 130, 133, 134, 137, 139, 141, 144, 145
  Sebald and 45–7, 55, 57–60, 67, 79
  subjectivity and 84
  supremacy 3, 21, 158, 159, 177
humanization 4, 18, 25, 28, 70, 135, 144
Hungry Tide, The (Ghosh) 164
hunting 142–3
Hutchinson, Ben 45, 49

India 6, 124–7, 129, 131–3, 135, 136, 138, 143, 156 n.3, 164, 167, 168, 170
industrial animal agriculture 6, 13–16, 47, 55, 56, 58, 59, 61, 66, 72, 114, 116, 117, 128, 141, 144, 160, 163, 167, 169
Infrahumanisms (Glick) 19
inhumanity 18, 134–9, 159, 163
Intergovernmental Platform on Biodiversity and Ecosystem Services 17
International Panel on Climate Change 16

James, David 80
Jameson, Fredric 25, 35, 147
Janes, Regina 85
Jude the Obscure (Hardy) 98

Kaakinen, Kasia 76
Kafka, Franz 32–3, 52, 103
Kennedy, Rosanne 81 n.5
Klein, Naomi 157–8
Köhler, Wolfgang 110
Kreilkamp, Ivan 26, 98

Lanser, Susan 27
Lazarus, Neil 147
literary animal studies 2, 4–5, 22–3, 86, 162, 171

literary form 1–2, 4, 6, 7, 10, 22, 25, 28, 29, 37, 41, 42, 62, 80, 88, 89, 108, 111, 130, 155, 158, 161, 162, 164, 168, 177
Livestock Revolution 15, 17
Living a Feminist Life (Ahmed) 115
Lonely Voice, The (O'Connor) 135
Long, J. J. 66
Lukács, György 39 n.15, 134

McCulloh, Mark 65, 81 n.1
Macherey, Pierre 24
McHugh, Susan 4, 23
McKay, Robert 22, 114
Mahasweta Devi 6–9
  activism 133
  adivasis 123–5, 127–32, 137–8, 140–8
  anaphoric formulations 153
  animality 137–43
  development 143–7
  double task 123–31
  'Douloti, the Bountiful' 138–9
  fiction 126, 128–30
  figuration and formal incorporation 147–8
  'Fundamental Rights and Bhikari Dusad' 132–4, 136–7, 160
  'The hunt' 142–3
  inhuman narratives 131–7
  literary de-extinction 147–52, 163
  literary project 125–7, 130, 134, 138, 149
  metaphorics of extinction 154
  Mother of 1084 135
  planetarity 152–5
  political imaginary 133
  postcolonial crises 126–7
  postcolonial justice 128
  Pterodactyl 6, 34, 123–4, 127, 130, 143–55, 160, 161, 163
  'Salt' 140–1
  stories 130, 132, 133, 135–7, 141–2
  tradition and modernity 135
  writing 131
Malabou, Catherine 52–3
Malm, Andreas 38 n.10
'man' 3, 18, 21, 32, 39 n.15, 85, 91
Marchesini, Roberto 38 n.8
Marcuse, Herbert 176–7
Marx, Karl 13–14, 37 n.1
mass extinction 17, 148, 159, 163

mass production
    and consumption 14–15, 169
    of farmed animals 17
    industrial animal agriculture 14, 16, 19, 160
    and mass extinction 2–3, 12, 17, 159, 163
Mbembe, Achille 19
Mehta, Tania 135
melancholia 9, 31, 33, 43, 44, 46–7, 80, 151. *See also* Sebald, W. G.
Menozzi, Filippo 168–9
metaphor 22, 32, 34, 42, 51, 66, 70, 91, 94, 106, 108, 110, 112, 119, 129, 138, 141, 148–50, 152–4, 163, 171, 172, 175
Mimesis (Auerbach) 39 n.15
Minima Moralia (Adorno) 36, 68, 71
Ministry of Utmost Happiness, The (Roy) 167–70, 175
Minor Creatures (Kreilkamp) 26
Mitchell, W. J. T. 149
modernity 1, 2, 4–6, 8, 9, 14, 21–2, 35, 75, 151, 157
    anthropocentric 80
    capitalist 8, 13, 14, 30, 31, 160, 162, 173, 176
    defined 44
    Holocaust to 44
    literature of 24
    nature and 45, 77
    quagmire 36
    Sebald and 42–7, 55, 56, 61, 62, 64, 66, 67, 69–71, 74, 75, 77, 79–81
    systematic domination 35–6
    tradition and 135
    zoo and 70
Mukherjee, Pablo Upamanyu 164, 177 n.2
Mullan, John 103
Müntzer, Thomas 13
Murphet, Julian 106–7

natural history 41, 42, 47, 55–62, 64, 66, 78, 113, 160, 169, 175
Negative Dialectics (Adorno) 36, 39 n.17, 57
neoliberalism 15, 59
Neyrat, Frédéric 66
Nineveh (Rose-Innes) 170–2
nonhuman 1–3, 5–7, 12, 14, 21, 23, 25, 26, 30, 34, 35, 45, 47, 59, 61, 67, 69, 71, 74, 75

animals 14, 21, 23, 33, 54, 67, 75, 90, 93, 111, 141, 163
    ecocide 148
    justice 67
    life 1, 9, 12, 19, 21, 29, 35, 45, 47, 79, 85, 87, 98, 113, 124, 137, 143, 152, 163, 173, 174
    sentience 75
    species 6
    specimens 77

O'Connor, Frank 135
Of Jews and Animals (Benjamin, Andrew) 67
One vs. the Many, The (Woloch) 94
One-Way Street (Benjamin, Walter) 32–3
Open, The: Man and Animal (Agamben) 27, 28
Ortiz Robles, Mario 22
Overstory, The (Powers) 173–6

Parry, Benita 91
Pick, Anat 33–4
planetarity 152–5
population
    animal 15, 71, 97, 113, 142, 169
    human 59, 98, 125, 129
posthumanism 3, 18–20, 23, 34, 81 n.5, 86, 87, 171
Powers, Richard 173–6
Prasad, Archana 137
Pratt, Mary Louise 60

race 19, 21, 35, 70, 141, 154, 171, 176
racialization 19, 94
Rajan, Romy 168
Rancière, Jacques 23–4
realism 7, 32, 89, 98, 99, 101, 105, 106, 108, 109, 120, 126, 127, 161, 164
Rise of the Novel, The (Watt) 25
Robbins, Bruce 101
Rose, Gillian 57
Rose-Innes, Henrietta 170–2
Roudinesco, Elisabeth 17
Roy, Arundhati 167–70, 175
Roy, Parama 126
Roy, Piyali 164
Ruti, Mari 34
Ryder, Richard 20

Said, Edward 79
Salgado, Minoli 131
Santner, Eric 33, 34, 47
Schreiner, Olive 98
Sebald, W. G. 5–9, 161
  archiving of life 74–81
  Austerlitz 41–3, 48, 67–80
  Holocaust 44, 66, 67
  humanity 45–7, 55, 57–60, 67, 79
  hypotaxis 47, 75–7, 80
  images 62–7
  inclusion of animals 47
  language and syntax 48
  literary project 41, 42, 46–8, 54, 66, 74–5, 80, 161
  longue duree 44
  modernity 42–7, 55, 56, 61, 62, 64, 66, 67, 69–71, 74, 75, 77, 79–81
  Nach der Natur 45–6
  narrators 42, 46, 48–51, 53–5, 57–61, 64, 68–70, 75, 90, 113, 160
  natural-history narration 55–62
  oeuvre 64, 65
  parataxis 47, 75–7
  Rings of Saturn, The 42, 46, 48–66, 72, 74, 75, 79, 80, 93–4, 117, 173
  texts 41–3, 45–7, 49, 52, 62, 81 n.5
  Unglück 52, 53, 81 n.7
  writing 42–5, 47, 56, 62, 76, 77, 81 n.1
  Zerstreute Reminiszenzen 43
Second World War 2, 8, 14, 35, 45
Shah, Alpa 137
Shiva, Vandana 156 n.4
Silent Spring (Carson) 1–2
Singer, Isaac Bashevis 117
Singer, Peter 20, 117
Sinha, Indra 164, 165, 178 n.2
Sixth Extinction, The (Kolbert) 17
Slaughter, Joseph 25, 129, 146
Soper, Kate 20, 38 n.10
South Africa 83–5, 92, 97, 98, 100, 106, 171
speciesism 20
Spivak, Gayatri Chakravorty 84, 89, 95, 130–1, 143, 147, 154
Steiner, Gary 38 n.8
Steller, Georg Wilhelm 45

Story of an African Farm, The (Schreiner) 98
subaltern 124, 128, 133, 135, 137–9, 153, 155 n.1, 164

Taylor, Sunaura 15, 19
Theisen, Bianca 51

vanishing mediator 147
vulnerability 11, 32, 34, 50, 51, 86, 137, 143, 150, 153, 159
vultures 169–70

Wadiwel, Dinesh 12
Walter Benjamin's Other History (Hanssen) 32
war against animals 2–3, 5–10, 17, 164, 173, 176, 177
  Benjamin 33
  capitalist modernity 14
  Coetzee 87–9, 105, 113, 115, 118, 159, 161
  Derrida 12
  Devi 129, 149
  mass death 14–17
  Sebald 42, 44, 54, 62, 71, 80
  Wadiwel 12
Watt, Ian 25
Weheliye, Alexander 19
What Is Nature? (Soper) 20
Why Look at Animals (Berger) 14, 72–3
Wicomb, Zoë 97–8
Wolf Border, The (Hall) 166, 178 n.4
Wolfe, Cary 19
Wolff, Lynn 76, 81 n.1
Woloch, Alex 94
Wordsworth, William 103
Wright, Laura 115
Writing Animals (Baker) 23
WWF report 17
Wynter, Sylvia 5, 18, 19

Xaxa, Virginius 125

zoo 6, 14, 42, 45, 63, 67–74, 80, 109, 167
zoonotic diseases 16, 38 n.5, 157, 169

www.ingramcontent.com/pod-product-compliance
Lightning Source LLC
Chambersburg PA
CBHW061829300426
44115CB00013B/2300